Praise for Dancing into Battle

'*Dancing into Battle* succeeds in placing Waterloo firmly in the social context of Regency England, and thereby provides a fascinating new perspective to one of the most famous conflicts in British military history' *Daily Telegraph*

'Foulkes has written a wonderful book. Drawing on a rich stock of memoirs from those who fought and those who partied at Waterloo, he creates a picture that is gaudy, sad, elegant and impeccably English' *Mail on Sunday*

'Not since Thackeray himself has a writer so powerfully evoked the mood of the British in Brussels before, during and after the Battle of Waterloo. The Duchess of Richmond's Ball saw the pinnacle of Regency romance, and in Nick Foulkes has found a scholarly researcher as well as a witty chronicler' Andrew Roberts

'[An] enthralling social history of the Battle of Waterloo' *Daily Mail*

'[An] entertaining chronicle … Foulkes's description of combat is as deliciously British as his vignette of teacakes and cream' *Observer*

'Entertaining … Foulkes captures the frenetic mood of nervous pleasure-seeking and growing tension in the city as the armies massed before the action. He also gives a clear exposition of the battle and its aftermath' *Literary Review*

'Foulkes uses colourful accounts that historians have neglected … While he never disparages the bravery of armies, Foulkes's presentation of such overlooked material about Waterloo makes this a welcome addition to its literature' *Times Literary Supplement*

'Foulkes is strong on the historical side of events, most interesting is what he observes about the mythologising of the ball as it blended seamlessly into the battle' *Sunday Telegraph*

'A well-researched social portrait … Foulkes entertainingly and gracefully brings to life the Regency upper class at war'
Simon Sebag Montefiore

Nick Foulkes read English at Hertford College, Oxford, and has spent the last twenty years working as an author and journalist. His writing has appeared in most of Britain's national newspapers. A regular contributor to the *Financial Times*, he is contributing editor to *Vanity Fair*, luxury editor of *GQ*, and a well-known columnist whose work has appeared in many magazines around the world. His biography of Count D'Orsay, *The Last of the Dandies*, was published in 2003. He is married with two children and lives in London.

Dancing into Battle

A Social History of the
Battle of Waterloo

NICK FOULKES

PHOENIX

A PHOENIX PAPERBACK

First published in Great Britain in 2006
by Weidenfeld & Nicolson
This paperback edition published in 2007
by Phoenix,
an imprint of Orion Books Ltd,
Orion House, 5 Upper St Martin's Lane,
London WC2H 9EA
An Hachette Livre UK company

3 5 7 9 10 8 6 4 2

ISBN 978-0-7538-2217-3

Typeset by Input Data Services Ltd, Frome

Printed and bound in Great Britain by Mackays of Chatham

The Orion Publishing Group's policy is to use papers that
are natural, renewable and recyclable products and
made from wood grown in sustainable forests. The logging
and manufacturing processes are expected to conform to
the environmental regulations of the country of origin.

www.orionbooks.co.uk

For Alexandra, Max and Freddie

CONTENTS

LIST OF ILLUSTRATIONS

Lt-Gen. Sir Edward Barnes by Thomas Heaphy (National Portrait Gallery)

Caroline 'Car' Lady Paget with their daughter Caroline by John Hoppner (courtesy Marquess of Anglesey)

Lord Paget by George Engleheart (courtesy Marquess of Anglesey)

Thomas Creevey (Private Collection)

Lt-Col. Andrew Hamilton (Private Collection)

Col. Sir William Howe De Lancey (artist unknown) and his wife Magdalene Hall by George Engleheart (National Portrait Gallery)

Wellington's officers: the Prince of Orange, the Duke of Brunswick, the Duke, General Lord Hill,General Sir Thomas Picton, Prince Blücher, the Marquess of Anglesey (BAL)

A Swarm of Bees by George Cruikshank (City of Westminster Archive Centre/BAL)

Quatre Bras, 16 June 1815, by Thomas Sutherland (BAL)

Plan of the battle of Waterloo (BAL)

Battle of Waterloo by Dighton (BAL)

Wellington at Waterloo by Robert A. Hillingford (BAL)

Private Shaw (Private Collection)

Wilberforce and Achilles (Guildhall Library/BAL)

Village of Waterloo after the battle by George Jones (Courtesy of the Council National Army Museum/BAL)

Baron Raglan (photo Roger Fenton)

Wellington in old age (National Portrait Gallery/Leeds Museums and Galleries (City Art Gallery)/BAL)

Heroes of Waterloo: Thomas Graham, Baron Lynedoch; Rowland Hill 1st Viscount Hill; Sir Thomas Picton; Henry William Paget 1st Marquess of Anglesey (artist unknown/National Portrait Gallery)

Waterloo banquet (Illustrated London News Picture Library)

Time and the Hero (Illustrated London News Picture Library)

INTRODUCTION

The battle of Waterloo is one of the most, perhaps even *the* most, discussed, analysed, written about and replayed armed clashes in the history of warfare. The fighting, which eventually involved some 200,000 men, 60,000 horses and more than 500 pieces of artillery, took place on a patch of ground roughly four kilometres by four kilometres (approximately two and half miles square). According to one historian: 'almost 200 years and two world wars later no subsequent battle has managed to cram so many men and animals into so small a space'.* It started shortly before midday and ended around nine hours later in the early evening, but the space it occupied in terms of time and geographical area are disproportionate to its ramifications. The world changed between sunrise and sunset on Sunday 18 June 1815. The battle brought the era of Napoleon to a decisive end and with it, over a quarter of a century of almost constant warfare in Europe. It raised the curtain on the nineteenth century and ushered in the modern, mechanised world. The next time British forces fought in a war in Europe it was with aircraft, machine guns and such weapons of mass destruction as gas and railway-mounted superguns.

The battle has been the subject of many distinguished books, and this is certainly not intended as anything other than a view of a familiar subject from a little-used vantage point. Andrew Roberts has recently published an excellent volume which combines brevity and accessibility with the author's flair for engaging history – along with Mark Adkin's excellent

* The Waterloo Companion, p121

Waterloo Companion, it should be in every household that has an interest in events that have brought us to where we are today. Those who have a particular interest in the Duchess of Richmond's ball, should, as well as reading this book, pick up a copy of David Miller's account of the most famous dance in history, which provides exhaustive statistical analysis of the ball and those invited to it.

What fascinates me about the battle is its unique situation straddling two centuries. In its role of closing the eighteenth century and heralding the nineteenth, the battle belongs to both eras: the barbarously elegant England of the Regency, with its relaxed attitude to sex, alcohol and violence; and the imperial England of Queen Victoria, with its improving zeal, conspicuous virtue and high (albeit occasionally hypocritical) moral standards. As well as what today might be called the 'global' view from the twenty-first century – as an event that altered the course of the political and economic development of the world – the drama of the event itself has long exercised a powerful influence over me. *Vanity Fair* is one of my favourite works of fiction: it has the many excellent qualities of the nineteenth-century novel, spiced with the author's cynicism. From the arrack punch which Jos Sedley drinks too freely in the Vauxhall Pleasure Gardens to the reinvention of Becky as the charitable benefactor of 'The Destitute Orange-girl, the Neglected Washerwoman, the Distressed Muffin-man',* the shifting values of the nineteenth century from its teens to middle age are mercilessly chronicled.

Thackeray understood the dramatic potential of Waterloo and the events preceding it in a way that nobody else has matched. Social forces, most notably the tendency of the British aristocracy to accrue debt, had filled Brussels with a frivolous crowd of British expatriates, who regarded the rapid military build-up in anticipation of a desperate struggle with the most feared military genius of the time as an opportunity to enlarge their social lives, rather than a cause for concern. As well as making up the expatriate community in Brussels, the British aristocracy supplied the British Army with officers, and the result was that the divide between civilian and military life became so blurred as to be virtually non-existent, with non-combatants riding out to 'enjoy' the battle. Indeed, the proximity of the battle to the city of Brussels both in terms of sheer geographical propinquity, and the ties of family and friendship, gave Waterloo a unique character whereby individuals stepped from the ballroom to the battlefield and back again. It had the effect of bringing warfare closer to the sporting activities associated with a house party in the country.

Vanity Fair, p877

Of course the life of the aristocracy, in peace and war, rested upon the efforts of what one Victorian prime minister would call 'the heroic men from the lowest classes of the community'. For the most part they too enjoyed the build-up to the battle: pleasant billets, plentiful food, good tobacco and strong drink perpetuated the sense of unreality that characterised life in the ballrooms and salons of Brussels.

All this made the battle – not that it was unexpected – more of a shock when it came. Almost as much of a shock is the callous plundering of the dead and dying: one of my favourite vignettes in *Vanity Fair* has Becky, now Mrs Rawdon Crawley, buying a sword hilt, some epaulettes and a cross of the Legion d'Honneur from 'one of the innumerable pedlars who immediately began to deal in relics of the war',* which are then sent back to Rawdon's aunt as trophies taken by her nephew, complete with detailed accounts of how he had won them.

I grew up during the 1970s, not a period immediately associated with the Battle of Waterloo, however even in that decade of the twentieth century, the events of that June weekend in 1815 were still being felt. Rod Steiger, Christopher Plummer and Orson Welles starred in an epic film of the battle which appeared in 1970, and in 1974 a Scandinavian pop group launched their own bid for world domination at the Eurovision Song Contest with a catchy number entitled 'Waterloo'. And in putting together this account of the events around Waterloo and their continuing effect, I suppose I was inspired by another product of the 1970s, the disaster movie: one is introduced to various characters, some of whom will be snuffed out by impending catastrophe, and as events unfold there will be instances of chivalry and cowardice, gallantry and self-interest. Waterloo has these elements in abundance, along with glamour, horror, sex, shopping, parties, drinking, gossip, gambling, racing, cricket, picnics and even art appreciation.

* *Vanity Fair*, p409

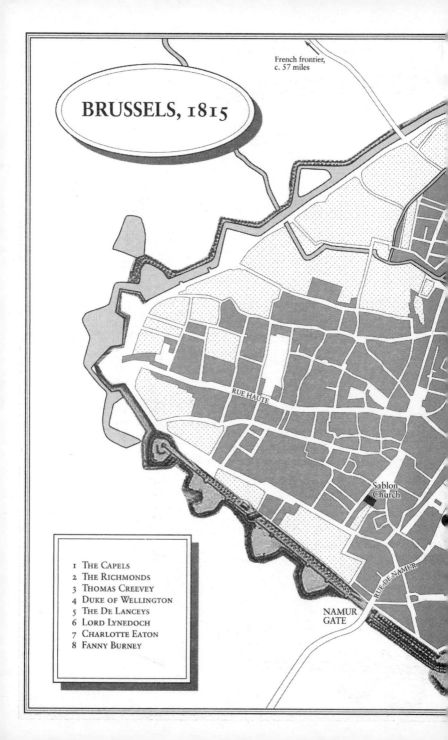

BRUSSELS, 1815

French frontier,
c. 57 miles

RUE HAUTE

Sablon
Church

RUE-DE-NAMUR

NAMUR
GATE

1 THE CAPELS
2 THE RICHMONDS
3 THOMAS CREEVEY
4 DUKE OF WELLINGTON
5 THE DE LANCEYS
6 LORD LYNEDOCH
7 CHARLOTTE EATON
8 FANNY BURNEY

NINOVE
GATE

ALLÉE VERTE

Warehouse

Antwerp,
c. 25 miles →

ANVERS
GATE

R. Senne

Saint Nicholas
Church

Hôtel
de Ville

GRANDE
PLACE

Theatre

PLACE
ST. MICHEL

②

RUE DE MARCHÉ AU BOIS

⑧

Saint Gudula
Cathedral

④   ⑤

PLACE DE
LEUVAIN

RUE ROYALE

PARC

⑥   ①   RUE DUCALE

N

Map by András Bereznay; www.historyonmaps.com

PROLOGUE

'At an early hour, a britchka was at the door of the Duke of Wellington's residence, to transport me and my vulpine companions.' It was a brisk morning early in March 1815 and the light Russian-style carriage was waiting outside a palace a short walk from the Hofburg in the centre of Vienna. The young man, more a boy really, with the 'vulpine companions' was fifteen-year-old Lord William Pitt Lennox, the seventh of the Duke and Duchess of Richmond's fourteen children. Through the nepotistic system of aristocratic preferment that characterised life among the ruling class of England, he found himself working as an aide to the Duke who, having become a British national hero after the Peninsular War, had embarked on a diplomatic and political career: first as ambassador to the court of the recently restored French monarch Louis XVIII and now as Britain's representative at the Congress of Vienna.

At the beginning of October the preceding year, delegates of the major victorious powers of Russia, Prussia, Austria and England, as well as numerous representatives of a panoply of little kingdoms, statelets, and principalities and electorates, crowded into the ancient city of Vienna, hub of what remained of the thousand-year-old Holy Roman Empire, to impose a new world order upon the wreckage of Napoleon's European dream. The former French emperor, who at one point had presided over an empire stretching from Moscow to the Iberian peninsula and from the northern shores of Europe to the Mediterranean kingdom of Naples, was exiled on Elba and pejoratively referred to as Robinson Crusoe.

Britain's gifted, ambitious and Machiavellian foreign secretary Lord

Castlereagh, who had initially headed the British delegation, had expected the whole thing to be wrapped up in a couple of weeks. After it became clear that it would take a good deal longer, Castlereagh returned to politicking in London, leaving the job of attending endless meetings, balls, masques and reviews to Wellington.

The Congress now had become a giant territorial bazaar. Monarchs installed during the Napoleonic era were in Vienna to lobby for maintenance of the *status quo*. German-speaking royals who had forfeited their micro-kingdoms, duchies, electorates and so on turned up hoping to have them restored. Nationalist activists saw a chance to shake off unloved rulers. The Church sought to reassert its power, somewhat bruised after Napoleon had kidnapped the Pope. And with each delegation came a small army of courtesans, lawyers, servants, and sightseers. Now, with negotiations entering their sixth month, a sense of boredom had set in that the innumerable balls, banquets, pageants and reviews could not assuage . . . which was where the 'vulpine companions' came in.

The British delegation had taken the precaution of bringing a pack of hounds to keep themselves amused, 'and during Wellington's stay in the Austrian capital, he went out constantly with them'.[2] Deer was the main quarry, but to be on the safe side bag foxes were brought along to prolong the day's sport, and today that duty fell to Lord William Pitt Lennox.

> Just before I got into the carriage, my brother *attaché*, Fremantle, gave me the hint that the 'Beau' – the name the Peninsular campaigners gave to their chief – might probably be unable to attend the hunt, and that I was to inform the Prince [the hunt was to take place at the country estate of Prince Esterhazy] that despatches of some importance had arrived, which called for his immediate attention.[3]

It was a good day's sport but the Duke of Wellington's absence was noticeable. Among those present was Prince Eugène de Beauharnais.

> 'Is the Duke coming to-day?' he anxiously inquired.
>
> 'It is very doubtful,' I replied; 'some important despatches were brought to him this morning.'
>
> 'That confirms all I have heard,' responded Eugène; then, turning to me, he abruptly asked, 'have you heard any rumour of Napoleon's escape from Elba?'[4]

1

'An economical plan'

As young Lord William heard the news of Napoleon's escape early that chilly March morning while out with hounds, 570 miles north-west of Vienna in the cosmopolitan city of Brussels, things were beginning to stir in the household of his father Charles, 4th Duke of Richmond. At 7.30 a.m. Lord William's three youngest brothers were woken by their twenty-three-year-old tutor Spencer Madan, so that by breakfast time at 9 a.m. they had already had morning prayers and begun their lessons. Schoolwork was recommenced at 10 a.m. and finished at 12.30, at about the same time as the Duke, having risen at 11 a.m., finished his breakfast and began his day.

In August of the preceding year, the Duke of Richmond had moved to Brussels, where his son and heir Lord March was Aide-de-camp to the Prince of Orange. Lord March, an intelligent-looking, clean-cut, handsome and popular twenty-three-year-old, had been assistant military secretary to Wellington during the Peninsular War. He was still carrying a musket ball in his chest from a wound received at Orthès, and was liable to pass out if the temperature dropped suddenly. This wound would have been a source of pride as well as pain, for the Richmond clan was strong on military tradition, as the present generation demonstrated. The Duke, a general, was often painted in uniform. Of his seven sons, six went into the Army, one rebelled and joined the Navy.

As a young man the Duke of Richmond had been rather dashing, famous for having fought a duel with the Duke of York in 1789. Now, twenty-five years later, aged fifty, jowly and with thinning hair, his kindly good looks were overlaid with a tired melancholy air; 'he is become the most Gloomy Melancholy person I ever met with,' commented the wife of an old friend, 'but still keeps his warmth & cordiality of heart.'[1] Some of his melancholy, and his jowliness, could have been ascribed to his habit of sitting up till early in the morning smoking and drinking. His drinking routine was recalled by his children's tutor.

> Our dining hour, called $\frac{1}{2}$ past 5 is usually 6, and the Duke, who never allows coffee to be announced, sits after dinner as long as any one will drink with him and when the company decline his pressing proposal for another bottle of claret, he orders coffee in the dining room or upstairs, after which liqueurs are handed round. When he is tired of the party of the night he withdraws, accompanied by a select few to smoke segars and drink punch till a late or rather early hour in the morning.[2]

The picture of a depressive heavy drinker, if not an alcoholic, was perhaps understandable to those who knew his wife, Charlotte. The Duchess of Richmond would have driven anyone to drink; arrogant, overbearing, capricious, snobbish, and ruthless in her schemes for marrying her seven daughters to rich aristocrats, she was a difficult woman who alienated everyone from her social peers, who described her as 'a difficult person to deal with and withal a dreadful *mischief maker*'[3] and 'a person not to be depended on',[4] to her children's tutor, who wished her 'at the bottom of the pond'.[5]

The Duchess's volatile temper was not improved by leaving England. 'A shade of ill-humour is superadded to her usual acidity of temper by the thoughts of going abroad,'[6] and this acid temper already exacerbated by xenophobic ill-humour was probably inflamed by snobbish contempt for the house her husband had rented for them in Brussels. By 20 August, when the Duke of Richmond had arrived in Brussels, all the smart houses available for rent in the fashionable upper part of the town around the park had been taken by English families who had arrived earlier. Friends anticipated that the Duke would have 'the greatest difficulty in getting a House large enough' that would also be 'in an Eligible situation'.[7] And they were right. The house the Duke ended up in may have had a large garden and spacious outbuildings, but it belonged to the son of a coachmaker and was in the unfashionable lower town with its light industry and muddy unpaved streets.

Towards the end of the preceding century, Jean Simons had enjoyed a reputation as a fashionable coachbuilder known for his '*voiture vitrée*'[8] and his house on the rue de la Blanchisserie, some way from the social hub of the park, had also been the location of his workshops and showrooms housed in the wings, their large galleried rooms illuminated by tall windows. The Napoleonic wars had killed his business and his son was happy to let the house to a visiting English aristocrat. A late-eighteenth-century engraving published in *Country Life*, now in the archives in Brussels, shows a pleasant house, with two large wings.[9] There was a separate cottage in the garden for the Earl of March and the large former workshops, now decorated with an appealing trellis wallpaper, served as a schoolroom and indoor games area for the younger members of the Duke's family of fourteen children. It was a big house: the garden was about 450 feet long, bounded on one side by the ramparts, and from the upper storeys there were views out to the Palace of Lacken three or four miles away. The rambling nature of the property would at least enable the Duke to keep out of his wife's way.

To understand what the Richmonds were doing in Brussels it is necessary to examine the events of the spring of the preceding year. In March 1814, Paris had capitulated to Allied forces, ending the rule of Napoleon across Europe. On 3 May the fat, gout-stricken Louis XVIII, brother of the guillotined Louis XVI, had made his ceremonial entry into the French capital. He had returned claiming that he had been King of France ever since the day his nephew, little Louis XVII, had died of tuberculosis in 1795. Even though he had spent over two decades in exile, it was almost as if the intervening years of Revolution and Napoleon's Imperium had never happened.

With 'legitimate' rule once more established in France, the occupying forces had departed and the British Army, which had fought since 1808 in the Peninsula, was shipped back to London from Bordeaux. That year the London season 'had been one of the greatest gaiety. Napoleon had abdicated the throne of the world – the Bourbons had been restored – Louis XVIII had quitted England – the warehouse for bonded sovereigns (as it had been called),' and just as Louis XVIII cleared off to reclaim his family's throne a quarter of a century after his brother had vacated it,

> kings, emperors, princes, potentates, had flocked to London, which was thronged with the votaries of fashion and pleasure. Fêtes, operas, balls, masquerades, dinners, concerts, illuminations, naval and military reviews, formed the order of the day and night. Everybody was dining out, supping out, driving out, and hunting the royal and imperial lions.[10]

When news of Napoleon's abdication reached England, curious and intrepid travellers made arrangements to visit the Continent, excited to go to Europe at such an historic time, 'eager to seize the chance of viewing the wreck of Napoleon's empire while the country was still ringing with rumours of battles and sieges'.[11] As soon as the French ports were open, hundreds began to prepare their journeys, travelling to London to get a passport, and asking influential friends and relatives to pen letters of introduction to those Britons abroad who might prove useful. Thus, on 5 June, a large family party of ten children, their parents and about half a dozen servants had invaded the Ship Inn in Dover.

The Hon. John Thomas and Lady Caroline Capel were connected to the highest social circles in England. John Thomas Capel was the son of the 4th Earl of Essex, half-brother to the 5th Earl of Essex; in time Capel's son Algernon would become the 6th Earl and his other children would, by royal decree, 'be granted the same title and precedence as if their father had succeeded to the Earldom of Essex'.[12] His wife was from an equally illustrious family; daughter of the 9th Baron Paget (a close friend of George III and Queen Charlotte) who had been raised to the title Earl of Uxbridge. Her eldest brother, Lord Paget, who inherited the title of Earl of Uxbridge on the death of their father, was one of the most dashing cavalry commanders of his age.

While undeniably in possession of a perfect pedigree, the Capels were, like quite a number of aristocrats, virtually flat broke. During the early nineteenth century, debt carried stigma and the threat of imprisonment. Moreover, Capel was addicted to gambling. During the eighteenth and early nineteenth centuries gambling was a mania that bankrupted many grand families. Even though he was not a first son and therefore had no estate to fritter away at the tables, by 1804 he had run up the very considerable debt of £20,000 (rather more than a million pounds today).

Precarious family finances were further prejudiced by the fact that there were very few occupations, in the modern sense of an activity that would return money, suitable for the half-brother of an earl, let alone one with a chronic gambling habit. As it happened, his wife's family had been able to arrange a couple of sinecures for him, which brought in around £2,000 per annum, and he enjoyed a private income of about the same amount. But even had he not been a gambling addict, he would have found it difficult to maintain an aristocratic way of life with an ever-growing family. During the years of war with France not even the upper class was insulated from the soaring cost of living occasioned by the expense of waging a protracted war.

For much of their married life the Capels had relied on the hospitality of Lady Caroline's mother – the dowager Countess of Uxbridge. The only other option would have been to seek a cheaper way of life abroad. However, with the brief exception of the phoney peace of Amiens of 1802, which ended abruptly but not entirely unexpectedly in May 1803, Continental travel had been an impossibility during the revolutionary and then Napoleonic wars that had convulsed Europe for a generation. The cessation of hostilities could not come soon enough for those, like the Capels, who were starved of the stimulation of foreign travel and desperately in need of a more forgiving financial climate.

For Capel, the defeat of Napoleon was the news he had been waiting for. And the French emperor had not even arrived on Elba before Capel had started looking for a house abroad where he and his family might live on what was politely known as 'an economical plan'.

Brussels had obvious benefits for the Capels and those like them, including their friend the Duke of Richmond. It offered cheap metropolitan living and the excitement of foreign travel relatively close to England: travelling with so many children (like the Richmonds, the Capels were philoprogenitive and would eventually have over a dozen offspring) and servants was a difficult, uncomfortable and, most alarming of all, expensive business.

There had been a scramble among the financially embarrassed upper classes, desperate to reduce their outgoings, as to who would get over to the Continent first to snap up the bargain properties. 'Capel would have gone to Brussels last week to procure a House,' wrote his mother-in-law, the dowager Countess of Uxbridge, on 22 April, 'but many Foreigners, and others, advised waiting a little while.'[13] It was as well to heed such advice, as what Capel had suggested would have been tantamount to going house-hunting in a war zone. Nevertheless it had become clear to old Lady Uxbridge that as soon as circumstances permitted there would be a huge exodus of impoverished British aristocrats to the Low Countries. 'We must make up our Minds to losing many of our friends; they will all fly to the Continent.'[14]

The Capels had been in the first wave of economic migrants to make the trip to Brussels. So keen were they to get away and ease the expense – doubtless part of the attraction for Capel was that in Brussels he would be beyond the reach of his creditors – that at Dover they crossed over with the Allied leaders coming into Britain for the victory celebrations in London, triumphal arches and eagles lining their proposed route.

The Capel family had been fortunate enough to meet up with Lord Rosslyn, the general commanding the south-eastern district, who was also an old family friend, and he had secured them a wonderful position from which to see the victors who landed at two o'clock in the afternoon on 7 June: the Capel children were delighted by a string of celebrities including the King of Prussia, the Emperor of Russia, the snowy-haired, fiery-tempered General Blücher and numerous princes.

Another family friend, Sir Charles Stuart, brother of one of the most able politicians of the nineteenth century, Lord Castlereagh, had been on hand to introduce them to some of the princes and generals, bringing them to the family's sitting room on the ground floor of the inn. But the moment the crowd had caught sight of Blücher shaking hands with and kissing the Capel children, they smashed the windows and broke into the room. A further visitor to the Capels was Admiral of the Fleet the Duke of Clarence, later King William IV.

While their parents had waited for a passage across the Channel, Caroline doubtless fretting over the expense of a protracted stay at the Ship Inn, the children had been kept amused by the excitement of a town packed with exotic foreigners – Cossacks and Junkers, princes and generals – all of whom who must have seemed like visitors from another planet. The rooms and corridors of the inn echoed to a cacophonous babble of different languages and dialects. 'If we stir out of this Room we must pass such a Phalanx of Foreigners of all Nations & Ranks – this is rather inconvenient as our sitting Room is on the Ground Floor,' wrote seventeen-year-old Maria Capel. 'But *I* think it *all* the best fun.'[15] Rockets had been fired, 21- and 100-gun salutes roared out, the horses had been unhitched from Blücher's carriage and it had been dragged along by an ecstatic crowd.

Bluff old Blücher was a particular favourite with the mob, and if they could not find the Prussian Field Marshal himself, they would seize upon any likely-looking foreigner, almost pulling him to pieces in their good-natured excitement. On hearing that Blücher was in a particular place, the mob had stormed in and hoisted on their shoulders a man they took for the hard-drinking, foul-mouthed, gambling-addicted Prussian soldier, almost ripping his coat off. The poor man was, however, the Prince of Liechtenstein and, having no idea why he was being carried bodily away by the mob, had cried out for his A.D.C. to hang on to him as tight as he could. Such scenes had been repeated throughout the summer of 1814 as the victors were received by rapturous crowds who, unable to make the trip to the Continent, had to make do with 'Emperor hunting'[16] around London, ripping the clothes off any unwary war hero they came across in a spirit of enthusiastic, albeit robust, souvenir seeking. 'Can the English ever be called cool and phlegmatic again?' wondered one lady who witnessed the tumultuous reception of the Allied leaders. 'It is really a pity some metaphysicianising philosopher is not here to observe, describe, and theorise on the extraordinary symptoms and effects of enthusiasm, curiosity, insanity – I am sure I do not know what to call it – en masse.'[17]

Through their connections the Capels had been able to enjoy a unique and privileged position at an historic moment and yet all the time the spectre of their poverty hovered over them. Every day that their sailing to the Continent was delayed meant further expenditure on accommodation in a town where rooms were so hard to come by that Blücher had slept one night in a rented carriage. 'If we are obliged to stay here we must live upon Mackerel for 9000 came in yesterday & they are of course very cheap,'[18] wrote one of the Capel daughters.

Eventually, after a week's wait, the Capels, their carriages, their servants and their luggage had made the crossing to Calais and then travelled by carriage to Dunkirk. Everywhere they had been followed by curious townsfolk, and their mood had not been improved by the fact that they wanted to travel to Bruges by canal barge but had been 'prevented from putting this economical manner of travelling into execution as the Carriages cannot be got into the Barge'.[19]

Frustration at the mounting expense of what was meant to be an economical plan had brought forth a string of complaints about 'odiously dull & stupid'[20] Dunkirk, and a landscape that was 'hideous, flat and like the ugliest part of Kent without its agriculture'.[21] And while the people had been grudgingly acknowledged to be very civil, 'their Horses are disgusting; and as for the Vehicles they *call* Carriages they would disgrace a stand of Hackney Coaches in London'.[22]

Out of England for only a few hours, and among the very first British civilian families to travel in Europe for over a decade, the Capels had already adopted the default position of the British aristocracy abroad: namely, reassuring themselves that everything at home is better and that there is no situation more fortunate than being born into the English upper classes. 'The little that I have already seen of the Continent makes me love & admire dear England more than I did before,' wrote nineteen-year-old Georgiana Capel. In fact the only thing that had kept them from turning back was that they might soon reach the promised land of the economical plan. 'We are all very anxious to reach Bruxelles which has, we hear from all quarters, every perfection . . .'[23]

2

'The English families rendered Brussels
very gay'[1]

Belgium had been one of the last places in Europe where Napoleonic rule had prevailed. While Paris had capitulated to the Allied forces at the end of March 1814, parts of the Belgian provinces still loyal to the French emperor had held out against the Allies into May.

The British had been campaigning in the Low Countries since the end of 1813, when a surprise Dutch rebellion against French rule presented Britain with the chance to seize the important harbour and naval base of Antwerp. However the British offensive in the Low Countries, led by General Graham (created Lord Lynedoch in 1814), was largely ineffectual, if not downright bungling.

The most positive complexion on events was that the British troops 'were, I believe, of some use in keeping the French garrisons of Antwerp, Bergen-op-Zoom, and other fortresses, within their walls'.[2] Indeed, it was only after Louis XVIII had assumed power, and therefore control of the armed forces, that French troops were ordered out of Belgium and British forces allowed to enter their strongholds.

However, within a couple of months Belgium had become like a Jane Austen novel that had gone on a Continental holiday. The topography of the town lent itself admirably to the re-creation of the pattern of life as led in a fashionable British spa town.

The dainty little park, where every morning troops paraded to the sound of a British military band, was the geographic and social hub of life in Brussels. 'Park is a misnomer,' wrote Cavalié Mercer, an artillery officer, 'consider it a *square*, in our acceptation of the term, and it is one of the most beautiful in Europe.' It may have been small, but it exceeded 'in beauty, if not in size, any of ours in London'.[3]

And those British émigrés who had been lucky and quick enough to get houses overlooking the park were charmed by

> [the] pretty lawns and thick shrubberies, with fine trees, etc., enclosed by a handsome iron railing, and surrounded by fine houses, the façades ornamented by Ionic pilasters, and painted in delicate tints of buff, green, etc., or white, and the whole forming a splendid spectacle and delicious spot. The park is laid out in walks winding through shrubberies and dingles, affording varied and pleasing scenery, some part of the ground being broken and uneven. In the centre is a sort of pavilion where refreshments are sold, and near it is a sheet of water, etc.[4]

The picturesque, elevated location was further enhanced by the old ramparts around which it was possible to walk, shaded by tall trees, and from which the view over the rest of the town and the surrounding countryside was very attractive.

The diversions the expatriate community had enjoyed since their arrival in Brussels would have been familiar in England. There was 'a respectable club',[5] also known as the '*Literary Club*',[6] where newly arrived British gentlemen would have themselves proposed for membership. Ostensibly a place to 'meet the best company in Brussels',[7] read the newspapers and enjoy 'an excellent dinner at 3 francs a head',[8] this respectable exterior was so effective at camouflaging its role as the local gambling hell that it took one British aristocrat's wife a year to find out that her husband had been gaming while she thought he had gone to read the papers.

There had been race meetings got up by the anglophile young Prince of Orange, his A.D.C. Lord March, the Duke of Richmond and other men who had brought racehorses over with them, with some of the owners riding their own horses. Reports of what were called the 'Brussels races' had even appeared in the English newspapers.

For those not keen on gambling and racing there was a part of the 'parc' called Vauxhall, with a small theatre and excellent displays of fireworks, just as in the London Pleasure Garden of the same name. The Windsor theatrical company had come over to put on an indifferent English play, which nevertheless had enjoyed a long run, and for four nights had played to a packed house, when the celebrated actress (and mistress of the Duke of Clarence), Mrs Jordan, appeared on stage.

There had been outings to the country, including one memorable picnic breakfast in the Forest of Soignes given by General Graham, who had turned out to be a better party planner than he had been invader of the Netherlands. As the band of the 52nd Regiment of Foot played, and horn music reverberated through the forest, guests ate under canvas and then, when the heat of the summer day had mellowed into the cool of evening, the General fearlessly led a cavalcade of twenty-six carriages on a drive through the forest. The only casualty during an otherwise faultlessly executed manoeuvre had been a carriage spring, which broke, throwing an unfortunate coachman to the ground.

Shooting parties and wolf hunting in the Ardennes had also become part of the social menu. One particularly grand wolf hunt had lasted a fortnight and had involved celebrated English visitors such as the Duke of Richmond and the Hon. John Thomas Capel moving from one grand chateau to another with an escort of Prussian cavalry. Once the hunters returned to Brussels after their two weeks of good living and good hunting, their bag had been hung in outhouses and for three days crowds jostled with each other to admire the animals' carcasses.

Very soon the social tensions that dominated life among the county families and London elite at home surfaced in the microcosm of fashionable English society that had sprung up on the other side of the English Channel. Once sufficient numbers of English people had moved to Brussels the same sort of social divisions that had kept factions of society apart in London became evident. 'The Ladies in the Park'[9] was the name given to the smart set, criticised for making the rule of visiting only those whom they had known in London. Perhaps the reason the 'The Ladies in the Park' kept themselves to themselves was that there had been enough bickering, affairs and elopements to fuel gossip among themselves, with one of them writing 'this is without exception the most Gossiping Place I ever heard of', that they had no need of others.[10] Indeed such had been the level of 'gossiping' that by definition a '*Bruxelles story* means a scandalous, or untrue one'.[11]

The inhabitants of Brussels were somewhat astonished by the behaviour of the British community that had established itself so quickly and become a dominant social force. Some, however, had professed to be, in the words of one British lady at least, 'delighted at the Brilliant Gaiety of Bruxelles which they all say they owe to the English'.[12] They had begun to adjust to the hours of the ever-increasing number of British aristocrats living in the city, with balls ending later and later. For their part, the English had brushed up on their ballroom manoeuvres. 'I must say that, in dancing, the English, both male and female, had to yield the palm to the *Bruxellois*,' recalled one officer stationed in Brussels. 'However, not liking to be outdone, even in dancing, many of our officers took lessons,' doubtless pleased by the reasonable rates charged by dancing instructors, 'and in time were able to make at least a respectable appearance, both in the quadrille and the waltz.'[13]

Some of the Bruxelloises wanted more than a waltz. The whiff of illicit sex with dashing officers had proved irresistible to some of the Brussels belles; 'the young ladies of the place had got a notion into their silly heads that Englishmen were prone to *enlèvements*,'[14] and far from being offended by flirtations, they were often upset that the amorous advances of the occupying forces were not more ardent.

But while the local girls may have been offended at the lack of attention, some young British women had been getting more than their share. At one time the young Prince of Orange was thought to be paying too much attention to the young women of the Capel household, in particular nineteen-year-old Georgiana, and her parents had to devise a stratagem to keep them apart.

Happily there were plenty of other young men to flirt with. Lord Erroll's dashing, young and 'very good-looking',[15] very well-dressed and impecunious son, James Lord Hay, was part of the Capel set and flirted with Maria, naming his favourite mare Miss Muzzy after her, while 'fire eating'[16] Major-General Barnes, who had proposed unsuccessfully to Maria Capel, spent so much time with them that people began to ask Lady Caroline, 'which of your Daughters is Genl. B to marry? Or is he to marry *them all*?'[17]

Certainly it was not to be Maria; she felt that while 'violent love' was not vital in such matters at least 'decided preference' was necessary and her preference had been for a General Ferguson. And it seems that the way in which this teenage temptress bestowed her ... ahem ... 'preference' raised a few eyebrows: 'above all, a young Lady, a Miss C___l, quite astonished me by a display of manners more *highly fashionable*,' wrote one scandalised observer, 'I conclude, than I was before at all aware of. I am almost ashamed to say that she appeared to be absolutely making love to a handsome General on whose arm she was hanging, and who, I am told, is not the first, second or third, who has been equally honoured.'[18]

It would seem that Caroline Capel had been either unaware of, or had ignored, the scandal surrounding her daughter. Perhaps she had been too overcome with relief at the ease with which they had set up their establishment to worry about anything else. For the first time in years it had seemed to her that their fortunes were looking up. If the Capels had anticipated any problems getting hold of a house that was smart and cheap enough, these worries had vanished when it transpired that General Graham had managed to instruct the mayor of Brussels to find the Capels a house and appoint someone to look after them. The military was at the disposal of certain civilian visitors: for instance, when their heavy luggage arrived from England a dragoon had been despatched at once to make sure that all was in order and four military baggage wagons had been made available to bring the luggage to Brussels. Once again the Capels' connections had helped them immeasurably.

By 23 June Lady Caroline had been able to write to her mother from a large house with not two but *three* staircases and a grand entrance hall, in the centre of town overlooking the park, about her favourite topic, the economy of life in Brussels: 'it is wonderful how cheap every thing [*sic*] is here and the exchange is improving every day.'[19] Successive letters had contained further evidence of the miraculous economies that were being made: 'I can really say that every Article of living is above half as cheap as in dear England,'[20] Lady Caroline had assured her mother, adding a mass of statistical evidence relating to her bills to reassure her ageing parent. From mutton to music masters, satin shoes to silk stockings, prices had struck Lady Caroline as miraculous.

However, not everything had gone smoothly. During the summer of 1814 there had been a spate of burglaries, all perpetrated against English residents. There had also been friction with local society.

> The inhabitants of this Town have now declared open warfare with the English residing here – The *Ladies* abuse every thing we wear & every thing we do – The *Gentlemen* are not so severe, & declare that their Countrywomen are burning with spite envy and jealousy at the superiority of the Englishwomen – this as you may suppose does not mend matters and it really is become very entertaining.[21]

Separated for so long, the two societies had developed along markedly different lines; for instance, the residents of Brussels found it remarkable that the British should stay up so late and drink so much. Balls in Brussels traditionally began at 8 p.m. and ended at what some English people thought the very tame hour of 1 a.m. Some British visitors had taken steps to enliven the rather staid and decorous local dances, as one visiting Briton recorded in a letter home to his brother.

> You would have been much amused had you been present at a public ball here last Saturday, some mischievous Wag put some quick operating

Medicine into a glass of wine, and gave it to a Belgian Lady, the consequences were natural enough, and more what Richard Weatherstone likes to happen to his horses when they trot to work off their physic, when the unfortunate B__ began to dance after Supper, the medicine operated in a way impossible to describe, the Waiters exerted themselves and brought perfume and S__ [Scent?] to take off the unfortunate (tho' horrid) smell. I was not present but I had the above report verbatim from undoubted authority.[22]

While the Bruxellois had found themselves faced with the crude lavatorial sense of humour and cruel practical jokes of the British, the visitors had been confronted with new patterns of eating such as the *déjeuner à la fourchette*, a meal that took place in the middle of the day and would eventually become known by the English as luncheon.

Nevertheless, unusual mealtimes and the spectre of 'foreignization'[23] had not deterred other English people from visiting Brussels, especially as the British garrison gave the place an English ambience; 'really it was a gratification in passing the gate to see a fat John Bull keeping guard with his red coat,'[24] noted one English visitor with relief when he arrived in Brussels.

Old Lady Uxbridge's prediction that there would be an exodus to the Continent had been right. The summer and early autumn of 1814 had seen the expatriate community expand hugely.

A very ill Lord Mountnorris had appeared on 21 June attended by his wife and two daughters. In July, Sir Charles Greville and his wife Lady Charlotte, daughter of the Duke of Portland, had passed through Brussels on a tour of the Continent and had been so enchanted with it that they had taken the last available smart house near the park with a view to settling there in September, Lady Charlotte quickly and enthusiastically adopting Continental fashions and becoming a prominent hostess. Among the most interesting visitors to have arrived at this time was Thomas Creevey, a Whig politician, who had recently been prosecuted and convicted for libel. Added to this personal humiliation was the fact that his political career was stalled as long as the Tory party was in power and the Whig opposition in disarray. Given these circumstances, his wife's ill-health and his stretched finances, he felt little inclination to appear at the House of Commons, and instead had taken a house in Brussels in the hope that the move would improve his wife's health and his own bank balance. Creevey's was a lively mind which sparkled in Brussels; he had a habit of speaking without thinking, was cheerfully candid and was the sort of intelligent, gossipy good company that made him a welcome guest in the salons overlooking the park. He responded to life in Brussels with enthusiasm, delighting in his social triumphs and taking a keen interest in everything and everyone around him.

What had started out as a desperate cost-cutting measure had become a fashion statement: Brussels had become an established stop on the itinerary of those British tourists doing the Napoleonic tour. As 1814 wore on, travelling to the Netherlands had become decidedly chic and in the words of one visitor hotels were 'very full of English, much too full'.[25]

3

'Austria has sold the Netherlands and Brabant to England'

The anglicising of Belgium had also taken on an important political dimension. Barely had the very earliest émigrés settled in Brussels, when a concerted diplomatic and political campaign was launched to bring the territory into Britain's sphere of influence. Inasmuch as England had anything approaching a 'European' policy, it was to foster closer links with the newly created United Netherlands: Britain's pied-à-terre on the Continent, a client state, a buffer between France and Germany and a corridor linking Britain to its Prussian Allies.

On the French invasion of the Netherlands, members of the ruling House of Orange had fled to England; the young Prince William of Orange, who was now a fun-loving man in his early twenties, had been just three years old. So, while he had been born in The Hague into one of the grandest European families, his upbringing had been entirely English; he had even joined Wellington's staff in the Peninsula and been promoted to the rank of major-general in the British Army. Nicknamed 'Slender Billy', on account of his long neck, or the 'young frog' (his father being the 'old frog'), Prince William was thoroughly anglicised, perfectly pleasant and rather stupid. His portrait by Copley shows him in a cocked hat, holding a sword. It has something of the air of a child in fancy dress about it.

It had been hoped that relations between England and the House of Orange would be strengthened by a politically propitious marriage between Slender Billy and Princess Charlotte, daughter of the Prince Regent and granddaughter of the reigning but raving King George III. News of the impending nuptials had been bruited about since May, but as the young frog had spent much of his time in England getting drunk, going to the races and, on one memorable occasion, returning from Ascot hanging from the back of a stage coach, Princess Charlotte had terminated the engagement. In this story the Princess had not kissed the young frog.

But, even after the young Prince of Orange had been jilted by Princess Charlotte, faint hopes of some sort of dynastic union had survived. On 1 September Lady Caroline Capel had written that 'there is a Party here who want the Duke of Cambridge [brother of the Prince Regent and son of George III] to marry the Duchess of Oldenburg, to have this Country ceded to England, & that he should reside here & have the Government of it'.[1]

In the absence of tying the Netherlands to Britain by means of marriage, the British were still keen to show their support and approbation for the fledgling United Netherlands. One rumour 'current all over the Continent' during the summer of 1814 had been 'that Austria has sold the Netherlands and Brabant to England'.[2] Such rumours could only have been further fuelled when, in August 1814, a couple of months after the more intrepid, and impoverished, British aristocrats had settled in Brussels, the Duke of Wellington paid a visit to this newest of European nations.

He had been on his way to take up his post as Britain's ambassador in Paris, but in a significant move, instead of heading direct to the French capital, he had travelled via the Netherlands and toured the country's fortifications. The message to France, and indeed any other acquisitive Continental power, had been clear – that the British intended to defend the sovereignty of the Netherlands. The timing, preceding the Congress of Nations that had been called in Vienna, had demonstrated quite publicly Britain's almost proprietorial feelings towards the Low Countries.

The United Kingdom of the Netherlands was the name given to the new country invented after the fall of Napoleonic France: a buffer state creating a barrier between Bourbon France and territorially ambitious Prussia. It incorporated Belgian provinces (the former Austrian Netherlands) and Dutch provinces, placing them under the rule of the House of Orange. However, the name could not have been more misleading. There was nothing remotely united about this small soggy stretch of northern European coastline. Fractured along religious, linguistic and political lines, the rule of the House of Orange was deeply resented by the Catholic majority in the south.

Many people, including, most significantly, Napoleon, viewed Belgium as a part of France: the language as well as the religious and cultural leanings of many Belgians inclined them more towards the French than their Protestant neighbours in the Netherlands. In his history of Europe, Norman Davies writes that 'Brussels and Paris shared the same language. News travelled fast between them. The 'Belgian Revolt', which continued to run long after the emperor's coup, was an essential component of the 'French Revolution'. 'Paris did not lead Brussels; Brussels led Paris.'[3]

In line with Britain's policy of strengthening the borders of the newly constituted country, British troops had been redeployed accordingly. Graham had handed over as commander-in-chief to the Prince of Orange, and the summer and autumn of 1814 had seen the remains of Graham's force moved from the Dutch part of the kingdom into the border towns that the Duke of Wellington had visited. Once there, they had found that preserving the country from external attack was not their only duty. Thomas Morris of the 73rd Regiment made this assessment:

> I believe the motive for quartering the British troops through the towns of Belgium, at this time, was to ensure the tranquillity of the people, until the annexation of Belgium to Holland should be carried into effect, as agreed on by the Allied Powers, in their settlement of the boundaries of the different states.
>
> Belgium, of right, belonged to Austria; but that power readily agreed to its being joined to Holland, on their receiving an equivalent for it. [Austria was to be apportioned part of northern Italy to compensate it for the loss of the Netherlands.] In another quarter, the proclamation of the (now) King of Holland, in reference to the incorporation of the two countries, was very unpopular; so much so, that where we were, they could not prevail on any of the inhabitants to assist in the reading of it; and that duty had to be performed under a guard of British bayonets. It was easy then to predict, that the union of two countries, different in religion, language, customs, and manners, would exist only as long as a foreign army should be there to enforce it.[4]

Consequently, there had been grumblings about naked British self-interest. 'Poor England is certainly not much beloved,' wrote one visitor, 'we are admired, feared, respected, and courted; but these people will have, and perhaps with some reason, that upon all occasions our own Interest is the sole object of consideration; that our Treaties have the good of ourselves and not the peace of Europe at heart.'[5]

However, while the rule of the House of Orange was being enforced at the point of British bayonets, and Britain's conduct was being bad-mouthed in public, the British aristocracy were living the good life in Brussels; doubtless feeling that their presence had been tacitly legitimised by the high-profile visit of Wellington, whose arrival in Brussels had been attended by almost as much public enthusiasm as the arrival of the Allied sovereigns had occasioned in England earlier in the summer. Wherever he had gone Wellington had been cheered and fêted. Indeed, the mere sight of Wellington's carriage had provoked a stampede of excitement, as the stage-struck Lord William Pitt Lennox had discovered to his acute embarrassment, when he found himself mistaken for the Duke simply because he had used his chief's carriage to get to the theatre and had occupied his box.

On 12 August, Brussels had been taken over by celebrations of the Prince Regent's birthday. There had been a birthday parade around the park, the Duke of Wellington had been rapturously received by an enthusiastic crowd, and in the evening Lord Clancarty, the British ambassador, had given a ball. After the Regent's birthday had been appropriately marked in Brussels, it had been time to celebrate the birthday of his brother, the Commander-in-Chief of the British Army, the Duke of York.

And then, having thrown parties in absentia for members of the British royal family, Brussels had at last seen a real live royal duke, in the person of Adolphus Frederick Duke of Cambridge, seventh and favourite son of George III. As well as paying frequent visits to his old friends the Capels, who referred to him as the 'dear old Duke of Cambridge' (he had celebrated his fortieth birthday in 1814) or the abbreviated and decidedly unregal nickname 'Cam', he had been, in effect, a goodwill ambassador: the acceptable, sane and relatively virtuous face of the British royal family.

Writing home to her grandmother in advance of the Duke of Cambridge's visit, Harriet Capel had hit upon the effect that his visit was intended to have.

> The Prince of Orange is expected here on Sunday – this creates great pleasure in *general*, tho' there is a strong Party against him – As long as we have an English Garrison here, I don't care for any thing, but the possibility of ever losing *that* is dreadful – I had a dear Letter from *Cam* the other day, & he speaks almost with certainty of seeing us here – this will be delightful – The inhabitants of Brussels ought to see him, as a *good* specimen of our Princes – hitherto they have only been acquainted with the *Duke of Clarence* [later King William IV] who does not do much honour to his Country. [6]

'Cam' had proved a hit in Brussels society – the town insisted on supplying him with a house during his stay and on his appearance at the theatre, the whole building was illuminated, the band struck up 'God Save the

King' and the audience took off their hats, cheered and applauded.

Next, Lord Castlereagh, Britain's gifted foreign secretary, had arrived in Brussels on his way to the Congress of Vienna and had invested the Prince of Orange and his son with the Orders of the Garter and Bath. In his speech 'he dwelt with admiration upon his conduct during the Peninsular campaign; adding a confident assurance that the same zeal would be displayed by him, in his newly restored country, should its safety or the repose of Europe be endangered'.[7] The Prince of Orange had been quite overcome with emotion.

Castlereagh's moving oratory had of course been a bravura piece of politically motivated diplomatic cant. 'The Prince is a brave young man, but that's all,'[8] had been Wellington's characteristically laconic appraisal of the military capabilities of the heir to the Dutch throne, which was not saying much, as Wellington considered courage a characteristic of the fighting man that was remarkable only when it was absent. Indeed, the only zeal that the young Prince of Orange had shown vis-à-vis his 'newly restored' (perhaps newly created might have been more accurate) country was for enjoying himself. He had thrown himself enthusiastically and energetically into a punishing party schedule: on one occasion leaving a wedding ball at The Hague at three o'clock in the morning and galloping eighty miles in five hours to be back in Brussels as soon as he could, where he flitted in and out of smart British households with an easy informality, refraining from being announced by servants and generally making himself as at home among the expatriate British as 'a *tame Cat*'.[9]

Nevertheless, the House of Orange was all that the British had to hand, and, having demonstrated their support for the new Kingdom in a most public and ostentatious fashion, Britain's emissaries had gone their various ways. The Duke of Wellington had set off for Paris as ambassador. Viscount Castlereagh had moved on to the Congress of Vienna as head of the British delegation. The Duke of Cambridge had headed back to his family's home town of Hanover.

Wellington's move to Paris had presented the opportunity of a diplomatic reshuffle. Sir Charles Stuart, who had been running the British Embassy in Paris, had been transferred to the Netherlands to replace Clancarty, who was off to Vienna as part of Castlereagh's delegation. Clancarty had been a popular and highly social appointment. His successor was a different man: more cynical, less sentimental, colder, harder, no less correct but far less social than his predecessor. 'He is a plain man, of some prejudices, caring little for politics and of very good practical sense' had been the way Brougham put it in a letter to his friend Creevey in Brussels.

You will find none of his prejudices (which, after all, are little or nothing) at all of an aristocratic or disagreeable kind. He has no very violent passions or acute feelings about him, and likes to go quietly on and enjoy himself in his way. He has read a great deal and seen much more, and done, for his standing, more business than any diplomatic man I ever heard of. By the way – as for *diplomacy*, or rather its foppery, he has none of the thing about him; and if you ever think him close or buttoned up, I assure you he had it all his life just as much. He has no nonsense in his composition, and is a strictly honourable man, and one over whom nobody will ever acquire the slightest influence.'[10]

Brougham had been spot-on in his analysis of this serious-minded man: four months into the job he had seen little of English high society in Brussels. 'Lady Charlotte Greville, Lady Caroline Capel, and the Duchess of Richmond are the principal English at Brussels,' Stuart had written, adding, 'I am so much on the road that I have not many opportunities of frequenting their society, and I think my gaieties are confined to two or three visits to Lady Charlotte.'[11]

4

~~~

'His Majesty has been graciously pleased to express his opinion that no sentence for corporal punishment should exceed 1,000 lashes'

As Stuart's example had shown, there was more to being British in Belgium in 1814 than the nexus of deracinated British aristocrats in Brussels who had turned the park and its surroundings into an Anglophone resort. Life in the border towns had also been affected, following the decision to garrison them with British and Allied troops.

For instance, officers in the King's German Legion, which had been formed as a force for non-British troops wishing to fight Napoleon, and was led by German and British officers (the latter often being too poor to be able to purchase a commission in a smart regiment), had found a scaled-down version of the charms of Brussels in the border town of Tournai, where there were weekly public balls and a theatre 'somewhat larger than our Country playhouses such as Richmond, Bexhill etc'.[1]

In Brussels the influx of fashionable British had been such that the normal social balance had been disrupted, resulting in friction between the expats and the Bruxellois. In Tournai, however, the locals had reserved their antipathy and social competitiveness for each other. British officers had been able to observe an animosity between the trades-people and the local aristocracy so fierce that 'it requires the nicest discrimination of deportment to preserve the good opinion and acquaintance of the two Classes'.[2] Nevertheless, as one King's German Legion officer wrote of his time in Tournai, 'the months I spent there were the most pleasing, the most instructive and the most amusing of any I ever enjoyed'[3] while serving abroad.

Even the lowest form of expatriate life, the British infantryman, had found agreeable diversions. The favourable cost of living on the Continent had yielded a dividend that was enjoyed by common soldiers as well as impoverished aristocrats running from their debts. Strong spirits, or hollands as they were known, were ludicrously cheap, eight pence a quart, and readily available at distillery strength. Thus, with no fighting to occupy them, they reverted to what the Duke of Wellington would have the world believe was their natural state, as 'scum of the earth'.[4] The Duke was famously of the opinion that given the raw material the British Army worked with, 'it is only wonderful that we should be able to make so much out of them afterwards'.[5] Wellington could hardly be accused of sentimentality when analysing the motivation of his men. 'The English soldiers are fellows who have all enlisted for drink – that is the plain fact – they have all enlisted for drink.'[6]

What would now be called alcohol abuse was a cherished national characteristic during the Regency. The British could be counted on to consume quite prodigious quantities of all sorts of alcohol; whether of the finest ports (half a dozen bottles a day was considered sufficient proof of one's masculinity) or the actively poisonous arrack punch served in the pleasure gardens of London. While the fashionable bucks enjoyed their sherry and Madeira, the poor anaesthetised themselves with gin. Many of those who died during the Gordon riots did so from excessive consumption of looted distillery-strength gin. By the beginning of the nineteenth century, with an estimated 50,000 public houses open all day ensuring that no one need ever draw a sober breath, Britain was a nation fuelled by alcohol.

A generous allowance of spirits was of course part of the rations given out by the Army. However, for most men in the ranks (and indeed their officers) it was nowhere nearly enough. During the autumn and winter of 1814, the cheapness of spirits in Belgium had given rise to a wave of drunkenness and crime among the British forces. As a result, quite brutal measures had been used to keep the consequences of this appetite for alcohol in check.

Discipline had been maintained with procedures that were little more than torture. At this time the cavalry specialised in a particularly ingenious practice called 'picketing'.

The victim had his hands strapped together and his boots taken off; a peg, about six inches long, was stuck in the ground, and the ball of his right foot was rested upon it, while his extended arms were fastened by a cord to a strong beam. In this position he remained for half an hour or more, suffering the most frightful torture.[7]

But picketing must have been reserved for only relatively minor infractions: during the Peninsular campaign the British Army under Wellington had established a reputation for quite savage discipline – the unauthorised shooting of a pig had been sufficient in one instance to send a man to the gallows. However, the gallows might be judged positively pleasant and humane when compared to the prospect of enduring hundreds of lashes, under which many perpetrators of relatively minor offences could, and did, die. It was not unknown for soldiers to commit suicide out of fear of the lash.

But just in case the mania for flogging was in danger of getting out of hand, the authorities did impose a limit on the number of lashes it was permissible to inflict, in a General Order issued in 1807.

> It appearing to his Majesty that a punishment to the extent of 1,000 lashes is a sufficient example for any breach of military duty, short of a capital offence, and even that number cannot be safely inflicted at any one period, his Majesty has been graciously pleased to express his opinion that no sentence for corporal punishment should exceed 1,000 lashes.[8]

His Majesty's gracious pleasure had been promulgated most vigorously in Belgium where the lash was the preferred method of enforcement. Public floggings with miscreants receiving 500 lashes were not uncommon.

Typical had been the corporal punishment of two soldiers accused of drunkenness and insubordination while stationed in the border town of Courtray, which had been visited by Wellington during the summer. The first man, a grenadier sentenced to 800 lashes, had received 500. Next it had been the turn of his fellow drunkard, a young, small and weak-looking drummer boy, to be tied up and whipped. Having recently been flogged for another misdemeanour, his back had barely healed and the first few strokes had shredded the skin, exposing the bone.

Just before being led out to his punishment he had been given a 'copious draught of hollands', which had sent him into a frenzy. 'Instead of wincing from the stripes, he abused the commanding officer, and sung a variety of scraps of songs. The major who commanded that morning was exasperated at the apparent levity of the prisoner, and abused the drum-major for not making the drummers do their duty more effectually; and for every stroke the drummer gave the poor wretch, he received one from the drum-major's cane, across his own shoulders. At length, the major suspended the punishment' but not out of compassion. Instead he 'selected one of the drummers; and formed what is called a "Drum-head court-martial". The drum-major swore that the man could punish more effect-ively, if he chose. He was found guilty of refusing to do his duty; was tied up there and then, and received one hundred and fifty lashes.'[9] After this interlude the original punishment had continued, but the small weak drummer-boy, having sobered up, had passed out from the agony and was untied and then carried to the hospital unconscious.

What had made these punishments more humiliating was that they were carried out in public on Courtray's 'Esplanade', which was overlooked by the houses of the town's more respectable citizens. Revolted by the particularly barbarous incident involving the drummer, they had com-plained, and thereafter more humane punishments such as extra guard duty and solitary confinement had been adopted. Punishment and drunkenness aside, troops had had to contend with a smallpox scare, but otherwise life could have been worse; military duties had been light, drink cheap, billets pleasant and some of the local women willing to embark on affairs.

A group of soldiers had spent the winter at a public house called the *Parrot*. The septuagenarian landlord of the *Parrot* was believed to have been so jealous as to have poisoned three of his wives. But although he had been investigated twice, nothing had been proven. Undeterred by her husband's reputation as a jealous man who punished infidelity with death, his latest wife (about forty years younger than him) had carried on an illicit and passionate relationship that was far more than a mild flirtation with one of the sergeants billeted at the *Parrot*, 'whose criminal intercourse with her was beyond doubt'.[10]

However, as spring stole upon the Low Countries, there would soon be much more for British troops to fear than jealous husbands and harsh military discipline.

5

'An enemy and disturber of the tranquillity
of the world'

News of Napoleon's escape stunned the Congress of Vienna. Despatches
from Lord Burghersh, the British minister-plenipotentiary to Florence,
confirmed that Napoleon was once more at liberty. The man who until
recently had been joked of as Robinson Crusoe had given his captors the
slip and set sail for mainland Europe.

The traditional course of events has Metternich, Austria's hugely influential foreign minister and the dominant personality of the Congress,
being woken early and dashing off to see the Emperor of Austria, the Tsar
of Russia and the King of Prussia, with the decision to wage war agreed
upon within an hour. However, given the spirit of the Congress and the
tempo of ballroom diplomacy, grace rather than rapidity was the order of
the day and things took a little longer to work out. It was not until midnight
of 13 March, a few hours short of a week after the news had first reached
Vienna, that the Congress issued its famous statement declaring Napoleon
an outlaw:

> Napoleon Bonaparte, by again appearing in France with projects of con-
> fusion and disorder, has deprived himself of the protection of the law, and
> in consequence has placed himself without the pale of civil and social
> relations; and, as an enemy and disturber of the tranquillity of the world,
> has rendered himself liable to public vengeance.[1]

Talleyrand, the club-footed but politically agile and flexible, if not downright elastic, statesman who served France before, during and after the
Revolution, had been a close ally of Napoleon. Subsequently the architect

of the Bourbon restoration and now Louis XVIII's representative in Vienna, he had preferred a harsher, more vindictive form of words for his one-time friend the former emperor ... little wonder that Napoleon neatly cut through court etiquette and called him a shit in a silk stocking.

But even this 'softer' formula left no one in any doubt as to what was intended for Napoleon, and it outraged the more liberal end of the political spectrum in England.

The tone of this statement underlines the seriousness with which the Allied leaders viewed the news of Napoleon's escape. His combination of charisma, ruthlessness, egotism, rapacity and military genius had kept Europe at war on numerous fronts for a generation. The thought that instead of buying lasting peace, the hard-won, bloody victories of the military forces of the rest of Europe had merely purchased a few months' respite from the slaughter, expense and disruption of the Napoleonic wars was too much for the delegates to bear. It must have seemed uncannily like the Treaty of Amiens of 1802, when an uneasy and fragile peace had lasted for a little over a year before the resumption of hostilities. After that treaty was breached, it had taken the combined Armies of, among others, Russia, Austria, Prussia, Saxony, Spain, Portugal and England over a decade to subdue Napoleon and the French. Now it seemed to be happening all over again.

Although he heard about Napoleon's departure from Elba on 7 March, the Duke of Wellington did not leave Vienna until 29 March, by which time Napoleon had been out of his island kingdom over a month. Part of the reason for this hiatus was that it took a very long time for accurate news to reach Vienna. By the middle of March Talleyrand would have been climbing the walls with frustration, had his dignity and his lameness permitted, at his ignorance of events in France as letters he fired off to friends and colleagues in Paris, pleading for even the tiniest scrap of information, went unanswered.

But then those French subjects loyal to Bourbon rule had other things to worry about than keeping their man in Vienna abreast of developments. They themselves were being rapidly overtaken by events.

Colonel Sir Neil Campbell, who had been given the ill-defined role of British resident on Elba – part jailer, part guardian, part shoulder for Napoleon to cry on, part coordinator of the visits of many prominent English liberals who came to pay their respects to the fallen emperor – had been off the island, in Florence, for a few days in the latter half of February. Napoleon took advantage of Campbell's absence and later that month he slipped out of Porto Ferrajo with a cadre of loyal supporters crammed into a flotilla of half-a-dozen small vessels. The flagship of this minuscule invasion force was the 300-ton 16-gun *Inconstant*, painted to resemble an English vessel.

The strength of his force was little over 1,000 men: grenadiers of the Imperial Guard, some Polish lancers, two cannon, three generals, a chest of gold coin and a carriage. Compared with the lavish displays and endless military parades taking place in Vienna, it was a pathetic ragbag of a force that sloped out of port and sailed slowly towards the European mainland.

During a lengthy voyage Napoleon's little fleet avoided capture by French naval vessels patrolling the waters between northern Corsica and Italy and outran the highly embarrassed Colonel Sir Neil Campbell, who upon discovering his charge's absence gave chase in the *Partridge*. On 1 March, Napoleon landed at what is now the end of the Croisette in Cannes, but what was then open countryside between Cannes and Antibes.

At first his return got off to a faltering start: the garrison at Antibes initially imprisoned the advance party. But by the end of the day, once the full force had landed, the garrison at Antibes capitulated and the period known dramatically, if strictly speaking inaccurately, as the Hundred Days had begun.

The column of men marched over the Alpes Maritimes and through Grasse, Castellane, Séranon, Digne, Volonne, Sisteron and Gap. It was now 5 March. Napoleon had been in France four days without encountering any resistance, and it was only on this day that the corpulent King Louis XVIII finally got to hear of the quondam emperor's arrival in France. Two days later, while Wellington was giving up a day's hunting to ponder Lord Burghersh's report that Napoleon had disappeared from Elba (initially he had been thought to be heading to Genoa, and in Vienna there was still uncertainty as to where he would land), Napoleon confronted French troops, nominally loyal to the king, a few miles south of Grenoble at the village of Laffrey.

In a charismatic display of courage typical of his dramatic personal style, Napoleon dismounted, walked in front of the troops blocking his way, stood still within easy range of their muskets, unbuttoned his trademark grey greatcoat and said: 'If there is any man among you who wants to kill his Emperor, here I am.'[2] None did. Instead, they cheered, broke ranks and joined him. That evening Grenoble fell without a shot being fired. Napoleon would later say: 'Before Grenoble I was an adventurer, at Grenoble I was a ruling Prince.'[3]

Three days later, in Lyon, he shed the role of ruling prince and started behaving as emperor, issuing decrees, appointing ministers, convoking a national assembly called the 'Champ de Mai'. Already the country was responding spontaneously to the emperor's return: there were riots, insurrections, anti-royalist demonstrations, and once more revolutionary slogans from the days of the tumbril and guillotine were being shouted. By the middle of March, as the Allies in Vienna pronounced him a fugitive from international justice, Napoleon in effect took over the rule of France, when the impetuous and headstrong Marshal Ney, Prince of Moscow, the bravest of the brave, who had vowed to his king to bring Napoleon back to Paris in a cage, defected to his cause.

On 7 March the king had written to Talleyrand about what he called Bonaparte's 'audacious attempt'. Louis seriously underestimated Napoleon's popularity and the electric effect that his return would have. The view from his deceptively comfortable position was of the caricature ogre, whose name had been invoked as a bogeyman to scare children in England – the country in which Louis had been exiled – making little more than a theatrical and suicidal gesture. It was with confidence that he wrote to Talleyrand that he was not at all disturbed by the news that he had received. He was confident that it would do as little to disrupt the tranquillity of Europe as it would his own; in fact he confided that he was in quite good spirits as his gout was bothering him rather less than it had been a day or two earlier.

At first there was optimism in royalist circles that the 'audacious attempt' would soon be crushed. Writing to his brother the Duke of Beaufort on 7 March, Lord Fitzroy Somerset acknowledged that while 'Bonaparte has actually put his foot upon French ground', he believed that support was minimal. Somerset was a loyal officer who had served on Wellington's staff since the expedition to Copenhagen, and now that Wellington was at the Congress in Vienna he was the acting ambassador in France. He had served in the Army for ten years and now aged twenty-six, he was England's man in Paris. He felt the importance of his position, but in some ways he was a limited person. In his letter he betrays more of the qualities that make a brave soldier than a wily, far-sighted and cautious diplomat:

> His force is about 1200 men & I don't hear that he has been joined by many people since he landed – Monsieur, and the Duke of Orleans are gone off to Lyons & Preparations are making to get rid of the monster and I hope to god they will kill him or that he is dead by this time – Paris is quiet, but a good many of the English are confoundedly frightened and wish themselves safe at Dover. I'll give as many of them passports as require them, for probably they will be better out of the way.

But neither Fitzroy nor his pregnant wife was concerned: 'Emily is very well and not at all alarmed.'[4] He was stout-hearted and Wellington's man to the core; Emily, his wife, was Wellington's niece.

However, over the following few days the situation grew much more serious as Napoleon travelled triumphantly through the country. On 11 March Fitzroy Somerset wrote: 'Affairs are nearly as bad as they can be.'[5] His Majesty King Louis had a relapse and took to his bed, where, wearing a nightcap, he met ministers and advisers, leaving one visitor with the unfortunate image of a colossal child. From his bed he continued to rule with his customary inertia. The novelist Fanny Burney, who was married to the royalist general and courtier Alexandre d'Arblay, declared in a letter: 'the histories daily recorded to me of the calm dignity of his Majesty's mind though exposed to every species of conflict, & of the imperturbable serenity of his manners, while suffering the most excruciating injuries, & most wounding disappointments, reflect equal honour upon his fortitude, his Temper, & his religious principles.'[6] Burney's is certainly one interpretation of the king's actions, or rather inaction. That he had no grip on the situation and was allowing himself to be buffeted here and there by events, as he always had been, is another.

In fact the monarch's placidity and complacency were almost lethal. Less than a fortnight after he had written to Talleyrand of his imperturbability, his last hope was gone. On 20 March Napoleon was in Paris; Louis XVIII had left at midnight the night before in one of six identical carriages (to deceive his pursuers), with his crown, his diamonds and little else. That night, across Paris, members of his government followed their royal master's lead and sprang from their beds into their carriages.

The need for immediate flight came as a surprise to many including Burney: 'till 19th March I had conceived no idea of the real danger of the state.'[7] And only that morning her husband had gone to a review of the Royal Household. She left Paris with the Princesse de Hénin at 10 p.m. on 19 March, heading for Brussels. As she drove through the French capital, the air was thick with a sense of expectancy. 'All at Paris then was quiet, – sad, dejected, & astonished. Every body had expected some great blow wd be struck, though nobody knew by whom, nor when, nor how.'[8]

And one who knew as little as anyone, if not less, was the king. As Napoleon settled into the Tuileries, its former occupant struggled across the muddy plains of north-western France. It had been mooted that Louis might establish a court in the city of Lille, a royalist stronghold with 60,000 inhabitants, close to the border with Belgium. But it was at Abbeville that he made his first stop, making it seem as though he was about to seek refuge in England again. His chief concern seemed to be that his luggage containing some shirts, a dressing gown and slippers, had gone missing. 'They've taken my shirts, and I was already short of them, but it's my slippers that I regret most,' moaned the almost inconsolable monarch, who complained that nobody understood 'what it means to lose slippers that have taken on the mould of one's foot'.[9]

However, those who thought that the king was heading into exile in England were wrong-footed, as the slipperless, gouty but legitimate ruler of France took a sharp turn right and headed towards Lille, which he reached on 22 March. The following day he set out for the border with Belgium and was conducted into the territory of the Allies by a British officer. On 30 March, the day after the Duke of Wellington set out from Vienna swapping diplomatic for military duties, Louis XVIII rolled into Ghent. By the end of the month he was installed in the spectacular residence of Count Hane Steenhuyse, where he set up his court in exile and waited placidly for the Allies to restore him to his throne ... again.

One reason that Wellington spent three weeks in Vienna after learning of Napoleon's flight from Elba was to help formulate a military plan. It was expected that during the summer of 1815 various Allied armies would mass along France's eastern borders, from the Alps to the Channel, and then crash through and crush Napoleon once and for all. An Austrian army of 210,000 was to move through Alsace-Lorraine, to be followed later by 200,000 Russians. To the south the armies of Switzerland, Upper Italy and Naples numbered 100,000 and were to punch into France along the Riviera. Meanwhile a Prussian force of around 155,000 was to attack from southern Belgium and an Anglo-Dutch force of about 110,000, to be created from a combination of British occupying forces left over from the campaigns of 1814 and Dutch and Belgian troops (some of whom had actually fought under Napoleon), would form in northern Belgium and drive along the northern French coast.[10] To the south-west, beyond the Pyrenees, waited 80,000 troops from Spain and Portugal; countries from which Napoleon's armies had been expelled by Wellington.

The numerical superiority of the Allies was immense; France had a standing Army of around 200,000, which had transferred its loyalty almost wholesale from Louis XVIII to Napoleon, but it was not nearly enough to wage war on the combined forces of the rest of Europe and nothing had been done to update, renew or repair its equipment for at least a year. Moreover Napoleon's domestic problems were considerable. He may have got to Paris without firing a shot, but royalist resistance continued throughout the Hundred Days. Although a 100-gun salute from all major fortifications in France on 29 April was supposed to signify that the last

Bourbon stronghold had been crushed and imperial authority had once more been established, the beginning of May saw the Marquis of Rochejaquelain come ashore in north-western France and stir up a royalist revolt in the Vendée that would tie up 17,000 of Napoleon's badly needed troops.[11]

At first Napoleon tried to convince the rulers of the Allied nations that he did not have warlike intentions. Nobody was prepared to listen. Typical was the British response to his overtures: the letter he wrote to the Prince Regent was returned unopened. Napoleon therefore immediately recalled those soldiers on leave, integrated the National Guard and mariners into the Army, mobilised various volunteer forces as well as veterans, initiated a general call-up, put the armaments industry on a war footing and arranged his forces as best he could, which was far from advantageously.

Against huge Allied armies, Napoleon was able only to post a token force. The border with Spain was guarded by two armies totalling 14,400 men. His eastern borders were similarly thinly defended. In the far south he was able to field the pathetically small Armée du Var with its strength of 5,500; the Armée des Alpes was posted near Lyon with a strength of 23,500; to its north were the 8,400 men of the Armée du Jura who were expected to link up with the 23,000 soldiers of the Armée du Rhin and hold back a combined Austro-Russian onslaught of 410,000 men. With 20,000 men assigned to protect Paris, and various other forces deployed around the country to keep down royalist revolts, Napoleon's striking force was the Armée du Nord, which he would command himself. It had a strength of around 125,000.[12]

He had two options. The first was to remain on the defensive while he built up his forces. The second was to strike first at the forces assembling in Belgium, hoping that he could defeat the Prussian and Anglo-Dutch Armies and dissuade the Austrians and Russians from attacking. The first would have been the more sensible; however it would have meant a protracted campaign and inevitable fighting on French territory, both of which might have had a serious effect on his domestic popularity. Therefore he chose the second option.

Napoleon judged he had until 1 July before the Allies were ready to attack. His plan would be to drive a wedge between the Prussians and the Anglo-Dutch Armies and defeat each Army separately, before they had a chance to join up. He hoped that a quick decisive victory would boost domestic support and provide a surge in the number of recruits. Moreover the defeat of the British force might well precipitate the fall of Lord Liverpool's Conservative administration in London and the election of a Whig government, which would be more disposed to a peaceful settlement.

Britain had been underwriting the cost of waging war on imperial France and in the absence of British cash, it might be possible, reasoned Napoleon, to conclude a separate peace with Austria and the minor German states.

Napoleon was to gamble on striking fast and striking first. The preparation and positioning of the vast Armies of Austria and Russia was not going to be accomplished rapidly, and it was unlikely that any unilateral attack on France would be made before all Allied forces were in place for a joint offensive. As Talleyrand wrote to King Louis XVIII from Vienna, the Duke of Wellington 'feels the necessity of not commencing operations until a general attack can be made everywhere by all the forces. Yet with the best will in the world, the distances to be traversed are so great, that the Austrians could not place a hundred thousand men on the Rhine before the end of May.'[13] And even Talleyrand would have had to admit that this was an extremely optimistic prediction . . . he himself was certainly in no hurry to leave the comparative safety of Vienna.

However, in spite of the lack of readiness of Russian and Austrian troops, the invasion of Belgium would be a huge gamble; nevertheless it was just this sort of startling coup upon which the Napoleonic myth had been built.

6

'Are you afraid of Bonaparte?'

At six o'clock in the morning of 28 February the cannon boomed out from the ramparts of Brussels, causing the citizens to wake up with a start. Bonaparte might have just embarked on his reconquest of France, but it was not to warn the Bruxellois of the return of their emperor that the cannon were roaring – news of his return would not reach Belgium for some time. Instead this salute was to mark news from the Congress of Vienna, namely that the Prince of Orange, the old frog, had been proclaimed king of the newly constituted United Netherlands. Britain's amalgamation of the Low Countries into a buffer state had received the official ratification and recognition of the European Powers. The Prince of Orange was now Europe's newest king.

In early March the first signs of spring were to be seen in the park. The weather improved and fashionable society resumed its habit of taking a stroll there after midday – 'the right time to walk in the Park as *every body* is walking in it then, and that makes it very pleasant'.[1] In fact the only barrier to their happiness that the expats in Brussels could envisage was that British troops would soon be withdrawn, depriving them of the help, attention and marriage proposals of the dashing officers. 'I am afraid that we shall very soon know what it is *to live abroad* as we have heard that by April the English Garrison will be gone and almost all the English Families that are here will go about the same time,'[2] wrote Louisa Capel to her grandmother at the beginning of March.

However, a few days later all thoughts of a British withdrawal had disappeared. 'The advance of Bonaparte to Lyons and the defection of the

French army have been made known to this Government by the arrival of a Courier with Dispatches from General Fagel,' wrote Charles Stuart to Lord Castlereagh on 15 March. He then went on to describe the emergency measures that were being taken:

> The Hereditary Prince sent General Lowe* [Major-General Hudson Lowe was the Hereditary Prince of Orange's Quartermaster General] to Aix-la-Chapelle to concert with General Kleist the movements which this unexpected change of affairs might render expedient ... H.R.H. will immediately concentrate the greater part of the troops under his command near the frontier with a view to occupying the Fortresses within the French line, in case the movement of the Garrisons should render the measure feasible ... The Dutch government will immediately direct the collection of provisions in Ostend, Ypres, Tournay, Maestricht, [sic] and Antwerp, and they have adopted my suggestion to make arrangements for the immediate advance of the whole disposable force, being about twenty thousand men, into Belgium. The public of this country have been depressed to a very alarming degree since the late accounts from Paris transpired.[3]

As Napoleon marched deeper into France, his popularity growing, the British in Paris made rapid arrangements to move to safety, and apparently as many decided to flee to Brussels as to Britain. By the middle of March every hotel in Brussels was packed with refugees. However, Caroline Paget did her best to reassure her mother that all was well. 'What annoys and worries me most at the Moment', she wrote, 'is the Idea that you will feel in a State of Anxiety at the News of the *Tyger* having broke loose; and as distance Sometimes Magnifies Evils [you] will perhaps think that there is cause for alarm on our Account, which I assure you there is not.'[4] Indeed Caroline had more on her mind than the imminent arrival of Bonaparte in Brussels. She was pregnant for the thirteenth time. What is more, Napoleon's sudden arrival in France had rather ruined her plans of getting a Brussels gown to her mother; Major-General Barnes was to have taken it in his luggage, but of course he was needed in Belgium.

Happily, old Lady Uxbridge's gown did leave Brussels on 23 March, carried under the greatcoat of a Major Trench. By then it was known in Brussels that Louis was fleeing Paris and that Napoleon was in control. Rumours abounded and even phlegmatic British households such as the Capels' and that of the Duke and Duchess of Richmond began to make arrangements for 'an easy retreat into Holland'.[5]

*Later Napoleon's jailer on St Helena.

Meanwhile relatives and friends in London bombarded the British in Brussels with letters asking anxiously after news. Creevey, the gossipy and clubbable MP in exile, was in touch with his friends in politics in London and was privy to the inner workings of the Whig party machine as it debated the merits of neutrality and speculated on whether British troops had already been committed to the royalist cause. Typical was the tone of a letter sent on 16 March by the Hon. H.G. Bennet, MP and friend of Creevey:

> The Gentilities seem inclined for war to keep out Bony, but you see Sam [Whitbread, a prominent and outspoken Whig] has declared for neutrality; it is generally credited – that we have offered Lewis Baboon our Brabant Army and that it is to be put in motion if wanted. If you can get any information on that subject, be so good as to let the faithful know it here as soon as you can, for it is of consequence. If Bony can hold his head up a fortnight, it is our opinion here that the Bourbons are done, which God forbid. Not that I like these personages, but peace with them is better than War with Napoleon.[6]

And while Creevey, who had retired to the Continent for the health of his invalid wife and his own bank balance, suddenly found himself at the centre of historic events and pestered by his parliamentary colleagues for scraps of information, their wives were writing to Mrs Creevey in much the same vein. 'We are *all* very anxious to know how you feel at this moment – are you afraid of Bonaparte?' wrote Lady Elizabeth Whitbread to Mrs Creevey on 22 March. 'I should rather GUESS that you are a little afraid,' she surmised, adding by way of encouragement: 'and you would be of little use in defending your Master if defence *was required*.'[7] With friends like Lady Elizabeth Whitbread, Mrs Creevey was in no need of a Job's comforter.

Only a fool would not have been 'a little afraid'. Brussels was in turmoil. As March progressed the number of British and royalist refugees arriving from Paris bringing with them news of Napoleon's inexorable advance increased; many of them had left in such a hurry that they had had no time to pack. 'I have no clothes!' complained Fanny Burney. 'I only possess a small change of linen, & 2 mourning Gowns! Ceaselessly but too late I regret not having had a better foresight of migratory destiny!'[8]

However, compared to some British she had been positively prescient in her planning. Fitzroy Somerset was genuinely taken aback by the speed at which the former emperor marched unopposed through France. He wrote to his brother the Duke of Beaufort that Napoleon was 'enabled to come on to Paris, with as little interruption as you would come from Badminton* to London'.⁹ Unable to get the necessary documents for travelling until 26 March, Fitzroy was in the embarrassing position of being British ambassador to the court of King Louis, stuck in a Paris occupied by Napoleon.

However, he and his pregnant wife were treated well. 'Nobody molested us at Paris after Bonaparte entered it, on the contrary the people who were before impertinent became civil to us,' he wrote to his brother, adding: 'I saw Bonaparte from the Garden of the Tuilleries, but I had not a very distinct view of him. He appeared short and fat. Emily saw him better, indeed she was near enough to be pointed out to him by the Queen of Holland, and he took his glass up to look at her.'¹⁰ Lord and Lady Fitzroy Somerset eventually got their passports and made it to Calais by 28 March, where they had to wait a day before sailing, on a French vessel, to Ostend. They arrived just in time to see the king passing through on his way to Ghent, where Somerset himself expected to be going as British ambassador to the French court in exile.

Lord Fitzroy was irritated to find that the British government did not think that the rump court of King Louis warranted its own British ambassador and had rolled that responsibility into Sir Charles Stuart's portfolio, who, in fairness, had been Wellington's predecessor in Paris. It appears that some members of the government were dissatisfied at Somerset's reports from Paris.

'It would have been but the act of a gentleman to have told me that they had thought proper to appoint Sir C Stuart to represent the king at the court of Louis,' wrote Fitzroy to his brother from Ghent on 6 April, smarting from what he took to be a gross public humiliation.

– It is clear enough that as soon as the court left Paris Ministers cared little what became of me or my feelings; & they have shown me, that the state of the Case, as nearly as it can be had, is not what they want; but that they must have favourable reports as long as my arm – Pretty encouragement this for a man, who has been brought up under a general who taught him to look upon a plain statement as preferable to a garnished sentence of speculation and falsehood[.] This act of Civility too could not have been productive of inconvenience, for they might have been sure that in the event of a war I should not be in the way, & that I should have insisted upon joining the Duke of Wellington. I am fully aware that it is

*The Duke of Beaufort's country seat.

very desirable for a Govt to receive intelligence Couleur de Rose; but if the fact is that the news is been noir, they ought to submit to the circumstance of the moment & believe what is told them by their minister or recall him as unworthy of their confidence[.] As I now stand Every person who hears I have been suspended & that the secrety [*sic*] of State has not made any communication to me since I left Paris, will have a right to argue, that I conducted myself so ill that they were obliged to adopt the expedient of begging Sir Charles Stuart to take charge of two Embassies at the same time rather than leave the interests of the British Nation at the Court of a man who has no kingdom in my hands a day longer – Pray reflect therefore on the consequences of Lord Castlereagh's inattention in this respect & yet five minutes trouble[?] would set all right. I have spoken to Pole on the subject who will probably hint to Lord Castlereagh that I expect such a communication – But at all events it will come late. Lord Harrowby did me the justice to tell Alava to day that I had not deceived the Govt in any one respect.[11]

While the indignity must have been very trying for Lord Fitzroy it is understandable that it was not at the top of the list of concerns occupying the British government. As refugees streamed into Belgium, British and Hanoverian troops were marching in the opposite direction towards the border, and many idlers and tourists who were not in Brussels on the economic plan left hurriedly for England. With no reliable information to be had, it was natural to fear the worst: after all, if he had moved so swiftly and so smoothly into France, would the scanty British and German forces be able to stop Napoleon rolling on into Belgium and liberating it from the newly inaugurated Kingdom of the United Netherlands?

Actually it is not quite true to say that there was no reliable information about the state of affairs: Creevey had a knack for finding himself in the know and he had the good luck that one of his stepdaughters was being courted by a Major Hamilton, a boyish-looking young man who was on General Barnes's staff and who enjoyed access to sensitive military intelligence. 'My Dear Mr. Creevey,' he wrote around about 18 March, '*If you will not blab*, you shall hear all the news I can pick up, bad and good, as it comes. I am sorry to tell you bad news to-day. General Fagal writes from Paris to say that Bonaparte may be in that capital ere many days,' ran his report, which continued in much the same vein, but ended on a bravely optimistic note: 'Fagal, take notice, is an alarmist, and I hope our next accounts will not be of so gloomy a nature.'[12]

His hope was to be unfulfilled. On 20 March he was writing to Creevey:

Bonaparte is at Fontainebleau with 15,000 men, every man of whom he can depend upon, because every man is a volunteer, and they have risked all for his sake. The Royal army is at Melun, consisting of about 28,000 men, National Guards, &c., &c., included – not a man of whom can be relied on. This is the critical moment; for if they allow him to enter Paris without a battle, all is over. I feel that I am not acting imprudently in thus stating facts, which naturally Mrs Creevey must be made acquainted with ... [13]

On 22 March he sent the ominous note: 'There is no news this morning. All communication with Paris is at an end,'[14] which was followed by bulletins throughout the day as the situation worsened. 'A Courier is just arrived from Mons, sent by Dorneberg [the commander of the garrison at Mons] to state that two emissaries of Bonaparte have been seized there this morning on their way into this country. Their papers are of con-sequence, and are before the Prince.'[15] This incident alarmed General Barnes sufficiently to warn his officers on the border to be extra vigilant, and he had the Guards ready 'to march on the shortest notice'.[16]

Tension increased as the scraps of news fed to Creevey indicated a deepening crisis. As well as recounting the inevitable entry of Napoleon into Paris, Hamilton voiced concern about the readiness and loyalty of the forces defending the border. The threat posed by Napoleon had become terrifyingly real; no one was calling him Robinson Crusoe now, and given the rapidity with which French forces had gone over to him *en masse*, the fear among British officers was that local troops on the border of the newly United Netherlands might do the same:

Matters are not so well with ourselves here as they might be, inasmuch as the Belgians at Mons evince a bad spirit. Dorneburg [*sic*], who commands that garrison, is a determined and good officer, and has corps of the German Legion near him should circumstances require aid. A letter from Lille speaks favourably of the good spirit prevailing amongst the inhabitants; but alas! if the soldiers do not hold to their allegiance, what can be expected?

'Pray do not blab,' he implores Creevey, 'for although all this may have come to your knowledge through other channels, yet it would not do for *me* to have the name of a news-giver.'[17]

But Hamilton was most certainly a news-giver. It would appear that he was in contact with other important British families in Brussels at the time; most certainly he was corresponding with the Duke and Duchess of

Richmond and it is difficult to imagine that at least the better-connected British in Brussels were not fully aware of how precarious the situation was. In those first few days after Napoleon installed himself in Paris, everyone was confused. As A.D.C. to the young Prince of Orange, Lord March was sent out to see if he could find the King of France: he returned without news. However, at least there would be ample warning of Napoleon's invasion should it come; '7000 Royalists from France, first to bleed, are outside the Belgic frontier; and will give us notice, *by their running away,*' wrote the doom-mongering Hamilton to Creevey, then tried to add a shred of reassurance with the words: 'but until WE begin to run, Mrs. Creevey need not fancy the French are in Bruxelles; and, *for her sake*, may they never be.'[18]

But some people were not about to wait for the British soldiers to evacuate Brussels before packing up and moving out: they were going to get away early. At the end of March Napoleon was reported to be at Lille with a large force, and panic ripped through Brussels. The mere rumour of Bonaparte's presence near the border was enough to terrify the western part of the United Netherlands and disrupt all aspects of life: 'every Banking House was shut up & not a Guinea to be procured – Those who could, fled immediately, leaving every thing that could not be immediately packed.'[19] British families that had until recently been revelling in the heady social life of the charming cosmopolitan town could not get out fast enough. They scattered to Antwerp, Ghent and Ostend, whence, if they could secure a passage on a boat, they could escape to England.

Even the better-informed, more confident British families, including the Capels, Richmonds and Grevilles, who decided not to join the general exodus, began to grow nervous. Ever mindful of the pecuniary ramifications, the Capels sent their plate to a friend's house for safekeeping and, their valuables thus protected, were ready to flee to Antwerp at a few moments' notice. Yet, even at this moment of crisis, so ingrained were the constant concerns about money that Caroline Capel, writing to her mother, was unable to avoid mentioning the financial implications of the panic. 'It is said that the Townspeople lose 50,000 Franks [*sic*] a Day by the departures that have taken place.'[20]

After a few days nothing had happened but the atmosphere was still tense, and some, including Lord Waterpark who had been so central to the merrymaking at the 'Literary Club' and the racecourse, were not taking any chances. He had cleared out of Brussels with his family but was keen to find out whether it was safe to return to collect some of the belongings he had left behind in his hurry to get away. Too scared to go himself, he sent his sister-in-law 'disguised in a French costume'[21] and travelling in a local carriage, to see what had happened. In a scene straight out of farce the woman was recognised by some of the Duke of Richmond's daughters 'and was obliged to confess the object of her mission, express[ing] surprise that any English persons were found still at large in this town'.[22]

At the height of the crisis the young Prince of Orange came to see the Capels:

> the dear little prince in the Midst of this tumult did not forget us – I never was more penetrated than by his coming into us at ten in the Evening with a most cheering Countenance & begging that we would not think of removing As long as his Head Quarters remained here, that we should always have twelve hours notice before it was necessary to move, that we must keep our things packed, & feel perfectly secure – This was the more goodnatured as he had sent to the Commandant the day before to get as many People off as he could in order to avoid unnecessary confusion.[23]

No matter how touching the young prince's concern for his smart English friends, his advice also demonstrates how ill-equipped this young man was to have command of the armed forces and the defence of the Netherlands. Charming socialite and enthusiastic dancer that he might have been, he was completely out his depth. A year earlier he had been nothing more than a brave, likeable member of the Duke of Wellington's staff, whose position there owed much to his father being a deracinated European royal with whom the British government was keen to forge lasting links. Now he was in overall command of a heterogeneous army, defending the uneasy amalgamation of Belgium and the Netherlands against the most successful military leader Europe had ever seen.

The young Prince of Orange had no idea of what to do and even before Napoleon had crossed the border, the Prince had, doubtless inadvertently, exacerbated the confusion by one day ordering the Commandant 'to get as many people off as he could', and on the next making personal visits that in effect undermined and countermanded that order, recommending that civilian families should stay and reassuring them that there were no immediate concerns for their safety.

He was not a commander to instil confidence in either the military or civilian populations. Everyone from the humblest British private to the grandest British aristocrat was agreed that the young Prince of Orange as commander of the Allied forces was a disaster waiting to happen. 'The Prince of Orange is in command of the Army,' wrote Private William

Wheeler of the 51st Regiment of Foot shortly after his arrival in the Netherlands.

> There can be no doubt but the Prince is well experienced in war, having served on the Duke of Wellington's staff during the Peninsular War but he is not the man for us. None but Wellington or Hill, or some one of the Generals who have served with us in the late campaigns can have our confidence. The Emperor will most assuredly command the French army, and it will require a General of uncommon skill to withstand so powerful a genus [*sic*].

'Wellington's the man that must lead us on,' was Wheeler's unsurprising conclusion. 'An hundred times a day, the question is asked, "Where is Wellington, surely we shall not be led to battle by that boy," meaning the Prince.'[24]

Nor was it just curmudgeonly infantrymen who muttered darkly about the young Prince's youth and ineptitude. One of the Duke of Richmond's daughters, Lady Georgiana Lennox, held the opinion that 'the Prince of Orange, although personally much liked, was inexperienced and rash'.[25] Nor was this a view formed by mere hearsay and gossip, but rather by first-hand knowledge and observation. Her brother Lord March was one of the Prince's A.D.C.s and the young Prince was exactly the sort of guest that the ambitious Duchess of Richmond would have been only too pleased to see at their house on the rue de la Blanchisserie with its large garden extending to the ramparts of the city. A military family such as the Duke of Richmond's would also have been buzzing with Army gossip. Thus with hostilities apparently imminent, the Richmonds found themselves at the nexus of military and social life in Brussels.

'During the Duke's [Wellington's] absence at the Congress of Vienna, the rumour arrived of Napoleon's intended invasion of Belgium,' recalled Lady Georgiana, 'and there was great anxiety among the English officers for the Duke's arrival, as the Prince of Orange would otherwise have been in command. The Prince himself was quite angry with me for sharing this feeling, exclaiming, "Why have you no confidence in me?" to which I replied, "Well, sir, *you* have not been tried and the Duke *has*."'[26]

And while young Lady Georgiana shared her lack of confidence in the Prince of Orange, strolling with him in the large pleasant garden off the rue de la Blanchisserie, the troops under his command became ever more jumpy as rumours about Napoleon and his troops poured over the border. 'While dressing to go out to a party, the girl came in pale and aghast telling me the cannon was planted "sur la grande place" with lighted matches, and that Boney was at Lille.' This was the entry for 2 April in the diary of Edmund Wheatley, a young officer in the King's German Legion, stationed in the border town of Tournai. Lille was virtually no distance from the border, and understandably this news caused considerable consternation. The garrison was thrown into turmoil, expecting an imminent attack. 'A sudden order came instantly to run to the Citadel and take the Guard there.'[27]

Those early days in April 1815 were an uncomfortable and uneasy time to be on the border between the United Netherlands and France. More troops were rushed to the border: within less than a week of Wheatley hearing the news of Bonaparte's alleged presence in Lille, the garrison at Tournai had tripled in strength and troops were moved out into the surrounding countryside. However, intelligence was very poor, and as one soldier put it: 'the most impenetrable mystery seemed to be observed in reference to Napoleon's future movements.'[28] So in the absence of a better plan, Allied troops were strung out along the border, where they waited.

Meanwhile in Brussels a brittle veneer of calm covered life in the city. A few of those who had fled Brussels during the panic returned. The newly crowned king and queen of the United Netherlands made a show of appearing in public, and even planned a lavish ball at the Hôtel de Ville, which boosted morale among the British expats. But all the time civilians and soldiers waited and waited for the arrival of the hero of the Peninsula, the only man judged by everyone, with the possible exception of the Prince of Orange, capable of delivering the United Netherlands from the threat of invasion by Napoleon. 'Lord Wellington is expected every hour – His name is a Host in itself,'[29] wrote Caroline Capel of Wellington's talismanic powers, to her mother at the end of March. But a week later the Duke, still expected on the hour every hour, had failed to arrive. 'Lord Wellington is not yet arrived but is expected every hour & is as much wished for by Foreigners as English.'[30]

7

‘Being in readiness for the riots occasioned
by the passing of the Corn Laws’

I was greatly oppressed by the first intelligence of Napoleon's Invasion. I
was afterwards re-elevated, and now I am tumbled down again.

To be sure, there never was such an execrable nation as the French. The
much more respectable Hindoos could not more meekly submit to any
conqueror that chooses to run through their country at the head of a set
of miscreant soldiers.[1]

Lord Sheffield's reaction to the news of Napoleon's arrival in France and
King Louis's flight from Paris, set down in a letter to his brother-in-law,
is eloquently expressive of the mood of apprehension, exhilaration and
exasperation that gripped Britain when it became widely known that
France had welcomed back its emperor.

At the end of the war, Britain had shipped its troops out of France,
demobilising some units and sending others across the Atlantic to join in
the war with America that had started in 1812. With the signing of a treaty
on Christmas Eve 1814 in Ghent, in Britain's client state the United
Netherlands, the war with America had ended. However, ratification of
the treaty and news of the peace arrived in America too late to stop further
clashes at sea and the battle of New Orleans in January, among whose
fatalities was General Sir Edward Pakenham, Wellington's brother-in-law
and erstwhile adjutant-general.

After the excitement of the visiting Allied sovereigns and the cessation
of hostilities with America, Britain returned to its introspective way of life.
There had been fear of a French invasion, but Napoleon had never come

to England, and for most of the nation the war, whether in Spain or America, had been a distant conflict in a remote country. So as soon as the fighting was over the country became obsessed by domestic issues. There was the continuing soap-opera afforded by the royal family: its insane paterfamilias; its spendthrift, gluttonous regent with his highly problematic domestic arrangements; and his variously corrupt and decadent brothers.

But the issue that gripped the country most tightly in February and March of 1815 was the Corn Importation Bill, a piece of protectionist legislation intended to stave off an agricultural downturn after the war. This bill had been put before parliament in February by a landowner called Frederick Robinson, later Earl of Ripon, who was typical of those with landed interests who backed the bill, which prohibited importation of cheap foreign wheat and also set minimum prices for other cereals. Robinson may not have known it, but his bill would ignite a debate on protectionism and free trade that would dominate political life in the first half of the nineteenth century.

The benefit to landowners was clear: a guaranteed price for their produce, and as the conservative administration was stuffed with landowners it would naturally be seized upon by radicals and reformers as a means by which the traditional ruling classes, the aristocracy and landed gentry, could control the rest of the population. Attempts were made to dress the bill in patriotic clothes; some supporters stated that the issue being debated was the very independence of Britain from foreign farmers who could, so it was argued, inundate the country with low-price grain and then, having driven domestic agriculture into ruin, either raise prices or cut off supply altogether. Another argument was that if farming became unviable, agricultural labourers would be paid less, which in turn would lead to a drop in demand for manufactured goods. This argument neatly sidestepped the fact that since the end of the war, with the release of servicemen onto the labour market and the scaling down of the armaments industry, both labour and iron were already cheaper than they had been during the war.

Opposition to the bill was lively, but as the interests of those opposing it were not, on the whole, represented in parliament, those who were not in favour had to find other ways to show their disapproval. Petitions were raised, which frightened parliament into rushing the legislation through the Commons and the Lords, which in turn infuriated those who would suffer most from a rise in the price of bread.

In the first full week of March, as Napoleon was marching deeper into France, the mood in London turned ugly. MPs making their way to the

House of Commons to debate the bill were jostled and manhandled by protesters, and parliament had to be surrounded by soldiers. The Radical MP Sir Francis Burdett spoke out in public against the bill and was carried aloft by the mob like a conquering hero. The windows of White's were broken, the houses of prominent supporters of the bill were attacked, and soldiers, drafted into London to maintain order, opened fire on rioters. At first, part of society was inclined to be amused by the disturbance, viewing it as a healthy display of the uniquely vigorous and physical nature of British democracy at work. 'We are rioting away here about the Corn Bill, breaking windows and battering in doors every night,' wrote one society lady quite cheerfully. 'If it were not that it must come to shooting a few and hanging a few it would be merely laughable, and, as it is, I can only consider it as an ebullition from that best political constitution that the world has ever seen, and which proves it is yet hale at the heart.'[2]

Even those in parliament who were the natural target of the mob's ire were inclined to be indulgent towards the rabble. One young officer on guard duty at St James's Palace wandered into St James's Square and saw 'thousands of the lowest of the London rabble' breaking windows and pelting the Life Guards with stones, mud and abuse. 'I beheld one man exciting the crowd to force the doors of the Bishop of London's residence. As the fellow was making a rush against it, I told him to desist, or I would immediately run my sword through his body.' With some satisfaction the young officer noted that this threat 'had the effect of calming the gentleman's ardour; he skulked away'.

Feeling rather pleased with himself the young guardee strolled towards King Street, whereupon he was accosted by Lord Castlereagh, who was back from the Continent and at that moment was calmly watching the mob breaking his windows. Castlereagh coolly thanked the young officer for his enthusiasm, but suggested that he exercise 'a little more discretion in future; "for the mob," said he, "is not so dangerous as you think."'[3]

Not everyone shared Lord Castlereagh's nonchalance. By Thursday the West End of London seemed to be under martial law, and older Londoners must have remembered the mood just before the worst excesses of the Gordon riots of 1780, when armed gangs had burned the houses of prominent citizens, stormed the jails, freeing violent prisoners, attacked the Royal Mint and very nearly succeeded in imposing mob rule on the city. This time the government was taking no chances. Infantrymen were stationed outside the houses of supporters of the bill and cavalry units were held in readiness to deal with rioters.

The man commanding the Guards and Household cavalry units to be deployed against rioters was Lord Uxbridge (formerly Lord Paget), eldest brother of Caroline Paget, who wrote from Brussels to her mother, concerned that the dowager Lady Uxbridge would 'feel nervous at Paget heading the Military in London – These commotions are, I trust, subsiding, & before this reaches you will, please God, be over.'[4] As it happened her prediction was entirely correct. Among the cavalry placed strategically around London were the 16th Light Dragoons, among whose officers was Captain William Tomkinson, a Peninsular veteran, who recalls being 'called up to the neighbourhood of Westminster Bridge for the purpose of being in readiness for the riots occasioned by the passing of the Corn Laws. During our stay here, Napoleon entered France from Elba, and placed himself again on the throne. Immediately on this account arriving in London, all disturbance about the Corn Laws ceased.'[5]

According to Captain Verner of the 7th Hussars, it was 'as though the ground had opened, and swallowed up houses, inhabitants and troops, there could not have been a more sudden termination put to Corn Laws, [for in] twelve hours, there was no more heard on the subject than if the panic had never existed, and in less than twelve hours the troops were on the march to their several destinations'.[6] That was that. Such was the powerful effect of the name Bonaparte that a highly important aspect of British domestic policy was influenced by just the idea of Napoleon; in effect he had helped pass the Corn Laws with much less trouble than if the British had been left to themselves to do it. He was no pantomime Corsican ogre, but a threat so large and so serious that every other concern was eclipsed.

The bill became law with a huge majority voting in its favour and with no more violent protest in the streets. The cavalry stood down, and like many of the units that had been prepared to quell riots, the 16th Light Dragoons 'returned to Hounslow to prepare for embarkation for the Netherlands'.[7]

8

'Eager to plunge into danger and bloodshed, all hoping to obtain glory and distinction'[1]

Early April saw the south of England busy with speculation and activity: a 'scene of bustle and anxiety seldom equalled – couriers passing to and fro incessantly, and numerous travellers, foreign and English, arriving day and night from the Continent, many travelling in breathless haste, as if fearful, even here, of Napoleon's emissaries'.[2] Rumours spread by these refugees heightened the air of confusion – according to some, Louis XVIII had been arrested in Paris, others said he was waiting at Ostend in the hope of being allowed to escape to England – and added an extra urgency to the preparations.

News of Napoleon's return reached the soldiers in various ways; but on the whole they reacted with enthusiasm to the news that they would be going back to war. Indeed, for many long-serving soldiers the news came as something of a relief: having fought for many years they were 'now more used to war and hardships than to peace and plenty'.[3] Many sources talk of peace being irksome to the hardened soldiers, and the observation of artillery officer Cavalié Mercer that his men were 'eager to plunge into danger and bloodshed, all hoping to obtain glory and distinction'[4] seemed to characterise the mood of many, particularly younger officers. One report has these young men 'looking ravenously forward to promotion' and being so happy at the news of the resumption of hostilities with France 'that they treated all the men to an extra glass of grog, to make everybody as lively as themselves'.[5] Their joy is all the more surprising in that this particular band of fighting men had been shipped to America and denied a respite after the war in Spain.

Particularly long-suffering was Harry Smith, who had served with the British Army in South America in 1806 and 1807 and fought in the Peninsula from 1809 until the end of the campaign in 1814, when he was shipped out of south-western France. By August 1814 he was fighting in America, where he became military secretary to Sir John Lambert, who took command after Pakenham was killed in the battle of New Orleans. After details of the ratification of the peace by President Madison reached them in March 1815 they sailed for England, but before Captain Smith had set foot on English soil again, he had heard the news of Napoleon's escape. However, instead of bitterness, anger and disappointment that a period of leave was to be cut short by yet another war, he was jubilant:

> As we neared the mouth of the British Channel, we had, of course, the usual thick weather, when a strange sail was reported. It was now blowing a fresh breeze; in a few minutes we spoke her, but did not make her haul her main-topsail, being a bit of a merchantman. Stirling [Captain Stirling, one of his comrades] hailed as we shot past. 'Where are you from?' 'Portsmouth.' 'Any news?' 'No, none.' The ship was almost out of sight, when we heard, 'Ho! Bonaparter's [*sic*] back again on the throne of France.' Such a hurrah as I set up, tossing my hat over my head! 'I will be a Lieutenant-Colonel yet before the year's out!' Sir John Lambert said, 'Really, Smith, you are so vivacious! How is it possible? It cannot be.' He had such faith in the arrangements of our government, he wouldn't believe it. I said, 'Depend upon it, it's truth; a beast like that skipper never could have invented it, when he did not even regard it as news: "No, no news; only Bonaparte's back again on the throne of France." Depend on it, it's true.' 'No, Smith, no.' Stirling believed it, and oh, how he carried on!
>
> We were soon at Spithead, when all the men-of-war, the bustle, the general appearance, told us, before we could either see telegraphic communication or speak any one, where 'Bonaparter' was.'[6]

Harry Smith could count himself lucky that he actually set foot on English soil, some of those *en route* from America were diverted straight to the Low Countries.

In Portsmouth, where the 51st Foot was stationed, news of Napoleon's dash for the throne of France elicited cheers. 'In an instant we were all wild – "Nap's in France again" spread like wildfire through the barracks – the men turned out and cheered,' recalled Lt Frederick Mainwaring.[7]

Stationed in garrison towns far away from the diversions of London, young men of good family were thrilled to have the chance to get back on campaign. William Hay seems to have been fairly typical. Born into a well-connected, if not aristocratic, family, he became a soldier at the age of sixteen and by the spring of 1815, then in his early twenties, he was quartered with the 12th Dragoons in Dorchester. 'It was the most horrid, dull, stupid inland town I had ever known,' was Hay's uncompromising verdict on the place.

> I may say that, until then, I never knew what it was to lead, what is commonly termed, a barrack-yard life.
>
> We had hunting, it is true, of an indifferent kind; and an old fellow, a yeoman farmer, who at the time was an Army contractor to supply the cavalry regiments in the place with forage, gave us some amusement in his meadows, where we used to hunt rats, to pass the dull hours.'[8]

Happily, as Hay saw it, the 'restless disposition' and 'symptoms of disturbance' occasioned by the debating of the Corn Laws meant that his regiment was to hold itself 'in readiness to march for the metropolis'.

> I for one was delighted at the prospect of breaking ground from Dorchester, be our destination where it would.
>
> Under such orders our mess establishment was broken up, and we dined at the inn; there was but one in the place and to that the mail-coach was driven on its arrival. The officers were waiting for the sounding of trumpets for dinner, at the said inn door, when the mail stopped. The guard, a good humoured fellow and a great favourite with all our officers, who had travelled to town by his coach, exclaimed: 'Well, gentlemen, I have brought you news to-day.' All exclaimed: 'What! the route?' 'Yes,' was the reply, 'the route in earnest, old Bonny [*sic*] has broken out again and got to Paris.' We were astonished, and indeed could not believe our ears; but on the delivery of the newspapers and letters the news we heard was not only confirmed, but an immediate order for us to march by Canterbury, *en route* to Dover, there to embark for Ostend, and, I must confess, the news gave me the greatest satisfaction, as I had no liking for the life of a soldier in idleness.[9]

'No liking for the life of a soldier in idleness'. These few words seem to characterise the mood of many officers who reacted with joy to the news that the war with France was back on after a hiatus of not quite one year. Of course the nature of a soldier is that he is paid, trained and, in part at least, lives to fight and kill for his country. Moreover some measure of retrospective jingoism and enthusiasm might be expected in the many personal accounts of soldiers who fought in the campaign of 1815 which appeared in print throughout the nineteenth century: doubtless an account of Waterloo that was not fizzing with manly emotions, leavened with a little sangfroid and underpinned by gallant patriotism would have found little favour with a Victorian publisher. Nevertheless the tone of enthusiasm is marked throughout numerous accounts.

What also stands out is the spontaneity of their excitement. In 1815 news was not a managed and manipulated commodity assaulting the public at every turn. Newspaper circulations were small, literacy was far from universal, and instead news was what one picked up in letters and in snatches of conversation with coachmen, sea captains, travellers from London and, if one were lucky enough to have them, friends at court or in parliament. The news of Napoleon's arrival in Paris reached people at a more human pace, the speed of its transmission depending on the tides, the weather, the speed of a horse and the quality of a road, so that it spread through Britain slowly, rather like ink seeping into blotting paper, with many soldiers first hearing of Napoleon's return as gossip. 'The news, so prevalent in Bath the day before I left, of the Emperor Napoleon's escape from Elba was confirmed beyond doubt when I arrived at Portsmouth,' wrote one sergeant, who returned to barracks to find his regiment 'undergowing [*sic*] an inspection by Lord Howard of Effingham, the Major-General in command of this garrison'.[10]

Details reached people at different times. Such was the uneven spread of news that some officers heard of the news much later than their men. Having left his regiment at Dover Heights, almost in sight of the Low Countries, Sir John Kincaid headed for Scotland to take 'a shot at the last of the woodcocks', and was thus enjoying himself 'when Buonaparte's escape from Elba once more summoned the army to the field'.

'The first intimation I had of it was by a letter, informing me of the embarkation of the battalion for the Netherlands, and desiring me to join them there, without delay.'[11] The tone is delightfully unmilitaristic. The sense is almost of Bonaparte – notice the slightly pejorative Corsican spelling of the family name – being ungentlemanly enough to invade France just while Sir John happened to be taking a little sport in Scotland; a terrible inconvenience, as the troops were several hundred miles away in Dover. Happily, Sir John was good-natured enough to accept their invitation to join them in the Netherlands.

Even the average private soldier in the Army seems to have greeted the news of Napoleon's return to France with little more than the irritated resignation of an agricultural labourer who has only just sat down to his supper when he is told that there is a fox in the chicken run.

One of the most charming accounts of learning about the arrival of

Napoleon in Paris comes from James Gunn. It is all the more evocative for apparently not having been published. Instead it has remained untouched, with its homespun wisdom, erratic phonetic spelling and mischievous recollections, in the Regimental Archives of the Royal Highland Regiment, better known as the Black Watch. Gunn's regiment, like several others, had been sent to Ireland after the cessation of hostilities with France in 1814. Although it would be more than a century before Ireland became independent of Great Britain, resentment against rule from London was a constant concern. In 1796 France had attempted an invasion of Ireland with a force of almost 15,000 men, forty-five ships and the Irish revolutionary leader Wolfe Tone. The attempt was thwarted by delays and bad weather, but it increased tension in Ireland and led to a brutal crackdown on Irish nationalists.

Gunn however was a cheerful man who took his pleasure where he could find it, and apparently found much to recommend life in what he calls the 'Blessed City of Kilkeny', where he was enjoying himself among 'the Kind Hearted Irish people and Defys any to say to the Conterary when one Morning what Should arive but the Rout for Cork and the News that Restless and ambisious Criket boney got back to France'.[12]

Quite how the emperor of the French would have reacted to being called a 'restless cricket' by a barely literate common soldier on garrison duty in Ireland would have been interesting to find out, but it is clear that morale was good and that some at least viewed the man who had waged war on Europe for almost a generation as little more than an irritating insect to be swatted.

Regiments were hurriedly inspected and declared fit for service. The confusion with which troops were being mobilised was compounded by the haste with which the army, so recently engaged in the Iberian Peninsula, had been disbanded. As the commander of a troop of artillery at Colchester recalled: 'the reductions necessary to put us on a peace-establishment had already commenced, when the order arrived for our being immediately equipped again for foreign service. To do this effectually, another troop, then in the same barracks, was broken up, and we got the picked horses of both, thus making it the finest troop in the service.'[13]

Within a few days ports on the south and east coasts were thronged with soldiers:

the little town of Harwich presented a most animated spectacle. Its narrow streets of modest houses, with brick *trottoirs*, were crowded with soldiers – some, all over dust, just arrived; some, who had already been a day or two in the place, comparatively at home, lounging about in undress; others, about to embark, hurrying along to the beach with baggage and stores.[14]

The crowds were further swollen by large numbers of well-wishers who gathered to cheer and see off the soldiers.

Some of those thronging the seaside towns were experienced soldiers, veterans of years of warfare, while others were in their mid-teens, and had grown up knowing nothing other than a state of near-perpetual war with France. The contrast made youngsters particularly conscious of their youth and inexperience. One fair-skinned, bashful young aristocrat, who had recently been gazetted as an ensign in a foot regiment but 'still wanted two months of sixteen' and felt that his complexion 'made me look still younger', was made acutely aware of his age and inexperience on his arrival at Ramsgate in late April, when the town was packed with soldiers. 'Observing the respect shown by the men to commissioned officers I donned my uniform and sauntered forth to come in for a share of the compliments due to my rank. There was no lack of salutes, but the irrepressible smile that accompanied them soon drove me back to my inn,'[15] where he consoled himself with a lavish and expensive dinner.

Although not yet sixteen, this fresh-faced young nobleman was certainly not the youngest boy waiting to embark for Flanders. Sir George Scovell, whose talent for cracking military codes and deciphering French despatches had earned him the sobriquet 'the cipher officer'[16] during the Peninsular War was a Lieutenant-Colonel who, on the resumption of hostilities, found himself attached to the Duke of Wellington's staff as an Assistant Quartermaster-General. On learning that he was destined for the Low Countries, he looked up Heeley, his old batman, who had been discharged on the general demobilisation in 1814, and engaged him as head groom. Heeley had a fourteen-year-old son who takes up the story. As well as being remarkable for the extreme youth of its author, Edward Heeley's reminiscences give an interesting insight into the personal retinue of an officer on Wellington's staff. As well as valet and groom, there were 'four good chargers and two baggage animals'[17] which needed looking after.

> Sir George seeing me asked my father what I was doing, and on being told I was doing nothing, only going to school, he replied 'I will take him with me if you like' but it was not settled till just as they were going to start, so that I had not more than half an hour's notice before I was on the road, and pleased enough I was, though my mother did not like it much.[18]

Having attached himself to Scovell's personal staff, in spite of his mother's reservations, young Edward set out on the road, finding 'plenty of company all making for Ramsgate for embarkation'.[19] He 'went along very merrily', although he does admit that 'as I was only 14 years old, I could not help now and then think that it must be dreadfull [*sic*] to go where there was war – and half wished myself at home again'. However his anxiety disappeared when he got caught up in the military preparations on his arrival at the Albion Hotel at Ramsgate, and 'there I had to begin grooming in reality, without being allowed even to grumble'.[20]

Heeley's mother's reaction was typical. John Haddy James, twenty-six-year-old assistant surgeon to the First Life Guards, admits that his mother would far rather have seen him 'settling into the quiet of some country practice', but adds that 'it is hard for the gentle sex to understand the love of adventure inherent in every man of parts'.[21]

9

'The rage for fighting'

A considerable part of the explanation of the British soldier's readiness and enthusiasm to go to war lies in the remarkable violence of the times. Apart from being drawn from a generation whose sensibilities had been coarsened by near-constant war, 'their souls were strong for war, and peace became irksome to them'[1] wrote one non-commissioned officer of the seasoned soldiers in his brigade just before the announcement of Napoleon's escape. Those who commanded and shaped the Army of the time had grown up in a culture where splendour and brutality, elegance and violence were juxtaposed and co-existed in a manner that might seem bizarre by today's standards, but which at the time was accepted as the norm.

Duelling was of course still an accepted method of settling disagreements between gentlemen, and even high-profile public figures used it as a way of resolving their differences; the Duke of Wellington involved himself in a duel with Lord Winchilsea as late as 1829. But more than this, there was a taste for violence. Quite barbaric 'sports' such as ratting and bull-baiting enjoyed a considerable chic at the time, being particularly popular with the Fancy (a loosely defined cadre of sportsmen who might today be called playboys). The all-male preserve of the public schools was the crucible of this sort of behaviour, and as leaders of fashion the aristocracy endorsed the violence and brutality that was endemic among the less privileged classes. Behaviour that today would be considered at best hooliganism and at worst criminal was tolerated if not celebrated; life was coloured with a callousness that at times was simply breathtaking.

One characteristic story of the time concerns a severely injured man who was brought in off the street into the hall of one of the clubs. Although bleeding profusely and clearly in danger of losing his life, he was refused medical attention because some of the members had placed bets on whether he would live or die, and, if the latter, exactly when he would expire. Then there is the famous story of the £1,000 wagered that a man could live twelve hours underwater: a 'low fellow was hired, and sunk in a ship by way of experiment – but the bet was lost'.[2] This was not a sentimental time and it created the sort of culture in which actions such as that of Lord Glasgow, who threw a servant through a window of his club and then said 'put him on the bill',[3] seemed far from extraordinary.

Nor were the young noblemen and gentry content to sit back and enjoy the spectacle of violent death, be it rats being torn apart by dogs, bulls set upon by dogs, an injured man bleeding to death or a 'low fellow' drowning. They were active and willing participants in violence. Regency England was one big brawl, and many of the aristocracy were members of a giant fight club.

> The autobiography of a Westminster schoolboy of the early part of the century would be incomplete without some mention of the rage for fighting with which the author of these memoirs, in common with the rest of his countrymen, was then afflicted, and which made him a performer in 'the fighting green', much oftener than he now cares to specify.

This is the Earl of Albemarle, writing much later in his life, when the standards of the Regency were thrown into relief by the public piety of the high Victorian era.

> The 'noble science of self-defence', was inculcated upon us boys as one of the essentials of a gentleman's education. It was the point upon which no difference of opinion existed either between masters and pupils or between sons and fathers.
>
> Carey,* who had been a good fighter in his day, did all in his power to foster this pugnacious feeling.[4]

Violence was not merely tacitly tolerated or looked upon with a blind eye, it was actively encouraged by schoolmasters and parents alike. One of the diversions open to pupils at Westminster was the rental of firearms from a certain Mother Hubbard. And at times a pugnacious nature was seen as more than compensating for a less than brilliant academic record. 'Well! If he is a good fellow and a good fighter we must not be too hard

* William Carey, headmaster of Westminster School from 1803 to 1815.

on him for Latin and Greek'[5] was the indulgent opinion held by one schoolmaster of an otherwise unremarkable pupil. The British public school system of the late eighteenth and early nineteenth centuries was not interested in broadening the minds of its pupils. According to one soldier who was educated at Eton at the end of the 1790s, 'the system was to drill into the heads of the boys strong aristocratic principles and hatred of democracy and of the French in particular'.[6] The result in the particular instance of this pupil was the opposite: he became a talented linguist, a great Francophile, and was buried in St-Germain. However he was very much the exception, and yet, even with his more liberal and intellectual leanings, he served in the Army from 1799 until 1822. The system of the public school and then military service was obviously a strong one.

The Earl of Albemarle was a typically diligent pupil when it came to the martial arts: as a youngster he ran with the mob and took part in the Burdett riots of 1810. The major disturbance took place on Saturday, 5 April, and as good fortune would have it 'Saturday was a Westminster half-holiday', so he could join the mob with a clear conscience that he was not neglecting his studies. He describes the squadron of the Horse Guards that was deployed against the rioters thus:

> The men and horses were of the same colossal form as are those of the same corps in our day [his memoirs were published in 1876]. Their height was considerably increased in appearance by the enormous cocked hats which they wore, what sailors would call 'athwart ships'. Their uniform was blue with buff facings which covered their chests. Over the coat were worn broad buff cross-belts. Their hair, greased and powdered, terminated in a pigtail which went half way down the back.[7]

The anachronistic appearance of these soldiers, with their dressed and powdered hair, given the unpleasant task of quelling public unrest, provides a piquant contrast to the rowdy mob of which this schoolboy aristocrat was a part. It was not unusual for gentlemen to be part of the mob, at the time of the Gordon riots, much was made of the elegant and 'gentlemanly' appearance of some of the rioters. The behaviour of the Horse Guards that afternoon earned the regiment the sobriquet of the 'Piccadilly Butchers'. Ironically, 'it was not till after its splendid achievements at Waterloo that it entirely lost the opprobrious name',[8] by which time the author of this set of memoirs was fighting with them rather than against them.

As has already been seen, the Army was held in readiness to quell expected disturbances about the Corn Laws, and after the Waterloo campaign the language of war would be echoed in the name given to the

'Peterloo Massacre' illustrating the interchangeable nature of violence at home and violence abroad and showing that when the Army was not fighting wars it was a frequent presence on the British streets.

And as if there was not enough violence in the spontaneous and lively clashes of rioters and soldiers, apparently the only way for the disenfranchised masses, denied the right of electing politicians to represent their needs, to express their views, there was of course the prize ring.

Of all the 'sporting' diversions of the Regency, prizefighting was the most bloody, spectacular and sensational. One commentator looking back on the Regency from the bourgeois comfort of the late nineteenth century remarked that 'it was a pugilistic age, and all classes patronized "the noble art of self-defence". Princes, peers and officials of the highest rank flocked to see a prize-fight or a set-to with' – or indeed without – 'the gloves as eagerly as they now rush to a boat-race or Lord's Cricket-ground. The best-born in the kingdom, in those days, were proud of recognition by one of the celebrities of the prize-ring.'[9]

The big news in the summer of 1811 was not the progress of the war in Spain, but the celebrated bout between Tom Cribb and Tom Molyneux. Cribb was a coal heaver, hence his nickname 'the Black Diamond'. Molyneux was a former slave who had been born in Virginia and quite literally won his freedom with his fists; beating another slave in a boxing match held for a wager of $100,000. The fight between Cribb and Molyneux lasted thiry-nine rounds, disfiguring the two combatants beyond recognition. In the end Cribb won, not without a little skulduggery and the invasion of the ring by racist spectators.

Their rematch, which Molyneux lost in the eleventh round, attracted a crowd of 25,000, an estimated quarter of whom were drawn from the nobility and gentry, and it was judged to be one of the great sporting spectacles of the nineteenth century. Boxers enjoyed a fame that transcended class and economic boundaries and was as great as that enjoyed by military heroes. 'Plaster of Paris models of the combatants in boxing attitude were carried about the streets by the image sellers – probably by the same men who a few years later bore on their heads the busts of Wellington and Blücher.'[10] Once again there is the sense that the violence of the ring and the battlefield are in some way pretty much the same thing to a public used to violence, and that the protagonists of either are heroes to be celebrated in souvenir form.

In at least one instance the ring and the battlefield were inextricably linked. John Shaw, a violent, hard-drinking, hard-hitting six-foot-six prizefighter, was also a trooper in the Life Guards. Six decades after his death he would be reinvented as an all-English hero: his life, and much more significantly his death, subtitled 'an exciting narrative', became fodder for the imperialist patriotism of the late nineteenth century as part of the wonderfully gung-ho 'Deeds of Daring Library'. The Library rhapsodises about Corporal Shaw, asserting that: 'Englishmen are proud of Shaw because he was essentially the embodiment of the national characteristics, in short, he was a representative man.'[11] And indeed Shaw was as much a man of his time as the bloodthirsty, public-school-educated, xenophobic sons of the aristocracy. Shaw was the kind of common man with whom a Regency aristocrat would have had no problem mixing: 'from his earliest childhood, ever ready with his fists',[12] he had what is euphemistically referred to as 'a pugnacious disposition'.[13]

It seems that Shaw would fight anyone over anything, and in early nineteenth-century England this was a valuable social skill. He participated in his first public bout at the age of sixteen and by eighteen he had enlisted in the 2nd Life Guards, where he 'found himself quite in his element, for pugilism was much cultivated by the Household Cavalry, and very few months had elapsed before he was recognized by his comrades as a bruiser of the first water'.[14]

At the time soldiers were subject to taunts from the public, hardly surprising perhaps when viewed in the context of the Army's secondary role as riot police (no police force existed until much later in the century). They were often called 'lobsters', a reference to the colour of their uniforms, or goaded with the words 'a shilling a day to be shot at' – except not all members of the armed forces earned quite that much per diem. Shaw did not react well to such abuse and would frequently take brutal revenge. Whereas today such behaviour might be a matter for a disciplinary tribunal, at the beginning of the nineteenth century it was enough to mark him for special favour.

Colonel Barton was an officer who fancied himself as something of a connoisseur of the art of pugilism. He took a special interest in Shaw, and presented him at Gentleman Jackson's rooms on Bond Street. Jackson was a prizefighter who had opened a boxing academy on Bond Street that was part gymnasium, part sparring ground, and altogether an extremely fashionable place to see and be seen. Jackson was the son of a builder, but through his proficiency with his fists had been accorded the status of *de facto* gentleman by his pupils, who tended to be his social superiors. At one time it is said that a third of the nobility frequented Jackson's rooms, to undertake gruelling training and strenuous exercise regimes under his instruction.

Such an environment could not have suited Shaw better. Under the patronage of Colonel Barton and the training of Gentleman Jackson he flourished as a fighter, beating professionals such as Molyneux and gentleman amateurs including a Captain Barclay, who once walked a thousand miles in a thousand hours to win a bet of a thousand guineas. By 1812 Shaw had cemented his fame, winning his first bare-knuckle bout in just seventeen minutes.

Now, on 18 April 1815, as the army mobilised, and started to move to the Low Countries, Shaw was to fight one of most important bouts of his career. From early that morning, the roads around Hounslow Heath, where the match was to take place, were clogged with every sort of vehicle, from smart carriages to crude carts, men on horseback and others trudging on foot, all heading to see Shaw the Life Guardsman demonstrate his prowess in the ring. He had just laid down his challenge to 'all England for the championship'.[15] His opponent, Ned Painter, had been released that morning from the Fleet Prison and was seconded by Tom Cribb. Within twenty-eight minutes Shaw had demolished him.

'The victory placed Shaw in such a position that, had he remained much longer in England, a fight for the belt with Cribb, the champion of England, must have taken place.'[16] However, Shaw was not to remain in England long enough to enter the ring again. Twelve days after his encounter with Painter, the 2nd Life Guards, among them Corporal Shaw, one of the most violent and celebrated men in England, left London to join the hurriedly assembled force heading for Belgium.

10

'The cool shade of the aristocracy'

The journey from Vienna had been an unpleasant one but at last ... at three o'clock on the morning of 5 April the Duke of Wellington's carriage rumbled into Brussels.[1] The effect of his arrival on the morale of both civilians and soldiers was electric. 'We are in as perfect Security here as you are in London,' wrote Lady Caroline Capel to her mother in early April. The reason for this sudden and remarkable change of mood? 'Lord Wellington is arrived in the highest Spirits & it seems generally believed that Napoleon never was in such a Scrape before.'[2]

On the day he arrived Wellington plunged into the business of preparing a credible force with which to meet Napoleon. Within days the Prince of Orange resigned his command. The Army was beside itself with joy. Private Wheeler captures the mood well in a letter home:

> Before we left we were delighted by a General Order issued by H.R.H. the Prince of Orange, in which order he 'Surrenders the Command of the Army into the more able hands of His Grace the Duke of Wellington'. I never remember anything that caused such joy, our men were almost frantic, every soldier you met told the joyful news.[3]

As the news spread across Belgium the streets of towns and villages echoed to the raucous cries of celebrating soldiers, shouting 'Glorious news, Nosey has got the command, wont [sic] we give them a drubbing now' and 'Drink hearty to the health of our old Commander, we dont [sic] care a d____n for all France, supposing everyone was a Napoleon'.[4] Such shouting was accompanied by much drinking of hollands.

However, the rejoicing was not universal. Although the young Prince resigned his command within a couple of days of the Duke's arrival, it would be some weeks before the ruler of the newly constituted Kingdom of the United Netherlands would announce the formal appointment of the Duke of Wellington as Commander-in-Chief.

For the recently crowned king on his insecure throne, the joy with which the Duke of Wellington's arrival was greeted must have been very galling. Moreover it further punctured the mythology of the United Netherlands' existence as an autonomous state. But the arrival of the Duke and his immediate assumption of the role of military commander and *de facto* military governor of the Netherlands was a *fait accompli*. All the piqued monarch could do was to withhold his official blessing to the existing state of affairs.

If, in the midst of the frenzied military preparation, he had time to think of this situation and how, by his mere arrival in Brussels, he had sidelined the local monarchy, Wellington must have allowed himself at least a chuckle of satisfaction. Wellington was the man to whom Europe turned when Napoleon threatened world peace, and he knew it. Now in his mid-forties, he appeared to have it all. With austere good looks, money, position, and dandiacal insouciance, he was irresistible to women and respected by men. Ladies' man, diplomat and soldier: he was a phenomenon. Yet Wellington the national icon, who arrived in Brussels in early April 1815 and took such decisive command of the heterogeneous forces in the Belgian provinces, was a very different person to the fifteen-year-old Arthur Wesley (the spelling 'Wenesley', which according to the current Duke dates from the family's arrival in Ireland during the 13th century, was revived around the turn of the 18th and 19th centuries) who had lived in Brussels in the mid-1780s.

Although from an aristocratic Anglo-Irish family, it can hardly be said that Wellington's own background was particularly glamorous. His father had been a professor of music at Dublin's Trinity College who had tried and failed to marry Lady Augusta Lennox, daughter of the Duke of Richmond, settling instead for a banker's daughter who, like him, was judged to be a little gauche and lacking in the sophistication of true high society. Moreover even before Wellington's father died the family was in straitened circumstances. And while his elder brother Richard distinguished himself at Eton and then Oxford, young Arthur was a shy, dreamy boy who liked poetry and distinguished himself in neither academe nor athletics. Instead he had inherited his father's musical ability and played the violin rather well.

After a couple of years he was withdrawn from Eton and travelled with his mother to Brussels, where he continued to play the violin. He was then sent to the Royal Academy of Equitation at Angers, a sort of finishing school that imparted a little French polish to the dim-witted scions of aristocratic families. According to one account of this part of his education he spent a great deal of time lounging on a sofa playing with his white terrier.

Then this sensitive and musically gifted, if indolent, young man was found a position in the Army, and it was as if he became a different person. The languid, poetry-reading violin player became a man of action; masculine, unemotional, laconic and cynical almost to the point of parody; clipped in his speech, seldom betraying a scintilla of feeling. He never played the violin again; a friend noted that Wellington thought fiddling about with a stringed instrument was 'not a soldierly accomplishment and took up too much of his time and thoughts'.[5]

One theory is that the catalyst for this abrupt change in his life was the rejection of his advances to Lord Longford's daughter Kitty Pakenham. As a younger son who had done little to distinguish himself he was not thought a suitable match. It was almost a rerun of his father's experience: another snub by a grand family. But Arthur would not take it as philosophically as his father; he vowed he would renew his addresses to the young lady when his prospects improved. Over a decade later he returned Major-General Sir Arthur Wellesley, with a fortune of around £43,000 (over £2,000,000 in contemporary values) and, without apparent enthusiasm, repeated his proposal of marriage. It was accepted. Then, casually and cruelly remarking to his brother the Rev. Gerald Wellesley who was to marry them, 'She has grown ugly by Jove,'[6] he wedded the woman whose family had at first rejected him. He then seemed to spend the remainder of their married life humiliating her with his amorous dalliances.

Perhaps, as he settled into Brussels, Wellington allowed his thoughts to wander to that pale romantic teenager who had played the violin, read poetry and played with his pet dog. If so, it is likely that he ruthlessly suppressed such thoughts; after all, that child had nothing in common with the chilly, snobbish autocrat who set about leaving his stamp on the ragged Allied Army. One of his first actions on arriving in Brussels was to dispense with Lord William Pitt Lennox, who had accompanied him from Vienna. 'A few days after our arrival, the Duke told me, in the most kind and considerate manner, that as he was anxious to replace on his staff those officers who had served with him in the Peninsula, he could no longer retain me.'[7]

The composition of his personal staff, or 'family', during the Peninsular War is eloquently indicative of his leanings towards the scions of aristocratic families. Writing in the 1860s, one of his aides recorded that 'The "family" was composed of the late Lord Raglan, then known as Lord Fitzroy Somerset; his nephew, the late Duke of Beaufort, then Marquis of Worcester; the Earl of March, Lords George Lennox, William Russell, Charles Manners and Clinton, the Honourable Fitzroy Stanhope, Honourable Henry Percy, Canning, Gordon, Colin Campbell, J. Fremantle, and the Prince of Orange'. Apparently the 'hunting field in England had made many of these gentlemen fully competent for an important branch of their duty – that of conveying orders to distant posts'.[8]

Indeed for many there seems to have been the sense that serving as a soldier on horseback was little different to a day's hunting. As Lawrence James puts it in his military biography of Wellington: 'A British cavalry charge had something of the wild quality of a hunt in full chase and it was observed that cavalrymen deliberately adopted the short stirrup of the "hunting seat" when they rode at the enemy.'[9]

While youth, an aristocratic pedigree and the distinction of having ridden to hounds may have struck the Duke as ample qualification to serve on his staff, others found it a little surprising. 'It was a matter of great surprise to the French officers, and one that they could not at all comprehend, that the British Commander-in-Chief should be attended by such striplings.'[10]

There is the sense that in surrounding himself with boisterous young men of impeccable aristocratic pedigree, Wellington was almost rewriting his own youth, or to put it another way, associating with the sort of young man he would have liked to have been, having conceived what seems almost like a contempt for the soft, soppy, sentimental little boy that he had been.

Even in an age when the aristocracy effectively controlled almost every aspect of life in Great Britain, it seems that Wellington's policy of surrounding himself with 'men of rank, fortune and station'[11] was remarked upon by his own side as well as those he was fighting. The defensive tone of this letter of 4 August 1810 to the military secretary Colonel Torrens suggests that he recognised this.

I have never been able to understand the principle on which the claims of gentlemen of family, fortune, and influence in the country, to promotion in the army, founded on their military conduct, and character, and services, should be rejected, while the claims of others, not better founded, on military pretensions, were invariably attended to. It would be desirable, certainly, that the only claim to promotion should be military merit; but this is a degree of perfection to which the disposal of military patronage has never been, and cannot be, I believe, brought in any military establishment. The Commander-in-Chief must have friends, officers, or the staff attached to him, &c., who will press him to promote their friends and relations, all doubtless very meritorious; and no man can at all times resist these applications; but if there is to be any influence in the disposal of military patronage, in aid of military merit, can there be any in our army so legitimate as that of family connexion, fortune, and influence in the country?[12]

The subtext is clearly that if a distinguished commander wanted to run his army as a private club for the sons of dukes and earls he was damned well going to do so. Although the views voiced in this letter are almost diametrically opposed to the prevailing wisdom today, they are views that Wellington clung to all his life, and it is rather charming that when, years later,

he resumed in 1842 the office of Commander-in-Chief of the Army, he appointed the present Duke of Richmond to be one of his aides-de-camp – a compliment highly gratifying to the feelings of his father. The son of another highly esteemed nobleman, the late Duke of Beaufort, also a member of the 'family', had the gratification of seeing his son, the present head of the Somerset family, installed in a situation which he had himself held in former years.[13]

As well as a dukedom and an estate, an influential job in the Army was something that could also be passed down the generations.

It must be remembered that British officers of the early nineteenth century bore little resemblance to the professional soldiers of today. Many were aristocrats who purchased commissions and swapped regiments on a whim; the question of regimental loyalty was not yet as highly developed as it would become by the end of the nineteenth century, and for many, fashion was the motivating factor in selecting one regiment over another.

Wellington had benefited from this system himself, achieving the rank of lieutenant-colonel by the age of twenty-five. He also expressed his admiration for the system of purchasing commissions, commenting that it brought 'into the service men of fortune and character – men who have some connection with the interests and fortunes of the country'. Conversely he was of the opinion that seldom, if ever, did good come of promoting from the ranks. 'I have never known officers raised from the ranks turn out well'[14] was his uncompromising verdict on what he saw as the folly of taking the lower orders and trying to make officers out of them.

Although Wellington was undoubtedly a conservative whose views ossified over the years, the stark divisions in society at the time would have ensured that the class-defined *status quo* of the military remained intact. Being an Army officer was one of the few acceptable careers for a gentleman who needed to fill his time. It was ideal for those second and subsequent sons of the aristocracy who would not inherit the family estate, in that it was an occupation rather than a trade, which would have been *infra dig* in the extreme. Hence a commission was also seen as a passport to social acceptability – a passport that could be purchased. In the first half of the nineteenth century, the base price of the rank of ensign in a Foot Regiment was £450 (approximately £22,000 in contemporary values).*

Commissions were purchased from and sold back to the government, but they were often perceived to be more valuable than the book price. There were fashionable and unfashionable regiments; indeed one's regiment was as much of a style statement as one's carriage and one's tailor. So to purchase a desirable and sought-after commission the buyer would have to lay out an additional sum of money. Although unofficial, and strictly speaking illegal, this practice was the norm, with the payment being pocketed direct by the seller – the sale being brokered by a shadowy figure known as the regimental agent. Thus the total investment required for an officer to reach a high rank, such as lieutenant-colonel, could amount to £10,000 (approximately £500,000) in both official and unofficial payments. Moreover if an officer died he forfeited the value of his commission (although in circumstances of extreme gallantry his family might be allowed to sell it). The custom was that an officer putting his commission up for sale offered it to the next most senior officer, so often if a high-ranking officer decided to sell up, a chain was established, not unlike those in sales of houses, right down to the lowest rank of officer.

Another route to officer status was patronage – often one or other of the

* The straight inflationary adjustment of around 5,000 per cent does not give a truly accurate picture of the value of money in Regency England. To convey an idea of contemporary expenditure, *A Practical Guide to the Peculiar Duties and Business of all Descriptions of Servants* published in 1825 informed its readers that a 'Widow or other unmarried Lady' with an annual income of only £100 'may keep a Young Maid Servant at a low salary'. So in other words the status of the lowest class of officer was worth about the same amount of money that would maintain a widow in genteel, albeit modest circumstances for four and a half years.

royal dukes or even the Prince Regent could be persuaded to give a friend's son his first commission as a present. However, given the decadent nature of the Regent and his brothers, such a system was wide open to abuse. In the early years of the nineteenth century there had been a huge scandal involving the Duke of York and Mrs Clarke, the latter being kept by the former, who was said to pay her £1,000 (around £50,000) a month. But the Duke of York was not very punctual in his payments, so she took to dealing in royal patronage, at one time managing to secure one of her footmen a commission in the Army. The scandal broke and eventually the Duke of York resigned from the position of Commander-in-Chief for a couple of years until the trouble blew over.

Only in times of war did the proportion of non-purchased commissions increase as new regiments were raised and as casualties had to be replaced rapidly. Therefore the prospects of advancement for the poorer officer were much increased if his regiment saw action. Often if there were no commissions to be had, a gentleman would join a regiment as a 'volunteer' serving as a private soldier, but the post was more accurately that of officer-in-waiting, as it was these volunteers who then made up the numbers of slain officers.

Very occasionally a deserving sergeant might get promoted to the rank of officer. Although one contemporary estimate that the odds were 100,000 to 1 against such an eventuality is doubtless an exaggeration, these incidents were certainly extremely few, very far between and tended to leave the recipient feeling less comfortable than he had been in the ranks. 'Indeed ... to obtain a commission places the individual in a worse position,' wrote one soldier:

> especially in what are termed the 'crack regiments'; the aristocratic officers of which, send every man to 'Coventry', who cannot, like themselves, boast gentle blood, and whose private purse is not sufficiently well filled to support all the luxuries and extravagance of the mess table. Besides, how is it possible, supposing a deserving non-commissioned officer is promoted to a commission in such regiments as the 10th or 11th Hussars, that he can provide his equipments, which, I believe, under the most economical arrangement, amount to upwards of five hundred pounds.[15]

One such story of discomfiture relates to a sergeant of the Guards who, upon being given a commission by the Duke of York, subsequently asked to be returned to the ranks as his fellow officers refused to have anything to do with him. The Duke of York then asked for the regiment to be readied for his inspection, whereupon he made a point of calling for the sergeant-turned-officer and walked arm-in-arm with him while the regiment was on parade. The mood of his fellow officers ameliorated immediately. While such blatant snobbery sounds comical it has to be seen in the context of the manners of the day, when it was seen as perfectly normal to 'cut', or ignore, close relatives and even parents, if one happened to think them socially inferior.

But even taking into account very particular social niceties and the very real, almost impermeable, class barriers that divided society, the system of purchase had its critics, leading to the famous maxim that the Army wilted under 'the cool shade of the aristocracy'. Gallant but incompetent was a prevailing and widely held opinion. As one ranker said: 'while I admit that I have known many brave and well-disciplined officers in the service, yet, on the whole I considered them the most inefficient of any officers in the European armies.'[6]

But its supporters, like the Duke, felt that it worked because it attracted men of independent means, which were needed, since an officer's pay was little more than an honorarium. And even though there might have been some radicals who voiced concerns about the purchase system, an Army staffed and run by rich aristocrats held little threat for the crown and government, as the majority of the aristocracy was dedicated to maintenance of the *status quo*.

Indeed, a sense of aristocratic responsibility similar to that felt by a landowner for his tenant farmers and servants carried over into military life. For those in command of a regiment there was much of the feeling of a personal fiefdom. Until the middle of the eighteenth century, regiments bore the name and title of their commanding colonel, and often might carry his coat of arms in the form of a badge. Even in 1815, the commander virtually owned his regiment, being responsible for clothing men and dispensing patronage among the officers. And of course the Duke of Wellington set the social tone by surrounding himself with A.D.C.s and staff officers of noble descent.

Another way in which the officers were set apart from the other ranks was in the manner of their dress: Wellington, so keen on discipline and obedience in all other aspects, let his officers dress how they wished. 'We might be rigged out in all the colours of the rainbow if we fancied,' wrote one officer, who recalled that 'scarcely any two officers were dressed alike. Some with grey braided coats, some with brown, some again liked blue,' adding with a note of pity that others, 'perhaps from necessity, stuck to the "old red rag"'. Add to this the plumed helmets, form-fitting trousers, fur-trimmed jackets and so on, and it is easy to see that one of the things that was so attractive about the Army in Wellington's day was the polychromatic variety of 'uniforms' – camouflage as a concept did not really take off until the following century. During the Spanish campaign Wellington himself dressed in a light blue frock coat (the colour of the Hatfield Hunt), which had been sent to him by a female admirer. According to his cook he wore the 'Blue Frock Coat and Mixed Coloured trousers, except on Grand Review, and then in Full dressed [*sic*] uniform'.[17] Nevertheless the Duke of Wellington did draw the line at his officers taking to the battlefield under umbrellas, feeling that it lent them an ungentlemanly air.

It was the Duke's mania for gentlemanliness that led to friction between various arms of the services. For instance, although the Duke of Wellington might have admired the martial prowess of the King's German Legion, he did not regard its officers as gentlemen. Nor was he particularly fond of the artillery. Perhaps this was because, unlike the infantry or cavalry, they were under the aegis of the Master-General of the Ordnance, rather than the Commander-in-Chief. Moreover Wellington must have instinctively revolted against the fact that artillery officers could not purchase commissions and that promotion was by seniority.

Wellington's pronounced prejudice against the artillery perplexed some. 'The Duke was not partial to our corps,' recalled one artillery officer who served in the Netherlands in 1815. 'It is difficult to say why, but his Grace certainly treated us harshly, and on many occasions unjustly.'[18] It was perhaps the professional nature of the Royal Artillery that was the greatest cause of division: since 1741, artillery officers had been trained at the Royal Military Academy (the Royal Military College for cavalry and infantry officers only came into being in 1802), making them, horror of horrors, professional soldiers rather than gentleman amateurs.

It also seems that Wellington's conservatism was at odds with some of the innovative techniques being pioneered by the artillery. Typical of the sort of issues that brought him into conflict with the artillery was the issue of Captain Whinyates and his rocket troop. Whinyates's rockets were erratic and caused little actual damage, but they had been used to considerable psychological effect in the war with America and in particular during the assault on Washington. Yet instead of seeing that these neo-logistic weapons might have potential, Wellington closed his mind to them. He 'looked upon rockets as nonsense, ordered that they should be put into store, and the troop supplied with guns instead'.[19]

Seeing one day that the Duke was in a good mood, a foolhardy colonel attempted to intercede on Whinyates's behalf. The exchange was brief and to the point. "'It will break poor Whinyate's [*sic*] heart to lose his rockets." "D____n his heart, sir; let my order be obeyed.'"[20] In the event Wellington did relent and allow rockets to be deployed, but his initial, instinctive reaction to such things was one of innate conservatism and suspicion. Another similar point of contention with the artillery was the issue of whether horse artillery should use six-pounders or nine-pounders; the use of heavier artillery was a progressive innovation, and once again Wellington reacted negatively towards it. It was only the reputation of the commander of the horse artillery and what is euphemistically termed his 'firmness of character' which eventually 'prevailed on the Duke of Wellington'.[21]

Wellington had enjoyed a stormy relationship with his artillery officers during the Peninsular campaign and he was not about to behave in a conciliatory manner towards them now. For their part, the gunners harboured a grudge.

Nor were truculent artillery officers going to be Wellington's only difficulty in his new command. As one of the most vocal advocates of the system of purchase, aristocratic preferment and patronage, he could hardly complain when he was overruled by a higher authority. Even though he was a celebrity he was not beyond the strict rules that governed social and military life. Just as he was once turned away from Almack's Assembly Rooms for being incorrectly dressed – wearing trousers instead of the stipulated knee breeches – so he could be thwarted in matters relating directly to his military command. Wellington was doing his best to rid himself of those officers he found antipathetic. Typical of his ruthlessness was the manner in which he got rid of the quartermaster-general he had inherited, Major-General Sir Hudson Lowe. Already prejudiced against those who had not served with him in the Peninsula, Wellington was further annoyed when, out inspecting troop positions, he asked Lowe where a certain road led. Lowe, uncertain, started fumbling among his maps and papers for the answer. Not waiting, Wellington barked out the crushing put-down 'Damned old fool'[22] and rode off. Lowe was not long in his job after that.

While he might have got his way over his own A.D.C.s and arrangement of the quartermaster-general's department, it was a different matter when it came to the cavalry. Wellington wanted his old cavalry commander from the Peninsular War, Sir Stapleton Cotton, who had just recently been made Lord Combermere – a solid, dependable and perhaps rather dull

11

'I'll take good care he don't run away with me'

The task of composing an army and a command structure out of the heterogeneous forces at his disposal was a complicated logistical, military and diplomatic jigsaw puzzle for the Duke of Wellington. The necessary but sensitive task of removing the headstrong young Prince of Orange from overall command had been tricky enough, but there were many other factors influencing the situation.

Wellington's ideal would have been to reassemble the officers with whom he had prosecuted the successful Peninsular campaign; but the complications of dispersed troops, disbanded regiments and forces still *en route* from America were far from being his only obstacles. For a start there were individuals right under his prominent nose in Brussels who expected a military appointment. Foremost among them was the Duke of Richmond, who as a personal friend, a soldier and a duke could not be fobbed off easily. For a while the idea being talked of was that the Duke of Richmond would command a body of reserve troops.[1] In the end his case was referred to the highest levels of government.

On 16 April, Major-General Sir Henry Torrens wrote from Horse Guards to Wellington explaining the decision:

> The question of the Duke of Richmond, which has been one of great embarrassment here, has been decided unfavourably to his wishes; and I enclose for your information the copy of a letter which I have addressed to him. I fear his Grace will be much dissatisfied, but I am commissioned by the Duke of York and Lord Bathurst to request your cooperation in

setting his mind at ease. In every point of view his employment would be unadvisable; and a due regard to his feelings, and a consistency towards the reason I have been authorized to assign for his exclusion, would prevent the possibility of any other full General being appointed to your command.[2]

The Duke of Richmond was far from placated. His children's tutor, Spencer Madan, wrote in a letter home: 'The Duke of R's offer of service has been declined by ministers, because he is senior to the Prince, and must therefore have a larger command than him. He is very much annoyed about it.'[3] Nor it seemed did he take much care to hide his feelings from those outside his family circle as John Somerset wrote to his brother on 23 May: 'I dined with the D. of Richmond, who is well, but I think looked old, & *I* believe (entre nous) he is rather hurt at not being employed with this army.'[4]

Presumably the decision and Torrens's request that he connive in the explanation made Wellington feel a little uncomfortable. The Richmonds' house was something of a refuge where he could relax. He was particularly at ease in the company of their younger children and would play with them quite unaffectedly, getting down on his hands and knees or sprawling on the carpet with them. He had been a frequent visitor from almost immediately after his arrival in Brussels – among the first invitations he had accepted was one to dinner with the Richmonds on 6 April, barely thirty-six hours after completing his marathon journey from Vienna.

And if his role as commander complicated his friendship with Richmond, his relationship with the man put in charge of his cavalry could have been seen as a potential disaster. Wellington might have been the most lauded and successful soldier in the British Army, but it could be argued that the Earl of Uxbridge was the most dashing and scandalous.

Wellington enjoyed surrounding himself with either the young pups of the aristocracy, who regarded serving under 'the Beau' as an adventure, or reliable commanders of the calibre of Lord Combermere who did as they were told. Lord Uxbridge, or Lord Paget as he had been until he inherited the earldom on the death of his father, was neither: brilliant where others were solid, mercurial where others were predictable and obedient, he was at times quite scarily gallant. His most recent post had been as commander of the forces stationed in London to restore public order in the event of large-scale violent protest against the Corn Laws, and now he was being talked of in connection with a senior command in the Allied forces gathering in the Low Countries.

'It is also said that Paget will have the Command of the Cavalry,' wrote Caroline Capel to their mother in early April, sympathising with her concerns. 'Poor dear little Soul, If this is true it will be another Source of Anxiety to you.'[5] And it seems that given her son's conduct on the battlefield, the dowager Lady Uxbridge's anxiety was completely justified. 'Lord Uxbridge – afterwards the Marquis of Anglesey – was a very fine cavalry leader, a sort of English Murat,' was one opinion (perhaps a little unfair, as he was cleverer than Murat), 'with all the dash, activity, and resource of that famous soldier. But he had too much fire in his temper for cool generalship. The tumult and shock of battle had the effect of champagne upon him. It kindled in his brain a sort of intoxication. So he took risks a cooler-headed soldier would have avoided.'[6]

While he may have lacked a cool head, Uxbridge was popular with those he commanded, a charismatic figure and, beneath the dashing exterior, an intelligent man. 'He is not only the cleverest cavalry officer in the British Empire, but unfortunately he is almost the only one with a cavalry genius,' wrote one Captain of Hussars. 'In this line all he does is peculiar to himself, and wherever he appears he invariably gains spontaneously the confidence of the whole of his profession.'[7] Uxbridge was clearly a talented man. Moreover he was his own man, who liked to do things his own way and he had particular views about how to lead cavalry.

At his most dismissive Wellington felt 'our officers of cavalry have acquired [the habit] of galloping at everything, and then galloping back as fast as they gallop at the enemy'.[8] He was suspicious and perhaps even slightly jealous of the gallantry and chic of the cavalry – it was a fact of early-nineteenth-century life that cavalry officers tended to have more fun. Some time later, on being told that the Prince Regent had appointed himself Captain-General of the Life Guards and Blues, he was quite caustic. 'His Royal Highness is our sovereign, and can do what he pleases; but this will I say, the cavalry of other European armies have won victories for their generals, but mine have invariably got me into scrapes,' he harrumphed, but even he could not deny their courage. 'It is true that they have always fought gallantly and bravely, and have generally got themselves out of their difficulties by sheer pluck.'[9]

Even when being more charitable he could only bring himself to describe the cavalry as 'the most delicate instrument in our whole machine. Well managed it can perform wonders, and will always be of use, but it is easily put out of order on the field.'[10] For Wellington it was an issue of control: he felt that the cavalry should be kept, pardon the pun, reined in. Lord Uxbridge's view was that a general of cavalry should 'inspire his men as early as possible with the most perfect confidence in his personal gallantry. Let him but lead, they are sure to follow, and I believe hardly anything will stop them.'[11] Much the same could be said of Lord Uxbridge's not-so-private life.

As well as having diametrically opposite views to him on the deployment of cavalry, Uxbridge had also eloped with Wellington's sister-in-law. Uxbridge's personal gallantry was something that appealed to the ladies. Pictures of him in his late thirties and early forties as Lord Paget show a handsome man, his dark wavy hair flecked with grey, whose physique is displayed to good effect in the dashing uniforms of the Colonel of the 7th Light Dragoons. Particularly fetching is an image of him with a short fur-trimmed cape slung over his shoulders, bearskin at a jaunty angle on his head, his feet shod in dainty tasselled boots out of which rises a pair of skin-tight breeches topped with a prominent cod-piece-like bulge. During his long life Paget fathered some eighteen children. He was the apotheosis of the moustachio-twirling officer of a romantic novel.

He served in the Peninsula, but while on leave early in 1808, attending one of his father's musical evenings at Uxbridge House, he fell in love with Lady Charlotte Wellesley. Although she was married to Henry Wellesley, Wellington's younger brother, and he was married to Lady Caroline Villiers, their attraction soon grew into a deep and passionate love affair. In a move worthy of a bedroom farce, the cuckolded Henry Wellesley, who worked as a Secretary to the Treasury, considered that Lord Paget, as a cavalry officer and a gentleman, was just the man to organise and accompany his wife on the course of riding that had been prescribed for her health. Only when she became heavily pregnant did the riding excursions cease.

A memorandum from Wellington, or Sir Arthur Wellesley as he then was, picks up the story: 'about this time Mr Wellesley had perceived the extraordinary attention paid to Lady Charlotte by Lord Paget, & had in consequence remonstrated with her on the subject.' The only thing for it, thought Henry Wellesley, was to move his wife out of town. 'Towards the close of the Session of Parliament of 1808 [in July] Mr Wellesley removed to Putney Heath [from Berkeley Square] & from that time till the return of Lady Charlotte to London in the Month of February 1809, Mr Wellesley had every reason to believe that no meeting took place between Lady Charlotte & Lord Paget.'[12] However, he was mistaken in that belief; Lady Charlotte and Lord Paget remained very much in touch and when Paget returned from another tour of duty in Spain they went for walks in Green Park, which was much more rustic than it is today, and on a number of occasions the footman who attended Lady Charlotte was told to leave and give the couple one or two hours alone together.

It seems that Paget's wife Car, as she was known colloquially (the rival for her husband's affections being nicknamed Char), was used to her husband's infatuations. Her brother-in-law Charles Paget noted in early 1808 at the start of her husband's most recent dalliance that she had 'as much or more reason to complain than ever'.[13] However she was not above consoling herself with a friendship with the Duke of Argyll. Had it been merely a case of the old-fashioned aristocratic pastime of musical bedrooms, with spouses turning a blind eye to each other's sexual exploits, all might have been well, except of course for the poor deluded Henry Wellesley, who by March 1809 had contracted a severe liver complaint to add to the misery of his wife's infidelity. But Paget was not content to leave his relationship with Lady Charlotte at the level of an extramarital fling that would pass. He was quite blunt about it and laid out the situation in clear terms to his wife. As his brother noted, he was under no illusion about Car's attachment to the Duke of Argyll.

Doubtless he rather hoped that Henry Wellesley might die of his liver complaint and save everyone a lot of bother. However Wellesley's constitution proved more robust than his wife and her lover might have hoped. Indeed one evening he staggered from his sickbed to his wife's bedroom where he found the door locked and heard the rustling of papers. Convinced that she was writing to Paget he confronted her, but although she denied it, he persisted and shouted that he and his wife could no longer remain under the same roof. This was the excuse for which Char had been waiting and the following day she went as usual to Green Park, dismissed the footman and disappeared.

The ensuing scenes are worthy of a nineteenth-century melodrama: husband fearing his adulterous wife has committed suicide; wife hidden in a black veil, which she wears at all times, even it is said in bed with her lover; lover, dressed in his oldest clothes to avoid recognition, meets the missing wife in a hackney carriage and takes her to the apartments of an old friend; old friend moves out into local hotel telling everyone that the couple in his apartments are friends visiting from the country who are unable to afford an hotel room; husband tracks down errant wife by following a delivery of linen; husband pleads with estranged wife to return to his side; however wife refuses, declaring 'that she could never think of returning home after the Iniquitous Act she had been guilty of with Lord Paget'.[14]

Although the bare facts of the affair and the farcical nature of the subterfuge would indicate a callous cuckolding by a known philanderer and a highly sexed woman, the affair seems to have caused genuine distress to all parties. Paget wrote to his father at one time admitting his part in the affair and telling how he had wished he had died in battle in Spain, and how when Lady Charlotte left her husband and he his wife, he was afraid to go to his own home in case the sight of one of his children might prompt him to commit suicide. Lady Charlotte wrote to one of her husband's friends, who was the conduit for communications between the estranged couple, that although they had had their differences and her husband might have been a '*little* too hard to me', she wished her correspondent to 'publish it to the World that in essentials and indeed in trifling subjects, he has ever been *kind to me to the greatest Degree*'. She describes her affair as 'this most criminal most atrocious attachment' and adds: 'could you know what are my Sufferings at this Moment you would feel for me.'[15] It was indeed a love affair, and one in which those at all three corners of the triangle were in pain.

However, private anguish did not translate into public sympathy. Old Lord Uxbridge was so incensed that he threatened to cut his eldest son off and had to be restrained from physically bursting in on the lovers. Lady Charlotte was widely seen as a temptress who had separated a man from his family and was called everything from a '*maudite sorcière*'[16] to 'a nefarious damned Hellhound'[17] or a 'stinking Pole Cat'.[18] She had left her husband on a Monday and by Friday her flight was discussed by 'the people in the streets' and even, *quelle horreur*, 'the mob'.[19]

So juicy was this scandalous and aristocratic liaison, involving some of the most prominent families in the country, one of the nation's most dashing soldiers and the relative of another, that it even replaced the scandal of Mrs Clarke and the Duke of York as the favourite topic of speculation in the press. One report claimed that the seriously ill Wellesley had somehow managed to kill Paget in a duel, while another had it on good authority that Sir Arthur Wellesley had chased the couple along the Oxford road and given 'the ravisher of his ailing brother's wife' a nasty wound.[20]

Neither report was true, but as the month of March wore on, the furore surrounding the affair gathered momentum. Supporters of the cuckolded husband became more vociferous in their denouncement. 'Damn her!' was the verdict of one. 'How Paget's stomach will heave in the course of six months, when she seizes him in her hot libidinous arms.'[21] So many challenges to duels were flying about that even one of the royal dukes became involved, threatening to pass information to Bow Street to have the participants arrested. For his part Paget refused to fight duels but said that any member of the families of either Wellesley or his wife would be more than welcome to visit him where he was lodging and shoot him.

By the middle of March it seemed that the affair might be brought to an end when a separation of a month was agreed to, with some quite desperate plans being mooted to slake Lady Charlotte's quite formidable libido. 'I wish I could get some huge Paddy to satisfy her lust and outdo Paget' was the suggestion of one self-appointed marriage counsellor.[22] However it seems that no such Irish stud could be found. The month's separation lasted a week and when Paget returned to those 'hot libidinous arms', another challenge awaited him from his lover's brother, Henry Cadogan, which he declined. By the summer, divorce proceedings were begun and by then the persistent Henry Cadogan had got his duel on Wimbledon Common, during which Paget did not aim to hit his opponent, saying he did not wish to inflict further harm on the family.

Eventually Char and Paget settled down and married, as did Car and her lover the Duke of Argyll, even though the latter relationship caused outcry in Scotland. But by the end of 1811 it seems that relations were remarkably cordial with Paget's children dividing their time between him and their mother and talking with 'filial tenderness of Mama Argyll and Mama Paget'.[23] Nevertheless the standards of the day would never allow Char to be accepted as a proper person for respectable people to meet.

However for Paget, or Lord Uxbridge as he was by 1815, it was a different matter. His complicated private life was no barrier to his military career, and although Wellington might have favoured the tractable Combermere as a cavalry commander purely because he was easier to manage than the flamboyant Uxbridge, he had no problem with the moral conduct of the seducer of his sister-in-law. Indeed Uxbridge's appointment seems barely to have caused the Duke to raise a quizzical eyebrow, which led some to wonder whether he had forgotten the elopement and scandal that had involved his brother.

'Oh no! I had not forgotten that,' one account quotes him as saying. 'That is not the only case, I am afraid. At any rate Lord Uxbridge has the reputation of running away with everybody he can' was Wellington's philosophical stance. He added with wry humour and a touch of cynicism: 'I'll take good care he don't run away with me: I don't care about anybody else.'[24]* However in the event the men got along well; as one observer of

---

* Another account has the Duke saying 'D____m him, he won't run off with me too.' Mackworth, *Army Quarterly*, Vol. XXXV, 1937-8, p.321.

Wellington and Uxbridge noted: 'They did meet and even appeared to be on the best possible terms.'[25] As far as Wellington was concerned, personal morality, or immorality, whether his own or his officers', was neither a social nor professional obstacle. Besides, he was enjoying himself far too much.

In the evening it was considered fashionable by the quality to stroll along the 'dark walk' close to the park. 'There his Grace of Wellington [*sic*] is sometimes to be seen with a fair lady under his arm. He generally dresses in plain clothes, to the astonishment of all the foreign officers,' remarked Captain William Frye, who was on furlough from service in Ceylon and had decided to come out to the Netherlands for something of a busman's holiday. 'He is said to be as successful in the fields of Idalia as in those of Bellona, and the ladies whom he honours with his attentions suffer not a little in their reputations in the opinion of the compères and commères of Bruxelles.'[26]

While Frye was merely casting an amused, if slightly jaundiced, eye over the Duke's Brussels flirtations, Caroline Capel was really quite exercised about the deleterious effect that the Duke's behaviour had on prevailing moral standards. 'The Duke of W_____ has not improved the *Morality* of our Society,' she wrote to her mother with unintentional irony, considering her own brother's contribution to the moral tone of the British army and aristocracy. Her main complaint was not that the Duke was giving a great many parties and dances while at the same time being faced with a grave international crisis, but that he:

> makes a point of asking all the Ladies of Loose Character – Every one was surprised at seeing Lady John Campbell at his House & one of his Staff told me that it had been represented to him her not being received for that her Character was more than Suspicious, 'Is it, by _____' said he, 'then I will go & ask her Myself'. On which he immediately took his Hat & went out for the purpose.[27]

The departure of Louis XVIII from Les Tuileries on 19 March 1815.

The arrival of Napoleon. The speed of Napoleon's march through France took the royal family by surprise: the King and his court escaped barely hours ahead of the arrival of the Emperor and his entourage.

Portrait of Wellington by Sir Thomas Lawrence: the classic image of the Duke at the height of his military, social and sexual powers.

(Left) The Duke of Richmond. He seemed financially and emotionally exhausted after his time as Lord Lieutenant of Ireland, and, given his demanding wife, *(right)* the Duchess of Richmond, can be forgiven for enjoying a drink.

The Duchess of Richmond's Ball by Robert A. Hillingford.

Before Waterloo by Henry Nelson O'Neil.

Lady Caroline Capel, aged twenty-one, and her daughter Harriet, aged one. Married to an aristocratic gambling addict, and sister of the Earl of Uxbridge, Lady Caroline had the unenviable task of maintaining an upper-class style of living.

The young Prince of Orange. Lady Georgiana Lennox held the opinion that 'the Prince of Orange, although personally much liked, was inexperienced and rash'. He was safer in the ballroom than on the battlefield.

Spencer Madan, who was tutor to the Duke and Duchess of Richmond's young children. He often experienced the temper of the capricious Duchess.

Lady Frances Wedderburn-Webster – a *femme fatale* who seems to have cuckolded her husband with frequency. The scandal of her affair with Wellington still rumbled on after her death, with him having to buy back letters that he had written to her.

The singer Guiseppina Grassini – a frequent guest at parties given by the Duke and Duchess of Richmond in their Paris residence. Her relationship with Wellington was so public that it was not unknown for a junior officer to seek Grassini's intercession on his behalf with the Duke.

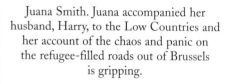

Juana Smith. Juana accompanied her husband, Harry, to the Low Countries and her account of the chaos and panic on the refugee-filled roads out of Brussels is gripping.

Novelist Fanny Burney, married to a royalist general and courtier Alexandre d'Arblay, was among those who left Paris in a hurry the night before Napoleon's arrival and took refuge across the border in Brussels.

Lieutenant-General Barnes – who had proposed, unsuccessfully, to Maria Capel – spent so much time with the Capels that people began to ask Lady Caroline, 'Which of your daughters is Genl. B to marry? Or is he to marry *them all*?'

Caroline 'Car' Lady Paget, with her first daughter, four-year-old Caroline.

Lord Paget. Charismatic, gifted and hot-headed, he was cavalry commander at the age of twenty-six.

The lively-minded Whig MP Thomas Creevey. He was a key member of the expatriate British community in Brussels.

Andrew Hamilton, who courted one of Creevey's stepdaughters and was a source of highly reliable military information for Creevey.

Colonel Sir William Howe De Lancey and Lady De Lancey. A distinguished soldier who enjoyed the confidence of the Duke of Wellington, De Lancey had just married the young Magdalene Hall when he was summoned to Belgium to stand in as the Duke of Wellington's Deputy Quartermaster-General.

12

'The Duke's orders are positive that no delay is to take place in landing the troops as they arrive, and the ships sent back again'

Lord Uxbridge was appointed commander of the cavalry on 15 April. Ten days later he arrived at Ostend and made straight for Brussels, where he found that a house had been made available to him by a Belgian marquis. However after one night under their roof he moved to an hotel:

> having made the Lady a very handsome Speech for the Accommodation he had met with, but declaring that he could not with any comfort take possession of another Person's House while it was possible to find Lodgings any where else – I believe they were truly sorry to part with him, for his remaining would have kept out others who may not make themselves quite as agreeable . . . [1]

Perhaps the less than agreeable nature of those being billeted on the Belgians could be ascribed to the altogether hurried, makeshift and uncomfortable nature of their transport to the Netherlands. In a way, the transport of troops to the theatre of war in the spring and early summer of 1815 was not unlike the situation of the British evacuation from Dunkirk 135 years later, albeit in reverse. Some travelled by military transports or converted commercial vessels (many of the 16th Light Dragoons made the crossing in small colliers capable of holding between ten and thirty-five horses); some took scheduled cross-channel services or packet boats, others had to make do with any vessel they could lay their hands on.

On arriving at Harwich with his wife, brother, two grooms, one lady's maid and five horses, Harry Smith struck up a conversation with the landlord of the Black Bull. 'He said I had no chance of embarking at

Harwich, unless I freighted a small craft that he would look out, and fitted it up for my horses.'[2] So the following day he struck a deal with the skipper of a small sloop, which compared very unfavourably with 'the 74's and frigates in which I had been flying over the ocean. We measured it, and found there was just room for the horses, and a hole aft, called a cabin, for my wife and self and brother.'[3]

The crossing itself was at best uncomfortable and at worst downright unpleasant; moreover the duration could vary from twelve or fourteen hours to several days depending on weather and the many logistical problems attending on the movement of so many troops. Embarking might take a whole afternoon, with troops boarding a vessel at around two o'clock and officers coming on board at the more leisurely hour of six o'clock.[4]

When on board many soldiers suffered dreadfully from seasickness; severe cases vomiting so much that the throat became so swollen as to make speaking difficult for a week afterwards. They found themselves rolling around the decks 'like dead-men' and being 'knocked about like so much lumber, nobody pitying or caring anything about them'.[5]

Perhaps the bad-tempered callousness of those who did not suffer from seasickness had something to do with the fact that as well as the stench of human vomit there was often an equine cargo to deal with. As one account puts it with unusual delicacy, 'there being above 40 horses below caused it to be extremely hot, and give forth not one of the most odoriferous of scents'.[6] Periodically grooms would have to venture below decks into the malodorous area where horses were crammed, to feed and water the animals and run the risk of being bitten by them.

After an uncomfortable, smelly and often rough crossing, their destination did little to raise the men's spirits. 'After a sail of about thirteen hours we made the coast of Flanders, which is not inviting in its aspect,'[7] wrote a regimental surgeon in his journal. However he can be considered positively lyrical in his description when compared with the initial reactions of others. 'Ostend is a dirty unwholesome place'[8] had been Edmund Wheatley's description of the port at which most of the British force disembarked. 'Nothing, certainly, could be more repulsive than the appearance of the coast – sand-hills as far as the eye could reach, broken only by the grey and lugubrious works and buildings of Ostend'[9] was artillery officer Cavalie Mercer's immediate impression of the country he was setting out to defend. The best that could be said about the place was that Ostend's 'usual dullness is however just now interrupted by the bustle of troops landing to join the allied army'.[10]

The spirits of British soldiers sank even further when the time came to disembark. They might have marched to their ports of embarkation in Britain, colours flying and regimental band pumping out stirring martial airs but, vomit-stained, queasy, hot and harassed, their arrival in the Low Countries was little short of ignominious. This typical account is one of many:

> Our keel had scarcely touched the sand ere we were abruptly boarded by a naval officer (Captain Hill) with a gang of sailors, who, *sans cérémonie,* instantly commenced hoisting our horses out, and throwing them, as well as our saddlery, etc., overboard, without ever giving time for making any disposition to receive or secure the one or the other. To my remonstrance his answer was, 'I can't help it, sir; the Duke's orders are positive that no delay is to take place in landing the troops as they arrive, and the ships sent back again; so you must be out of her before dark.' It was then about 3 p.m.; and I thought this a most uncomfortable arrangement.[11]

The recently enlisted child groom, fourteen-year-old Edward Heeley, recalled: 'We had scarcely got safe on shore before we saw our horses swinging in the air, so that we were obliged to go again into the sea up to our middles to catch them as they came on shore.'[12]

The chaos was appalling. Up and down the beach such scenes were replicated many times as dozens of vessels of varying types and sizes were unceremoniously unloaded by men obeying orders with a bloody-minded literalness that exasperated those commanding the troops on the boats. Heeley recounted:

> People who have not seen such sights must draw them in their own minds, for they are past describing clearly – fancy between 20 and 30 ships discharging a somewhat similar cargo to the *Scipio's*, all on the beach – the luggage thrown in all directions, numbers of horses running loose – and when we got a little together not knowing where to go, getting a civil answer from no one – and a thousand other disagreeablenesses.[13]

Instead of an orderly disembarkation, 'the scramble and confusion that ensued baffle all description. Bundles of harness went over the side in rapid succession, as well as horses. In vain we urged the loss and damage that must accrue from such a proceeding. "Can't help it – no business of mine – Duke's orders are positive," etc. etc., was our only answer.'[14]

After a long hot voyage, horses were taken from a crowded hold and dumped overboard or just thrown into the chilly sea. Guardsmen and grooms, some stripped totally naked, dashed into the water doing their best to calm the frightened animals and bring them safely to shore, but inevitably some beasts escaped and cantered up and down the beach adding to the chaos, or just galloped off, not to be seen again. As the tide came in it was all some officers could do to stop over-zealous mariners from flinging artillery and ammunition into the sea where it would sink, be washed away or rendered useless by the water.

The impression of leaderless disorganisation was redoubled when artillery officer Cavalie Mercer went into Ostend itself to try to find some military authority. The town's quays and streets were packed with all the manpower and paraphernalia of an army on the move, but the Assistant Quartermaster-General who would have been in charge of the logistics had made himself very scarce. Moreover the British commandant in Ostend, Lieutenant-Colonel Gregory, was apparently unaware of who was arriving and when. He 'had no other orders but that the troops of every arm should march for Ghent the moment they landed, without halting a single day in Ostend'.[15]

At times the disembarkation was further hampered by heavy rain and storms, prompting many officers to form up their men on the beach and march off to the nearest sheds, stables, warehouse, or whatever other shelter could be found. Often the first choice would already be occupied and they would have to march on until, eventually, they found somewhere to rest. The following morning would find the men and horses in poor shape: 'Our noble horses, yesterday morning so sleek and spirited, now stood with drooping heads and rough staring coats, plainly indicating the mischief they had sustained in being taken from a hot hold, plunged into cold water, and then exposed for more than seven hours on an open beach.' If anything the men were worse off: 'jaded, their clothes all soiled with mud and wet, the sabres rusty, and the bear-skins of their helmets flattened down by the rain'.[16]

The most distressing sight on the beaches was that of 'disconsolate-looking groups of women and children ... seen here and there sitting on their poor duds, or roaming about in search of their husbands, or mayhap of a stray child, all clamouring, lamenting, and materially increasing the Babel-like confusion'.[17] While senior officers travelled with their wives much as if on a Continental holiday, spouses of lower ranks had an altogether tougher time.

A quota system operated whereby a certain number of wives were allowed to join their husbands on active service; often the decision as to who would sail with their spouses was made by the drawing of lots or the throw of dice at the quayside. Families would follow their men to the very point of embarkation only to be told that they would not be able to continue. Although cruel, such a system did at least discourage desertion, it being more difficult to abscond from the quayside in full sight of officers and NCOs than if the decision had been taken days in advance.

For women with young children, it was considered best to limit the number of children joining their father on campaign to two; it was harsh either way. Scenes of farewell at the docks were terrible, and there is evidence of at least one woman dying with her newborn child as she was parted from her husband, who did not even have time to bury her before he sailed. But the quality of life for a private soldier's wife on active service was little better than for those left behind. Such an existence was physically and emotionally demanding in the extreme; women travelled with the baggage, were expected to work hard and were subject to rigorous discipline.

In the event of being widowed, women were quickly remarried, proposals sometimes being made at the funeral. And there were the inevitable sexual tensions arising from having a small number of women living closely with a large number of men on active service. In his memoirs Edward Costello recalls how in Spain, during the Peninsular War, a grenadier discovered that his wife, a vivacious and 'very pretty-looking Englishwoman', was having an affair with a sergeant called Battersby, and confronted her for having abandoned him and left him with a three-year-old child. Her view was that she was with a man who knew 'better how to treat me than you'. He asked if she was determined 'to continue this way of living'. She replied that she was.

> 'Well, then,' he exclaimed, holding her firmly by the left hand, which she had extended for him to shake, while he drew his bayonet with his right, 'take that', and he drove it right through her body. The blow was given with such force that it actually tripped him over her, and both fell, the bayonet still sticking in her side.[18]

But he was soon on his feet, and bracing a foot against his wife's corpse, he pulled the bayonet free. Having polished her off he went after the amorous sergeant, who made good his escape.

When the cuckolded murderer faced his colonel for disciplining he said in 'a rough and manly tone of voice' that 'I have done the deed, but sorry her seducer has escaped'.[19] The colonel was a compassionate man. The grenadier was sentenced to three months' solitary confinement, but doubtless in consideration of the extenuating circumstances, served only a month for this *crime passionnel* before being ordered to return to his regiment, to die fighting in the Pyrenees. Battersby got off scot-free. He survived the

Peninsular campaign and in early May 1815 was ordered from his barracks in Dover to Ostend, where he would have been able to practise his charms on the disconsolate-looking groups of women on the beaches, before moving on to try his chances with the unhappy wives of other soldiers.

If the experiences of one Army wife in the Low Countries at this time are anything to go by, the smooth-talking sergeant would have found plenty of opportunity to exercise his charm. As well as being forced to work and subjected to Army discipline, they often found themselves at the wrong end of their husbands' drunken temper. For instance Sergeant Burton of the 73rd went with his wife, and Thomas Morris, who tells the tale, to the town of Soignes to purchase some shoe leather. Business concluded, refreshment was taken with the currier who had sold them the leather. 'Mrs Burton ... though accustomed daily to take a *small* portion of her husband's allowance of spirits, exhibited unequivocal symptoms of having now taken a little drop too much; not that she would admit the fact, but attributed her slight indisposition to the heat of the weather.'

With the pass that allowed this leather-buying party to be absent from their quarters until 9 p.m. almost expired, there was a half-hearted attempt to sober up on coffee and bread and butter before they commenced the journey back. Drunk in a foreign country, they soon lost their way, and their predicament worsened when they were then caught in a rainstorm. Finding shelter in an inn, Sergeant Burton took the only sensible step, ordered more hollands and declared that he 'would not stir for all the officers in the country'. Mrs Burton felt differently and worried about the consequences of being absent without leave (bear in mind that wives were subject to Army discipline too and were often given corporal punishment). By this time Morris was getting increasingly frustrated in his role as mediator between the bickering couple.

> His wife, at last, left the place by herself; and I was trying to prevail on him to follow: when, finding she was really gone, he hurried out in a state of great excitement; and, before I could overtake them, he had drawn his sword and inflicted a wound on her head, cutting through her bonnet and cap. As soon as I came up, I caught her, fainting, in my arms, and found the blood from the wound trickling down very fast. Burton was instantly sobered, and sorry for what he had done, he assisted me in conveying her back to the inn.

Mrs Burton survived the sword attack by her husband and the following morning the sergeant was 'sadly chagrined at having struck his poor old woman, who had so long been the companion of his journeys, but they made the matter up'. Moreover, no one had missed them at their quarters. With almost comic understatement Morris says 'we began to get tired of the monotony'.[20] Given the violent nature of life in the early nineteenth century, it is perhaps not surprising that when not fighting the French, soldiers used their martial skills in the marital arena.

13

'We are in excellent health and spirits
and have the best of quarters. The people
are remarkably kind to us.'

The chaos of Ostend was an unpleasant start to the campaign, but it only heightened most men's appreciation of life in the United Netherlands. It seemed as though they had arrived in the land of Cockayne. Those from agricultural parts of England were struck with wonder at the fecundity of the alluvial land. 'I could not help remarking the cornfields today,' remembered one:

> they had (as I thought) a much finer appearance than I had seen in England, the rye in particular, it stood from six to seven feet high, and nearly all the fields had high banks around them as if intended to let water in and out, or to keep water out altogether – but the rich appearance of the country cannot fail to attract attention.[1]

As the season wore on the cereals in the fields waxed taller, causing one cavalry officer to write: 'I never saw such corn 9 or 10 feet high in some fields and such quantities of it. I only wonder how half of it is ever consumed.'[2]

Time and time again, accounts of those first days in the Netherlands refer to the high crops and the 'rich and highly cultivated'[3] agricultural land: 'The country flat, but highly cultivated and abounding with everything';[4] 'the country through which we passed is rich, and in all the fresh beauty of spring'.[5] 'Far from wearing the appearance of the theatre of war, it seemed to be the abode of peace and plenty.'[6]

To this abundance was added the novelty of the scene. Just as the impecunious aristocrats and men of fashion who had flocked to Brussels a year before to escape the high cost of living had been amused and diverted by the exotic timbre of life on the Continent, so the soldiers disembarking from Britain were taken with their new surroundings, bearing in mind that for many men this was their first time travelling out of Britain. Even for those who had served in the Peninsula, the lush, tranquil prosperity of the Netherlands was a considerable contrast to the arid war-torn landscape of Spain.

Perhaps because they were actually educated and qualified for their tasks, rather than merely having the money and family background required by a fashionable regiment, artillery officers seem to have taken an intensely academic interest in their new surroundings. Cavalié Mercer for example is almost anthropological in the detail he goes into on subjects as diverse as the 'clumsy ornamental collars'[7] worn by horses or the large gold earrings and sabots with rabbit-skin padding at the instep favoured by Flemish peasant women.

Nor was it just the inhabitants who were a source of curiosity. The Belgian provinces of the United Netherlands were filling up with troops of other nationalities too. The septuagenarian, hard-drinking, heavy-gambling and vehemently Francophobe Prussian Commander Marshal Blücher, 'by all accounts a vandal . . . actuated by a most vindictive spirit',[8] had set up headquarters at Namur, and the surrounding countryside was filled with foraging parties of Prussian lancers.

Whereas the British soldiers generally behaved well towards the locals and paid their way – Lt George Woodberry of the 18th Hussars even records changing English banknotes into the local currency and receiving eighteen silver francs for one pound sterling[9] – the Prussians were often considered little better than a rapacious army of occupation.

One British officer, upon stopping for coffee at a peasant's house on the roadside, was regaled with stories of the excessive demands of Prussian soldiers. 'Not content with exacting three meals a day, when they were only entitled to two, and for which they are bound to give their rations, they sell these, and appropriate the money to their own use; then the demand for brandy and *schnapps* is increasing,' noted Captain Frye, adding the rhetorical question: 'But what can be expected from an army whose leader encourages them in all their excesses?'[10] Whenever a Belgian complained, Prussian officers simply pretended not to understand what was being said. It is interesting to see how much the character of the respective commanders, Blücher and Wellington, shaped the behaviour of the forces they commanded. When it came to billets, English soldiers were greatly preferred.

However, for all their unpopularity with the locals, the Prussians' austere mien and powerful singing voices left a lasting impression. Captain Frye, the holidaying soldier from Ceylon, was one of the most sophisticated, sensitive and scholarly Englishmen in the Low Countries at the time. A Francophile and a liberal, he knew Greek and Latin as well as every major European language. In later life he lived in France, even publishing a volume of verse, some his own, some his translations into French from German, Italian, English, Swedish and Danish. He was most struck by the sight of a group of Prussian lancers:

> They were singing some warlike song or hymn, which was singularly impressive. It brought to my recollection the description of the Rhenish bands in the *Lay of the Last Minstrel*:
>
> 'Who as they move, in rugged verse
> Songs of Teutonic feuds rehearse.'
>
> The Prussian cavalry seem to be composed of fine looking young men, and I admire the genuine military simplicity of their dress.

According to Frye this Prussian dress contrasted favourably with the flashy elegance of the British cavalry, earning them the sobriquet of 'Hyde Park soldiers'. 'One sees in it none of those absurd ornaments and meretricious foppery which give to our cavalry officers the appearance of Astley's* men.'[11] Stirring singing seems to have been something of a feature of the German military man. Edward Heeley, the teenage groom, recalled that 'we could hear the Germans long before we came near to them, for they kept on singing, a great number together, I think it was hymns they sang.'[12]

What with a stream of transports hurriedly disgorging their cargoes into, rather than at, the harbour of Ostend; German units singing loudly and terrorising the local peasantry for being too French in their leanings; and intrepid tourists drawn to the Low Countries by the brisk social life, the low cost of living and the excitement of the military build-up, the eastern portion of the small Kingdom of the United Netherlands was becoming rather congested. From the 'meretricious foppery' of the English cavalry to Maria Capel's description of the Brunswickers, the Brunswick Corps, formerly known as the Duke of Brunswick's Black Legion or Black Horde, who with 'their Dismal Black Uniforms & Deaths [*sic*] head Caps†

---

* Astley's Amphitheatre, later the Royal Amphitheatre, was on the Westminster road and according to *The Panorama of London or Visitors Guide* of the 1820s/1830s, 'feats of horsemanship, form the grand attraction of this house'. P.313.

† This 'pretty' design was later adopted by another German military organisation, the SS.

look so pretty',[13] 'the streets [were] continually full of all sorts of uniforms.'[14]

But perhaps the most picturesque ornaments of this rich sartorial pageant were the Highlanders, in what the locals termed their 'jupes'. The kilt was a source of much comment and there were those who were quite scandalised by its appearance. One French lady 'had seen some and expressed her utter surprise', wrote a British tourist in a letter home from the Low Countries, 'and as if she was speaking to one who doubted the fact, she repeated, "C'est vrai! actuellement rien qu'un petit Jupon – mais comment!" and then she lifted her eyes and hands and reiterated, "petit jupon – et comment," concluding, as if she almost doubted the evidence of her own senses, "Je les ai vus moi-même."'[15] When the Gordon Highlanders arrived in Ghent's marketplace on market day, 'the novelty of the scene made as great an impression on the Highlanders as their garb did on the country people, who treated them very civilly.'[16]

The civility of the local peasantry was reciprocated: the Highlanders were apparently favoured as lodgers as they were said to be well behaved and 'cheerfully assist the different families on whom they are quartered in their household labour' – behaviour which had Frye beside himself with hyperbole. 'This reflects a good deal of credit on the gallant sons of Caledonia. Their superior morality to those of the same class either in England or Ireland,' not to mention the voracious, demanding and down-right dishonest Prussians, 'must strike every observer.'[17]

However helpful the 'gallant sons of Caledonia' were around the house, the ever-increasing number of troops began to make life a little more difficult. The cost of living was still reasonable; Cavalié Mercer was surprised to find a market well stocked with Indian goods, 'particularly silk pocket-handkerchiefs, which we found of the very finest quality, and at about half the price they sold at in England'.[18] Given Britain's unique links with the subcontinent, British soldiers must have been very surprised to find goods from one of their colonies cheaper in Europe than at home. Nor was it just the sartorially minded who snapped up bargains: private soldiers and officers alike marvelled at the cheapness of alcohol.

'Liquor is so cheap here, the people give them it,' grumbled one officer, who regretted the damaging effect that cheap gin and hollands had on discipline. Another went so far as to describe it as a 'villainous kind of spirit', blaming in part the quality of the local beer, 'which more resembled a mixture of cow-dung and water than anything else',[19] for driving the English soldier to gin. But the disapproval of their officers did little to dissuade common soldiers, who could get 'royal' on the stuff for tuppence. Besides, officers wrote approvingly of the price of higher quality intoxicants compared to England, where of course the Napoleonic wars had rendered French wine a highly prized commodity. 'Champagne, too,' wrote Captain Tomkinson of the Light Dragoons, 'at 4s. per bottle, was a new thing.'[20] 'Rhenish wine, 2s. 3d. per bottle, of most excellent quality,'[21] noted George Simmons, an officer in the Rifle Brigade.

But some prices did begin to rise. For instance, when buying a pony, which he named Cheerful, at a cost of 13 Napoleons, Lt Woodberry noticed that the cost of any kind of horse had risen tremendously, in fact had almost doubled, since the cavalry's arrival in the Low Countries.[22]

The swelling of numbers also had an effect on accommodation. When Woodberry and the regimental surgeon went into Brussels on 7 May, they were unable to find accommodation even for one night at the Hôtel de Flandres, the Hôtel d'Angleterre or the Hôtel de Clarence. Only with a great deal of difficulty, and presumably expense, were they able to find room for themselves and their horses at the Hôtel de l'Impératrice. However, their mission was social rather than military; they went for a stroll in the park, a ride out through the Anvers Gate, where among the fashionable throng they caught sight of the Dukes of Richmond and Wellington, before going to hear Catalani sing at the Opera.

After the urgency of their departure from England and the chaotic nature of their arrival, the British forces were beginning to enjoy their new posting. One thing that particularly pleased officers was the opportunity to travel between towns in canal boats, which seemed more like sumptuously appointed floating restaurants, often equipped with a small band or orchestra, than a form of public transport. It was a means of travel that one officer likened to 'gliding in the Carthaginian style between flowery meads and smiling lawns'.[23]

Horse artillery commander Sir Augustus Frazer was particularly taken with this mode of transport as he criss-crossed the newly founded kingdom, making his arrangements for the country's defence and dispositions of men and materiel at various fortresses and other defensible positions.

Nothing can be pleasanter than travelling in these canal boats, which are large and commodious vessels. At either end is a cabin, nicely fitted up. In the middle is a kind of public house; on one side an excellent kitchen, on the other, larders and store-rooms for all manner of eatables. The stern cabin, which is considered the best, is fitted up with looking-glasses, sofas, and chairs; and the sides, as well as ceiling, very prettily painted. There were six windows in the cabin of the boat yesterday; and at 1 p.m. we sat down to an excellent dinner, well put on the table. For this excellent dinner and carriage from Bruges, the price is five francs, that is, 4s. 2d. Wine, coffee and liqueurs are paid for separately. We were fifteen in the stern cabin; there might be twenty people in the middle part of the boat; and there were eighteen in the fore cabin; yet there seemed no difficulty in providing good cheer for all. There were several pretty and very agreeable women, and altogether no journey could be more pleasant.[24]

The other ranks were also enjoying a period of unaccustomed luxury. According to Captain Tomkinson, 'The men are better off than I ever remember. They receive a pound of meat a day, a pound of bread, and a pint of gin to six.'[25] And the men varied their diet when they 'clubbed their rations of bread, meat, and *schnapps*, with the vegetables, cheese, butter, and beer of their hosts'.[26]

Indeed, given the nature of the more hastily pulled-together units, their appearance was decidedly unmilitary. In later life, the Earl of Albemarle recalled that the third Battalion of the 14th Foot, in which he found himself as a fifteen-year-old Ensign, was a formation that 'in ordinary times would not have been considered fit to be sent on foreign service at all, much less against an enemy in the field'.[27] Many of the men were just teenagers like himself, 'Buckinghamshire lads, fresh from the plough, whose rustic appearance procured for them the appellation of the "Peasants"'.[28] And finding themselves billeted upon agricultural labourers they soon shed whatever little military manner they had acquired and reverted to their natural condition. The mood was anything but that of an army on active service abroad, and veterans of the Peninsula were able to tell new recruits that, compared to their earlier experiences, this was more of a holiday than a military campaign. Private Wheeler of the 51st Regiment of Foot wrote to his family in Bath at the end of May:

We are in excellent health and spirits, and have the best of quarters. The people are remarkably kind to us. I with one man are quartered at a tobacconists, so we do not want for that article, we eat and drink with the landlord and family, coffee stands ready for use all day long, when we get our rations we give it to the Mistress of the house, except our gin, this we take care of ourselves. I will tell you the manner we live. As soon as we rise a cup or two of good coffee. Eight o'clock breakfast on bread and butter eggs and coffee. Dinner meat and vegetables, dressed various ways, with beer, afterwards a glass of Hollands grog and tobacco, evening, sallad [*sic*], coffee, etc. then the whole is washed down by way of a settler with Hollands grog, or beer with a pipe or two, then off to bed. There are some

14

>⌒

'Balls, not wars, engage our every thought'

Across the border Napoleon may have been building up an army, but life in Belgium continued as if in a meta-universe. The presence of a large number of troops might have been expected to cause a measure of concern; in fact the opposite was true for the many British families who had settled in Brussels. One colonel's wife put it rather well when she said: 'the numerous English families appeared to consider the arrival of the army as the commencement of a series of entertainments.'[1]

Wellington may have been furiously firing off despatches to Horse Guards complaining about the size and quality of his Army, but his outward air of unconcern was infectious and was felt throughout the Army.

To understand the unique charisma of Wellington, so different to the emotional appeal of Napoleon, it is important to grasp the significance of the personality cult that had already grown up around him. It is important to bear in mind that even before his famous clash with Napoleon, he was already looked on by his subordinates with awe; and almost universally, if not by Napoleon, with respect.

On Wednesday 17 May, just after he had moved into new, more impressive quarters at a house on the rue de la Montagne du Parc, near the corner of the rue Royale, Wellington gave a dinner for the young Prince of Orange and some ambassadors, with music audible from the park – it was fashionable for bands to play outside the houses of grand expats who lived around the park. He fancied going for a post-prandial stroll, and Fanny Burney, who was also in the park with the Princesse de Hénin and the Duchess of Ursel, watched him carefully:

after the repast, the Duke & his Company came into the Park, to gratify the awaiting multitude, that were swarming about his door & windows. He walked by the side of the Austrian minister, Vincent; he looked remarkably well. All [*sic*] the mob followed quietly, & well behaved, his every step; all the better sort stood still, when he passed, in a row, as when the King walked on the Windsor Terrace. Quel beau rôle que le sien! Since his return to military command, he has an Air the most commanding, a high, superiur [*sic*] *port*, & a look of animated spirit. I think he is grown taller![2]

In a letter written later that month Burney recounts seeing Wellington at an evening at the Great Concert Rooms, where Catalani sang. 'I have a faith in him so great that, at his sight, I feel all courage.'[3]

The very physical presence of the Duke had a hugely reassuring effect. Officers and those they commanded drew inspiration from their chief and his phlegmatic disposition. They too adopted a similarly philosophical view of their situation. Private Wheeler captured the feelings of many of the common soldiers when he wrote to his family in Bath:

I cannot give you any certain account of the enemy, you will be better informed about them from the newspaper, than from anything I can say about them, there is no doubt but they are assembling a great force. This does not trouble us, we are commanded by Wellington, we have plenty of the good things of this life, so the best way is to enjoy ourselves while we can, it will be time to bid the D__l good morning when we meet him.[4]

Lieutenant, later Captain, Sir John Kincaid, whose shooting holiday in Scotland had been so rudely interrupted by Napoleon's resumption of the throne of France, was similarly sanguine. 'As our division was composed of crack regiments, under crack commanders, and headed by fire-eating generals, we had little to do the first fortnight after my arrival, beyond indulging in all the amusements of our delightful quarter.'[5] The amusements afforded the British officer were varied and almost always free of charge, 'other than the theatre and even there he pays only half price'.[6]

For the more reflective souls, arrival in this curiously relaxed theatre of war offered an opportunity to gorge on the cultural feast offered by the Low Countries. It was the educated artillery officers who were the hungriest. In between his tireless work shoring up the defences of the so-called United Netherlands, travelling by well-appointed canal barges and convincing the Duke of Wellington to allow him to change his six-pound guns for nine-pounders, Sir Augustus Frazer found time to visit cathedrals and art collections galore. His letters home to his wife are full of observations about ecclesiastical architecture, stained-glass windows, and artists living as well as dead. He was particularly pleased with a day spent in the company of a Colonel Gold in Antwerp touring the Rubens House, calling on a descendant of Rubens, studying some of Rubens's best portraits and finally visiting the artist's tomb. 'I was delighted with my visit to Antwerp. I wished, when there, to have pushed on to Amsterdam, which capital I have not yet seen.'[7] However his duties as commander of the horse artillery impeded his sightseeing.

Another artillery officer, Cavalié Mercer, who had made such meticulous and detailed notes about local peasant dress, had a little more time on his hands. He frequently attended church services, and although he may have approached them in a cynical mood, describing the rituals as 'childish mummery'[8] and affecting a worldly tone ('one goes to these Catholic ceremonies as to any other show'),[9] on at least one occasion he found himself having a spiritual experience. 'Puerile as these exhibitions may be, the effect on me was exciting; and as the last notes were faintly re-echoed through the building, I left in a frame of mind far different from that in which I had entered.'[10]

Mercer soon found himself settled in the chateau of Strytem, where he continued his contemplative way of life. After dinner he would go and smoke a cigar under the avenue of beech trees at the back of the house, before moving inside to his snug chambers and sitting in front of the fire with a book, interrupted only by the ticking of his watch as it lay on the table in front of him and the croaking of frogs in the moat. It is hardly surprising that he admits 'the charms of a country life have so occupied my brain as to chase from it all recollection of being a soldier'.[11]

But Mercer's contemplative and introspective way of passing the days in the Low Countries was not shared by all his comrades. Brussels was the chief centre of entertainment and, following the day's duties, many officers would ride in to enjoy themselves during the evening. By early May it became necessary for an order to be issued instructing all officers to rejoin their regiments and forbidding them to visit the city unless they had the authority of their general.

Although the lower ranks were castigated and often flogged for drunkenness, officers were also in the habit of partaking too freely of what for them were heavily discounted wines. And as Private Wheeler, billeted at the Grammont headquarters of General Hill, writes, there were occasions when the other ranks could feel morally superior to those who commanded them.

> Since we have been here I have not heard of a single fall out between any of our men and the people, but I am sorry that a few of our officers one night in a drunken frolic gave cause for offence, and that the people were not a little vexed at the time. What follows was the cause. In the great square, opposite the Guildhall, there is a fountain, in the middle stands a naked boy, apparently about four years old, his left hand rested on his hip and with his right he held his little c__ out of which the water flowed into the bason [*sic*] or more properly the well, for it is some twelve feet deep. One night some of our officers had been indulging themselves rather too much, they sallied out in quest of adventures and they managed to get a rope around the neck of the little urchin and pull him of his pirch [*sic*]. He being made of lead, down he sank to the bottom of the well.[12]

The townsfolk of Grammont were rather proud of their version of Brussels's more famous urinating sculpture and were put out by the vandalism. Happily, a couple of days later the pissing putto was reinstated and relations improved.

As well as drinking, many officers were chasing women, often each other's. One particular case related by Lt Woodberry seems to have the ring of a melodramatic novel about it. It concerns a woman who had been living with a Captain S_____ of the 16th Light Dragoons.

> This woman, a widow, had been kept for several years by Captain S_____ and B_____, having seen her recently, offered her 200 pounds a year if she would come and live with him and leave her lover, which she accepted. Captain S_____ sent his thanks to Mr B_____ for having taken the woman off his hands, adding that he had done so, moreover, more honourably than could a man of breeding. Some say that Mr S_____ should call Mr B_____ out. For my part, I think he acted quite correctly.[13]

Nor were the local women any more principled than the women that the officers brought with them. Describing them as 'the most shameless creatures', Woodberry said, 'I have seen such scenes in public, on the street, that I am rendered completely stupefied by them. How the women of my country would blush to see them behave.'[14] If the antics of the widow who moved from Captain S_____ to B_____ for a financial incentive is typical of the women of his own country, the locals must have been very bad indeed. On the whole it seems that British troops struck up relationships with local women quite rapidly.

When they could tear themselves away from wine and women, officers indulged themselves in that other great love of the English gentry and aristocracy: horseflesh. As soon as there was a suitable cavalry presence in Belgium there were inter-regimental races. As time went on and more British cavalry were dumped into the harbour at Ostend these races became ever larger and more elaborate. On 30 May, for example, there was a race meeting in which hundreds of riders, most of them officers, hoped to participate. These events soon became very popular with the fashionable set in Brussels. If hedonistic officers could no longer visit Brussels without the express permission of their General, then the *haut ton* of Brussels would simply visit the fun-loving officers. 'We have races once a week,' wrote Lt-Col Murray of the 18th Hussars to his wife, '& race dinners where people get very drunk, & ride home across the country.'[15]

Even rainstorms could not dampen the merriment. Woodberry describes a race meeting at the beginning of June, which was extremely well attended. The racing included amusing contests between mules and ponies, but it was stopped by a sudden and persistent downpour. Woodberry and his comrades took shelter in an old house where the mayor of Ninove had arranged for about seventy of them to enjoy 'an excellent cold dinner, washed down by a lot of champagne'. The mayor soon had cause to regret his generosity.

In two hours, the whole lot had time to eat and get drunk together: I seem to remember that a bad character from the 10th Hussars [the ill-bred Capt. B. who bought Capt. S.'s girlfriend was apparently from the 10th, so it might have been him] standing on one of the tables, set out to break, with a large stick, all the plates and dishes, all the bottles and all the glasses; that the remainder of the company took part in this fatuous entertainment, and that, throwing themselves on to their horses, went back to the racecourse, half of them falling off on the way, and many of the horses galloping to the stables without their riders. The maddest rushed headlong into a race to the bell tower, across the fields, at night, and gave the peasants some idea of the independence of the English Hussars by shouting in the village streets 'Long Live Napoleon!'

It seems that Woodberry himself was pretty far gone at this point as he is unsure as to whether he saw or dreamt the next outrage which involved overturning a couple of carriages, terrifying 'the women who were inside' and 'charging their husbands or protectors in a truly Cossack manner'. But he ends on a positive note: 'I injured my horse Dick, as well, through steeplechasing; but though I left the saddle three times, I was not the slightest the worse for it."[16]

Others were not so lucky. In early April Lord William Pitt Lennox, the Duke of Richmond's teenage son who had accompanied the Duke of Wellington to the Congress of Vienna, was playing a game of cricket when an ensign in the Guards asked him, 'as the lightest weight, to ride a match round the lake. Unfortunately for me, I consented, little knowing the nature of the animal, a Cossack horse, I was to mount.'[17]

So Lord William left the cricket pitch, tied a silk handkerchief around his head, vaulted into the saddle and was off. All went well until:

> [the] clattering hoofs of my opponent at his [the horse's] heels presently caused him to bolt into the wood, and dash between two trees. The result, as I afterwards discovered – for I was insensible for more than seventy-two hours – was, that my head and arm came in violent contact with the trunk and branch, and I was brought to the ground.
>
> Two medical men, belonging to the brigade, were soon by my side, and I was removed to a summer-house in the park, where they had recourse to the process of trepanning. So hopeless was my case deemed, that my arm, broken in two places, was scarcely attended to.[18]

A soldier was left to look after him, but Lord William was plainly not expected to come out of his coma. So it was with considerable surprise that on the third morning after his accident the soldier saw him sit up and ask where he was. While he hovered between life and death, fashionable society had been following his predicament very closely. The Duke of Wellington had written to Lennox's sister to inform her of the accident, and in spite of his many duties took a close interest in the news and how it was broken to the family:

> My dear Lady Sarah, – It is true that William has had a fall from his horse, which appeared yesterday rather a serious one. I am waiting for March to go down to the Duchess to let her know it, and you had better say nothing about it till I shall arrive.
> Ever yours, most sincerely
> Wellington.[19]

General Sir Peregrine Maitland, the brigade commander in whose care Lord William found himself, took a particularly keen interest in the young man's state as he was courting Lady Sarah, although at the time the affair was kept secret, given that the attentions of a soldier who was neither titled nor rich would not have been viewed at all positively by the snobbish and ambitious Duchess of Richmond.

For a few days Lord William's fall was the chief topic of conversation in smart circles. Lord Saltoun who had just arrived to take command of a detachment of guards, dashed off a note to his wife:

> I have no news to give you, except that Lord William Lennox, in riding a race on a horse he could not manage, got thrown off against a tree, broke his arm in two places, and so hurt his head, that he now lies in Maitland's quarters in a very dangerous state, as he has a good deal of fever, and the doctor will not be able to tell before to-morrow, whether his skull is fractured or not. From what I hear I am rather afraid of [*sic*] him; however, he is very young, and that goes a great way in these cases.[20]

It was indeed the youth and relative inexperience of so many of the officers that accounted for the holiday atmosphere that prevailed in the United Netherlands at the time. They may have been assembled to fight the most daunting military commander of the age, but in many cases the regiments were filled with and run by boys still in their teens and on their first trip abroad. They were young, they had foppish uniforms and they were having the time of their lives. The unfortunate accident that had almost killed Lord William, and from which he would only partially recover, causing him to lose the sight of one eye and remain on the sick list for two months, did not deter other young men of fashion from trying their luck at the races. Nor did it move those in command to think about banning the practice, even though the Army was preparing for war.

In fact race meetings continued right up until the final hour. 'Races on a grand scale came off at Grammont on the 13th June,' recalled the Earl of Albemarle, whose sixteenth birthday fell on that day.[21] Thousands gathered for the event. 'Everybody seemed determined to make the most of his holiday.'[22] One particular young man who stood out on that day as typifying the spirit of the British Army was Lord Hay, an ensign in the first regiment of Guards and A.D.C. to General Maitland. James, Lord Hay, son of the Earl of Erroll, a title dating back to the first half of the sixteenth century, was the apotheosis of the glamorous young officer – 'very poor I hear,' noted one young lady ruefully, but 'very good looking I know & particularly Gentlemanlike'.[23] His peers held him in awe. 'I had hardly ever seen so handsome a lad,' recalled the young Albemarle, who seemed to have a bit of a schoolboy crush on the young aristocrat. 'He was beaming with health and spirits, as he took his place in the scales in his gay jockey dress.'[24]

Young Lord Hay had become something of a hero for his spirited horsemanship around Brussels, where he delighted in taunting the local authorities. 'Never was there a finer fellow than James Lord Hay,' was the verdict of the convalescent Lord William Pitt Lennox, another of the youngsters who looked up to Hay as to a god.

> At the time the British army were quartered at and near Brussels, Hay's amusement used to be to 'lark' over the fence into the park, and, when chased by the keepers, charge the fence again into the street. Having done the above feat upon more than one occasion, a trap was laid for him by some of the *gens-d'armes*, who placed themselves in the different alleys and summer-houses in the enclosure, unarmed, that nothing should interfere with their pedestrian powers in the chase. A signal was also arranged, and every preparation made for catching the intruder. Hay, however, was too canny a Scot, and too good a sportsman to be caught. No sooner, after leaping the barrier, did he hear the yell of the keepers, the shrill noise of the whistle, and the numerous body of his pursuers, than he sought the stiffest part of the enclosure. So impracticable it appeared, that no one except an Englishman would have thought of attempting it, and, in consequence, it was left unguarded. Away went Hay in rapid flight, pretending to be approaching a gap, where he must inevitably have been taken, then, turning short round, made for the stiff part, charged, cleared it, and was safe from his pursuers.[25]

It was only when a complaint was made to the Duke of Wellington that Hay reluctantly stopped jumping the railings of Brussels.

15

'The sooner we put things in the order
they are to remain, the better'

To imply that the whole British Army was doing nothing but getting drunk, vandalising public statuary, riding around terrorising the locals and going to the races would be a distortion of the truth. Of course there was an element of military preparation too. The Royal Engineers were busy supervising work on the frontier forts and ensuring that each division had appropriate engineering support for the proposed invasion. Captain Oldfield of the Royal Engineers was able to write: 'The British never before had so complete an Engineer Establishment. We had twenty thousand peasants besides strong military working parties employed on the frontier.'[1]

Uxbridge too was a conscientious commander. According to one source, 'his natural anxiety was to have them [the cavalry], as a body, as efficient as his ardent and able spirit could make them; therefore, about twice each week the whole, to the number of about ten thousand men, assembled for field-day exercise; it formed a splendid sight from the village where our headquarters were stationed.'[2] But not everyone was in such good shape. The confusion of their arrival in the Netherlands left troops disoriented to such a degree that soldiers were unaware of the name of the place they were stationed and 'equally unacquainted with the direction of the roads going out of their own quarters'.[3] On 11 May, an order was issued to the 18th Hussars, directing that 'officers must take every means to make their Troops acquainted with the name of the village where they are stationed, and of the Head Quarters of the Regiment'.[4] Given that officers were out buying and selling their mistresses or getting drunk at the races, it would be interesting to know how many were in a position to communicate this information to the men under their command.

The Prince of Orange however was taking his duties as a commander rather more seriously than one of his young officers, Ensign Edward Macready, would have liked; drilling his men from 'three in the morning till six in the afternoon'. However they soon devised a stratagem to put an end to this unduly taxing part of their stay in the Low Countries: at the time the Prince was passing the line, a man would drop, pretending to faint. 'This had always a good effect and we soon marched home,'[5] noted Macready approvingly.

There were rather more successful and serious parades and inspections than those attempted by the Prince of Orange. For instance, on 22 May there was a review of the Duke of Brunswick's troops at Vilvorde. In all there were about 7,000 men, and the Duke of Wellington 'galloped down the Allée Verte in great style'[6] clad in his field marshal's uniform and attended by Lord Uxbridge, the rest of his staff and his friend the Duke of Richmond, who brought along one of his daughters. At the time it was noted that the Duke of Wellington had been seen in the company of sixteen-year-old Lady Jane Lennox a great deal. It is this constant intermingling of the civilian and the military and the presence of so many figures from English high society that heightens the air of unreality surrounding the preparations for the war against Napoleon.

According to one source, by this time 'it had been generally understood that our army would advance into the French territory on or about the 20th June',[7] and yet at this review of the Brunswick troops, Lord Uxbridge spoke for a long time to Sir Augustus Frazer about further changes to the arrangement of the British forces. 'The sooner we put things in the order they are to remain, the better,' wrote Frazer impatiently, noting that 'a fifth and sixth division of the army have been formed' and that the horse artillery was to be remodelled, about which he was to see Lord Uxbridge at his headquarters.[8] Following his meeting, he noted that as he was not getting heavier guns, 'we are sadly in want of men and horses'.[9]

Even so, the constantly shifting state of the British Army and the disarray of various of its units was anything but apparent on 29 May, when the Earl of Uxbridge staged a review of the British cavalry near his headquarters in Ninove. It was a splendid event, both from a military and from a social perspective. It figures prominently in many accounts of the campaign and made an enduring impression on both spectators and participants alike. It was the major set-piece spectacle of the build-up to war, and to make sure that the event passed off without a hitch, Uxbridge had rented some picturesque meadows by the river Dender. Contemporary sources estimate that he paid up to £500 to the farmer who owned them. If it seems odd that Uxbridge had to rent the space for his review, it has to be remembered that at this time Belgium was small, crowded and covered with crops. 'This Country is so universally cultivated,' wrote Lord Fitzroy Somerset, 'that at this time of year, it seems impossible to find any space for Troops to assemble upon.'[10] And while the Prussians might have simply requisitioned the ground for their use without compensating the farmer, that was not the British way.

The day before, Blücher and several Prussian generals rode into Brussels for a dinner with Wellington, the Duke of Brunswick and the King of the United Netherlands, and then there was the obligatory promenade in the Allée Verte, followed by a supper given for Blücher by Wellington.

On the morning of the review, the weather was perfect. Those taking part were up early, and the whole town of Ninove was decorated with green branches of trees that gave it the impression of a bosky grove. Added to these sylvan accessories, a trifle presumptuously perhaps, were laurels and even a triumphal arch. In the meadows, with 'grass up to the horses' knees',[11] troops prepared for the afternoon's review.

> The different corps had no sooner formed in their position, and dismounted, than off went belts, canteens, and haversacks, and a general brushing and scrubbing commenced; for the Duke, making no allowance for dusty or muddy roads, expected to see all as clean as if just turned out: accordingly, we had not only brought brushes, etc., but even straw to wisp over the horses.[12]

Once tidied up and formed in lines almost three-quarters of a mile long, the British troops, between 6,000 and 7,000 in number, presented an impressive front both militarily and aesthetically. 'It was a splendid spectacle,' Mercer recalled.

> The scattered line of hussars in their fanciful yet picturesque costume; the more sober, but far more imposing line of heavy dragoons, like a wall of red brick; and again the serviceable and active appearance of the third line in their blue uniforms, with broad lappels [*sic*] of white, buff, red, yellow, and orange – the whole backed by the dark wood of the declivity already mentioned – formed, indeed, a fine picture.[13]

Others were equally impressed with the scale and quality of the review: '46 of the finest squadrons of cavalry ever seen were drawn up in a place in their lines, with 6 troops of Horse artillery and a Brigade of Rockets, in all about 6,500 men.'[14] And of course anywhere there was a gathering of troops, especially the dashing, colourfully clad cavalry, there was a congregation of persons of fashion. There were literally thousands of spectators: military personnel from all sorts of Allied countries; curious locals 'of the country for ten leagues around';[15] and 'all the *haut ton* of Brussels'.[16]

Well not quite all the *haut ton*. Sadly Lord Uxbridge's sister Lady Caroline Capel was unable to attend as she was in the midst of her thirteenth pregnancy. The discovery that she would be having a child had been made during the uncertain period between Napoleon's arrival in Paris and Wellington's appearance in Brussels, and her mother had urged her to come back to England. But once the mood had settled down, Lady Caroline had decided to have the child in Brussels and had found that there were a number of British women in a similar condition. 'Lady Fitzroy Somerset is going to stay on & to be confined here in May'– Lady Fitzroy gave birth to a girl on 16 May after a labour of three and half hours. 'Ly. Emily James is to do the same thing at the Hague, where She expects a Woman from England to attend her; As the time would suit exactly She has written to ask her terms & whether she would come on to Brussels to me afterwards,'[17] she wrote reassuringly to her mother.

Nevertheless she was irritated that her advancing pregnancy restricted her social life. 'Nothing ever was so fine or so Magnificent as the review of English Cavalry 3 days ago,' she wrote wistfully of her brother's review to her mother. 'It was 30 Miles off, & Capel thought it too great an Undertaking for me or I certainly should have gone, For I could have done it free of expence [*sic*],' – always an important consideration in the Capel household – 'Lord Hill having offered me Quarters, & General Barnes relays of Horses; the Day was tremendously Hot however – & part of the Road bad, and as Capel was generous enough not to go himself as I did not, there was nothing to be said.'[18] Lady Caroline Capel is clearly put out at having missed one of the major social occasions of the summer, especially as she could have enjoyed it for free. The potential cost of the outing seeming a far greater barrier to attendance than any injury to her unborn child.

The weather was lovely, the uniforms clean and colourful, horses exquisitely groomed, discipline perfect and troop dispositions exemplary. In fact only one thing seems to have been imprecise on that glorious early summer's day in the Low Countries so long ago: timekeeping. One detail that still eludes history and historians is the precise time at which the battle of Waterloo began. The answer seems to be the rather oblique one that timing in an era before the introduction of internationally recognised time zones was a subjective business. Each separate community had its own time as dictated by the shadow cast by the sun at the local meridian which gave local noon. Hence in a field in the middle of Belgium there was no exact local time. Instead officers would have had their watches set to the local time of the place where their journey had begun, while the accuracy of the watches – already questionable – would have been further disturbed by the constant motion of the ride to their destination.

What was true for the most famous battle of the nineteenth century was equally true of the cavalry review that preceded it by a little more than a fortnight. Depending on which account one follows, the Duke of Wellington, attended by various Allied commanders, the Prince of Orange, Prince Blücher and numerous dukes including, of course, the socially ubiquitous Duke of Richmond, arrived at this riparian meadow to take the review at either midday, half past twelve, 1 p.m. or 2 p.m.;[19] they were greeted by a salute of either nineteen[20] or twenty-one[21] guns. The Duke and his delegation only further embellished the splendour of the scene. As George Woodberry recalled, there was a 'large number of Russian generals, Prussians and Saxons' some of whom 'were so covered in stars, orders, gold braid and magnificent plumes that I almost wished to be at war with them in the hope of ransoming even one of the least important'.[22]

For their part the visitors were equally impressed by the warlike mien and excellent appearance of the British forces. Mercer was particularly proud that instead of passing through the ranks of his artillery battery, as he had done others, the excitable old Prussian commander inspected every horse, muttering that he had 'never seen anything so superb in his life, and concluding by exclaiming, "Mein Gott, dere is not von orse in dies batterie wich is not goot for Veldt Marshal."'[23] Yet the ever-sensitive Mercer noticed that while the Duke of Wellington enquired whose battery it was, he never allowed a single compliment or word of recognition to pass his lips, confirming his contempt for, or insecurity around, the artillery and its officers who did not, strictly speaking, come under his jurisdiction and who were of course trained professionals.

The apparent snub detected by Mercer aside, the whole review was judged to have passed off brilliantly, 'without a check, an error, or an accident'. It was plain to see that 'the cavalry had fallen into the hands of a master'.[24]

And with the review finished, it was of course time for a party. Uxbridge lived in what was variously described as an abbey or a monastery, the chief benefit of which was not its religious associations but rather that its rooms were large and 'well calculated for the princely feast',[25] a celebratory banquet for a hundred guests, which gave the Duke of Wellington and his gaudily dressed entourage the opportunity to meet Uxbridge's commanders socially. Dinner started about five o'clock, although given the notoriously imprecise nature of timekeeping this is best interpreted catholicly.

One thing not in dispute however was the quality of the catering: many courses, 'all served on plate', noted one guest approvingly, and of course the 'finest wines of every kind'[26] cascaded down the throats of thirsty diners who had spent all day under the sun. As host, Uxbridge sat at the head of the horseshoe-shaped table, flanked by Blücher and Wellington. And as soon as the excellent pudding had been served, double doors swung open to reveal a band which played 'God Save the King', presaging a torrent of toasts and the opening of the doors to allow the local gentry to come and gawp at the feast.

The combination of military might and luxury provoked philosophical contemplation from artillery commander Augustus Frazer: 'Many feelings are excited on days and in sights like this, in which one sees all this world has to show of splendour and of luxury – all that is prepared for the gratification of this life, – and for the destruction of it.'[27] All in all it was an apt appraisal of the whole campaign, where the gaiety of civilian life and the concerns of high society were inseparable from the misery of war and the serious military business of tackling the French leader.

This was not a late night however; after coffee the party broke up as dusk was beginning to fall, at about 8 p.m. according to one officer's pocket watch – too early apparently for the hard-drinking Marshal Blücher who seemed to be enjoying himself hugely. And as the laurel-garlanded streets of Ninove echoed to the sound of squibs and fireworks let off by the enthusiastic inhabitants, the officers of the cavalry and artillery returned to their usual routine of life in the Low Countries: racing, flirting, wife-swapping, socialising or just being busy relaxing in a tranquil country billet.

16

'Monsieur is a high-bred prince, but he is no soldier'

Before returning to his pleasant country chateau with its moat full of frogs, Mercer noted something strange in his account of the evening. Among all the splendid guests of various nationalities, there was 'not one Frenchman that I recollect'.[1]

Although the Allied Army was assembling with the aim, yet again, of reinstalling a Bourbon monarch on the throne of France, French involvement in the military build-up against Napoleon was non-existent. Given that with its usual perversity liberal British opinion had swung towards Bonaparte when he had been exiled on Elba, the trail of *bien pensant* British who had made the pilgrimage to see the former French emperor in his Mediterranean exile must have encouraged Bonaparte in thinking he could return to mainland Europe. Then there was the ribald commentary that greeted the pusillanimous way in which France had once again succumbed to Napoleonic rule. All but the ghost of respect for the exiled monarch and his court had vanished.

The official British position, vis-à-vis the rump of the French court that had accompanied the gouty monarch into exile in Ghent, was articulated by Lord Castlereagh in a letter to Sir Charles Stuart, the British ambassador to the United Netherlands.

War is now too serious a question for Etiquette, and altho' it is very fit that the Princes of the Blood should expose themselves, it is not right that they should expose their Armies, nor the cause for which they contend, by taking upon themselves a charge for which they are wholly incompetent.

Just in case he was not making himself crystal clear, Castlereagh departed from the obfuscatory language of nineteenth-century diplomacy and added: 'Monsieur is a high-bred Prince, but he is no soldier.'[2]

Wellington agreed with this view of the French royal family; 'he is, I believe, a well-meaning man,' he said of the king, but also: 'he is the most difficult person to deal with I have ever met.'[3] His view of the exiled monarch's court was less charitable still: 'He is surrounded by persons who have been in the French service. It is very well to employ them, but I would not trust one of them out of my sight, and so I have told him.'[4]

As might be expected, Wellington was characteristically blunt in his assessment of the military value of the rump Bourbon Army. Shortly before or after the review at Ninove, Wellington was talking to Ambassador Stuart outside the latter's house on the park in Brussels. Thomas Creevey happened to be taking a stroll there with his stepdaughters at the time, and once the Duke and the ambassador had finished their conversation, Wellington joined Creevey and walked with him. The British papers had arrived that morning with news of debates in parliament about the likelihood of war, and after some banter about political life, Creevey asked him what he thought the outcome would be. The Duke stopped and answered in a most natural way: 'By God! I think Blücher and myself can do the thing.'

With Wellington it is impossible to know how much was bravado and sangfroid put on for the benefit of a notorious gossip – he would have known that Creevey was in contact with half the House of Commons – and how much was serious assessment of the military situation. Creevey pressed him. Did he count on any desertions? 'Not upon a man,' was the Duke's instant reply, almost revelling in the situation, and adding humorously: 'we may pick up a marshal or two, perhaps; but not worth a damn.' Perhaps the Duke was counting on support from the French forces in the United Netherlands loyal to the king? At this, it was as if Wellington had just discovered that he had trodden in a dog turd. 'Oh!' he said, freighting this one word with all the surprise and contempt that characterise the classic chilly put-down of the English aristocracy, 'don't mention such fellows!' No, for Wellington the answer to the problem was simple. He looked around the park, and soon his eyes alighted on what he wanted. 'There,' he said, indicating a private soldier from a British infantry regiment, 'it all depends on that article whether we do the business or not. Give me enough of it, and I am sure.'[5]

The sentiments that were this clearly expressed at the very highest levels of government and the Army were also felt in the lowest ranks of the armed services. While ordinary British soldiers respected the martial prowess of Napoleon they felt no common cause with the regime that they were notionally prepared to fight, kill and if necessary die to reinstall. At best theirs was an unquestioning understanding (or lack of understanding) that they were being called in to sort out another fine French mess, at worst they showed outright contempt for the largely discredited French monarchy as was demonstrated on the day of the great review at Ninove.

At some stage during the preparations of the review, while all the men were either cleaning their kit or brushing their horses, a cavalcade of brilliantly uniformed individuals was spied and the cry went up that the Duke was coming. But it was early in the day and Wellington was not expected for some time, even accounting for the inaccuracy of the officers' watches. It was soon discovered to be a false alarm; it was indeed a duke, the Duc de Berri, but not *the* Duke, not Wellington. Laughing with relief at their mistake the men returned to the serious business of preparing their kit and their mounts for Wellington's arrival. Meanwhile the Duc de Berri galloped towards the point where he imagined he would take the salute, 'reined up and looked haughtily and impatiently about him'[6] while thousands of British soldiers pointedly ignored him and continued to prepare themselves for the 'real' duke. Even at a distance de Berri's mounting fury was obvious. When it became plain that he was going to receive nothing like the salute to which he felt entitled, he charged off, leaving his retinue to catch up with him as well as they could, to the amused guffaws of the British who had not even interrupted the brushing of their horses for a member of the French royal family.

It was not the first time that 'the little Duke' as he was pejoratively known by some, had let his temper get the better of him. Indeed, while he was in Paris, Lord Fitzroy Somerset recorded that the king had needed to talk to Berri about his behaviour: 'the Wigging was chiefly directed to the Duc de Berry [*sic*], who has behaved on more than one occasion very improperly, aping the style of Napoleon both in Violence and Expression. I fancy the little Duke, though a good natured Man, is as hot as Pepper without any judgement whatsoever.'[7]

The Duc de Berri was apparently a pompous, self-aggrandising fool fond of throwing his weight around, who, when not giving in to a tantrum if not accorded the respect he considered his due, spent his time drilling his small number of troops (what Mercer memorably describes as 'Louis XVIII's phantom of an army')[8] and fiddling his expenses. 'He draws rations from the British army, and is said to receive an allowance for ten or twelve horses (per diem), which he profits from by only keeping a couple,'[9] noted one British officer caustically. And to judge from Fitzroy Somerset's opinion of the manner in which Berri left France, it would seem that he would not be of much use in battle: 'The Duc de Berri, shewed the White Feather rather than the white cockade, & was very nearly lost in the mud because he did not venture to take a road where it was possible he might be in some degree opposed.'[10]

In Ghent the only reason that, from time to time, the British were keen to form part of the guard of honour to King Louis was that the duty came with no responsibilities other than to participate in the horseplay practised by the youngsters who formed His Most Christian Majesty's *Garde du Corps*, and who, like so many of the English officers, were little more than boys. Moreover British members of the guard of honour could look forward to enjoying excellent food. Even in exile, whatever the prevailing view of their conduct, the king and his court ate well. 'The King retains his composure & his appetite. Nobody ever eat [*sic*] so much, but his Maison tread in H. M. steps in that respect as much as they can, though in others they differ, having lost their head & heart early in the business.'[11]

At best the exiled French monarch, or *'notre Père de Gand'* (Ghent) as he was mockingly known, was a tourist attraction, a sight to be ticked off the list of noteworthy objects in the Low Countries that summer. Seeing King Louis seated at the dining table was a highlight of any visit to Ghent at that time, as one visitor recalled:

we saw Louis the Eighteenth dining, as it is justly called, 'in public;' for the windows of his room were thrown open to the populace, who were eagerly staring at him as he sat surrounded by about 30 officers, enjoying, or affecting to enjoy, better appetites than under such circumstances might have been expected.[12]

Otherwise Louis spent his time driving out in the afternoon, meeting his ministers and generally behaving much as if he were taking a small holiday, apparently sublimely indifferent to the huge and rapid build-up of military force intended to restore him to the throne of his ancestors. Much as he may have looked like a gouty man-mountain oblivious to his surroundings, Louis XVIII was nothing if not a survivor, and while he might have appeared magnificently imperturbable, his experiences as a refugee and indigent monarch in exile had taught him to be prepared. It was said that 'he had engaged all the post horses in the town, to be ready to carry him away the moment there should appear to be any necessity for retreating'.[13]

Harry Smith was one of the few British people to come away with a favourable impression of the king: 'He was very inactive, but impressive in manner. He laid his hand on my shoulder to support himself. His great topic of conversation was how delighted he was to see us, and how much he was indebted to our nation. A more benign countenance I never beheld, nor did his subsequent reign belie the benignity of his expression.'[14] Fitzroy Somerset was more noncommittal, describing him as 'a nice old Man'.[15]

Rather more typical was the commentary of a civilian visitor to Ghent at that time, Charlotte Eaton, who was supremely unimpressed:

> The City of Ghent seemed to be restored to some traces of its ancient grandeur by the temporary residence of the Bourbon princes, and the little expatriated court of Louis XVIII. I had never been able to feel any extravagant degree of attachment to this unfortunate royal family: their restoration had not given me any enthusiastic joy, nor their fall much sorrow; and even the honour of paying my devoirs to Louis le Désiré, and exchanging some profound and reverential bows and courtesies with his most Catholic Majesty, failed to inspire me with much interest or admiration for this persecuted, princely race. These bows, by the way, cost the good old king considerable time and labour, for he is extremely unwieldy and corpulent, and gouty; and he looks very lethargic and snuffy; and it is really a thousand pities that an exiled and dethroned monarch should be so remarkably uninteresting a personage.[16]

If the king was famous for epicurean habits, corpulence and gout, his brother and heir, Monsieur le Comte d'Artois, had acquired a certain celebrity status for his piety and devoutness. In fact seeing Monsieur at prayer was almost as much of a tourist attraction as seeing *notre Père de Gand* gorging himself at the breakfast table. Mercer happened to be in Ghent on a Sunday when a mass was celebrated expressly for Monsieur. 'Expecting something grand I repaired to the cathedral in company with several other officers.'

They were welcomed, seated in the stalls and the organ loft, and to their surprise found that they formed the entire congregation until the 'illustrious communicant' made his entrance surrounded by his courtiers. Like his brother he was unimpressive to look at:

> a small man of good figure, but of no very distinguished appearance. He was dressed in a blue uniform coat with silver embroidery, white breeches, and silk stockings. He advanced with a quick pace to the steps of the high altar, where a single chair had been placed for him, bowed very low, crossed himself most devoutly, bowed again, and, kneeling on the chair with his

arms resting on the back, buried his face in his hands, and in this attitude remained throughout the ceremony. His suite, military and civil, ranged themselves across the choir behind him. A few found chairs, and knelt on them, but the greater part remained standing, and seemed little interested in the service. At length, to my great joy, the last taper was extinguished, and, tired to death, I made my escape, resolved never again to attend a royal mass.[7]

If Mercer's boredom seems disrespectful, it is nevertheless positively restrained when compared to the jaundiced view of Frye. His view of the king – 'his devotions at the table are more sincere than at the altar' – was uncompromising. However his most blistering contempt was reserved for what he saw as the 'religious cant' of the heir to the French throne, whom, like Mercer, he studied while attending a service in the cathedral.

Monsieur has all the appearance of a worn out debauchee, and to see him with a missal in his hand and the strange contrite face he assumes, is truly ridiculous. These princes, instigated doubtless by the priests, make a great parade of their sanctity, for which however those who are acquainted with their character will not give them much credit.[18]

Monsieur's devout display may not have convinced the cynical Frye, but upon the death of his brother Monsieur became the notoriously God-fearing Charles X, whose behaviour while king would achieve what neither the Revolution nor Napoleon could achieve, the destruction of the Bourbon monarchy in France. In 1830, as the last Bourbon king of France, he would be forced into exile.

It is remarkable that in the space of about a century, the Bourbon dynasty had dwindled from the mighty Sun King Louis XIV to a decrepit trio of exiles in the Low Countries: a gouty glutton, a religious maniac, and an angry, arrogant young cavalry commander who practised petty fraud on the Army that was assembling to return his family to the throne of their ancestors.

And yet in spite of the uninspiring nature of the cause for which they were about to go to war, and for which many would sacrifice their lives, Allied forces continued to pour into the Low Countries.

17

꙳ ꙳

'He kept making everybody dance to the last'[1]

When Wellington first arrived in Brussels, Creevey had reason to expect that he would be snubbed by the Duke. Half a dozen years earlier Creevey had been a bitter critic of Wellington's brother Lord Wellesley, who had served as Governor-General of India, so he was pleasantly surprised when he met the Duke towards the end of April at Lady Charlotte Greville's. In common with many British residents, Lady Charlotte regarded the military build-up as a social bonanza and was in the habit of 'having a party of all the principal persons then in Brussells [*sic*] of all countries every evening'.[2]

At the time the chief topic of conversation was the likelihood of an armed confrontation with Napoleon. The very fact of the Duke's presence indicated that the British at least thought a military showdown inevitable, and yet Creevey was so struck by what he took as the Duke's naïveté that as soon as he got home he made a note in his diary that, according to Wellington, 'it would never come to fighting with the Allies' and 'that he was confident it would never come to blows'.[3] Accordingly Creevey came away with the impression 'of his [the Duke] having made a very sorry figure, in giving no indication of superior talents'.[4]

Lady Charlotte Greville's salon was well frequented; Creevey continued to bump into the Duke there and always came away with the same poor impression. The diarist's opinions seemed confirmed when he attended a ball given by Wellington: 'The Duke during this period was for ever giving balls,* to which he was always kind enough to ask my daughters and myself; and very agreeable they were.'[5]

This ball was held shortly after the news of the outcome of the Champ de Mai reached Brussels. Since early April builders in Paris had been working on an amphitheatre opposite the École Militaire, the structure intended for an event called the Champ de Mai, which was meant to be a national congress to be held during May. Instead it took place on 1 June and, as it transpired, was the sort of state fancy dress pageant that Napoleon had gone in for throughout his career; conflating religious, political, military, historical and nationalistic themes with the cult of Napoleon. Dignitaries appeared in elaborate robes, heavily embroidered cloaks and feathered hats, presided over by Napoleon in a black hat accessorised with ostrich feathers and a giant diamond, which must have clashed terribly with the 'Roman Emperor's robe'[6] he was also wearing. It seems that Wellington had hoped that this event would prove to be the undoing of Napoleon and that political in-fighting in the imperial circle, together with a national weariness of war and bloodshed, would somehow derail the train of events that appeared to be leading to war.

As it happened, the Champ de Mai passed off well as far as Napoleon was concerned and, catching up with the Duke at his ball, Creevey asked what he thought of the turn of events in Paris. It is easy to imagine the elaborate insouciance of the Duke, looking out over the dancers, his eyes darting between the prettier young women, with the annoyingly insistent Creevey at his side. 'I asked him what he thought of things now at Paris,' recalled Creevey, 'upon which he laughed and seemed not in the least degree affected by the event.'[7]

To be fair to Creevey he was far from alone in his opinion of the Allied commander. Given that Creevey was already underwhelmed by what he had seen of Wellington, and being the pathological gossip that he was, he could not resist commenting to the next important person he saw on what he considered to be the Duke's irresponsible indifference to the much-increased likelihood of war. A ball at the Duke's house was bound to have numerous celebrated guests, and Creevey soon found himself chatting to the British ambassador, Sir Charles Stuart. It seems that Creevey may have been rather caustic in his assessment of Wellington's grasp of the situation, as the ambassador replied in a 'curious

---

*Creevey might have been hyperbolising. According to the Duke's cook, James Thornton, who was with him in Brussels from the middle of May, 'The Duke had large dinners nearly every day and three large balls during our stay in Brussels.' (Thornton, p.94)

blunt manner: – "Then he is damned different with you from what he is with me, for I never saw a fellow so cut down in my life than he was this morning when he first heard the news.'"[8]

Wellington's flippancy and blithe confidence were a front that he presented to British expatriate society in Brussels. The slightly desperate tone of his letters to Horse Guards and the misgivings, concerns and even fears that he shared with a very small circle (including, it seems, Stuart) indicate a completely different man to the public image projected as he danced at balls, flirted in salons and strolled in the park. Wellington was surprisingly skilled in public relations where they helped achieve a military end.

He maintained fearsome discipline among his soldiers which, as well as making for an obedient and well-drilled fighting force, helped win the hearts-and-minds campaign that the British had been fighting since their arrival in the Low Countries. While the near-lawless Prussian forces were perceived as little better than bandits, British forces were tolerated and indeed liked, thanks in great measure to Wellington's policy of discouraging the sort of theft, extortion, plunder and other forms of 'reparation' usually exacted by an army of occupation, which was in effect what the Allied force was. Doubtless this approach assisted Britain's policy of nurturing the nascent state of the United Netherlands, and having fought alongside guerrillas in the Peninsula, Wellington wanted to do his utmost to ensure that even if they did not join him, the population would not rise against him.

His masterly performance of insouciance, which seems to have taken in the observant and quick-minded Creevey, was part of the same strategy. Although he may have pretended indifference, he was aware of the huge effect of his personality. Wellington the phenomenon had arisen out of the need for a protagonist of stature to match Napoleon. Although he might not have been a head of state, Wellington was the receptacle of the nation's hopes and fears; he knew that he was under constant scrutiny and that in this closing period of the phoney peace, how he appeared was as important as what he did. He was Britain in the way that Napoleon was France. The French emperor used pomp and theatrical pageantry to broadcast his message and personal style to his subjects and to wrap his military ambitions in a cloak of national interest; so Wellington did something to achieve a similar end, albeit in a completely different way. He set about creating the myth of British imperturbability, the famous stiff upper lip that would come to be identified as the national characteristic of Britain as the century wore on. He may have been concerned, probably even scared, by Napoleon but he knew that it would have been dangerous to show it. At the time the world was on a knife edge, and anything he could do to defuse the tension would help. Hence his apparent fondness for giving and going to balls, such little touches as referring to his rival using the dismissive pronunciation Buonaparte, and such charades as the apparent insouciance during the walk in the park with Creevey and his stepdaughters. All these psychological tricks played their part in creating an image of unconcerned confidence for consumption locally and in Britain. In this the British civilians in Brussels were invaluable: the society ladies and their competitive party-giving created a social smokescreen and fostered an air of unreal calm, as if the salons of Mayfair had been transported to the edge of the battlefield.

The Duke's apparent lack of concern and his attendance at suppers and salons, dinners and dances almost every night would also have been analysed across the border in France. Wellington could be sure that his behaviour was being relayed to Napoleon who, the Duke hoped, might underestimate him as much as Creevey had. Given the proximity of the opposing forces, the sympathies of many inhabitants and the porous border between France and its former territory, spying was rife. Wellington had his conduits of information from France and there was a British presence with royalist supporters there, while, as June progressed, the exploits of French spies in Allied territory became increasingly daring.

Mercer describes one such covert operator, who rode in disguise into the middle of a village occupied by British forces and started to question them about troop dispositions, claiming to be on a mission from Lord Uxbridge.

> He was dressed as our hussars usually were when riding about the country – blue frock, scarlet waistcoat laced with gold, pantaloons, and forage-cap of the 7th hussars. He was mounted on a smart pony, with plain saddle and bridle, was without sword or sash, and carried a small whip; in short his costume and *monture* were correct in every particular. Moreover, he aped to the very life that 'devil-may-care' nonchalant air so frequently characterising our young men of fashion.[9]

The spy had a marvellous time ordering people about and extracting information from both soldiers and civil authorities before making himself scarce when the commanding officer returned to the village. 'Our friend deserved to escape,' commented Mercer indulgently, 'for he was a bold and clever fellow.'[10]

Outwardly at least Wellington was every bit as relaxed as the counterfeit hussar. On 2 June he wrote to General Sir Lowry Cole congratulating him on his imminent marriage to the Earl of Malmesbury's daughter on 15 June. Cole was to have commanded a division, but as it was judged that there was not much happening, he was spared a few weeks' leave to get married and take a honeymoon. As a result he missed the fighting altogether.

Wellington was also in contact with Graham, now Lord Lynedoch, who had failed to storm Antwerp at the end of the last war with Napoleon, but had organised such a lovely picnic in the woods near Brussels. Lynedoch wrote to the Duke of Wellington on an extremely urgent matter that could not wait: he wanted to start a club and invited the Duke of Wellington to be a founder member.

'My Dear Lord,' wrote Wellington 13 June, 'I have received your letter of the 7th instant, and I shall be very happy to belong to the military club proposed to be established, in which will, of course, be included the Peninsula Club, respecting which we before corresponded.' He then proceeds to tell Lynedoch:

> There is nothing new here. We have reports of Buonaparte's joining the army and attacking us; but I have accounts from Paris of the 10th, on which day he was still there; and I judge from his speech to the Legislature that his departure was not likely to be immediate. I think we are now too strong for him here.[11]

At this point it is difficult to decide whether Wellington was merely playing it very, very cool, or whether indeed he did believe that he was sufficiently strong to discourage Napoleon from attacking and that in a few weeks, at a time of his own choosing, he would move over to the offensive and invade France. It certainly seems that there were officers who believed invasion of France was imminent. In the latter half of May, long before Uxbridge's splendid cavalry review, Mercer wrote: 'For some time past it had been generally understood that our army would advance into the French territory on or about the 20th June.'[12] Edward Somerset had obviously heard a similar rumour, as he wrote to his brother on 8 June: 'Our army still remains in status quo, but it is expected that some movement will be made before the expiration of next week,' adding the inevitable observation about Wellington's active social life: 'In the mean time the Duke of Wellington is very gay at Brussells, & gives a great Ball & supper at least once a week.'[13]

However a few days later Somerset was writing to his brother again to say that he had been mistaken in his prediction of early action: 'I have reason to believe our operations will not commence quite so soon as I expected a few days ago, as it was then thought the army would move this week; but that does not now appear probable.' His letter is dated 13 June and includes further evidence that the British contingent were making themselves as comfortable as possible rather than preparing for imminent war. Having passed on the news that Fitzroy Somerset's wife and child were doing well he added that 'Fitzroy's curricle is arrived here from England in a sad state; the carriage is knocked about very considerably, & the Bar has been lost or left behind. The coach master says it will be necessary to new paint it.'[14] For a fashionable officer, a carriage in Brussels was a necessity; General Barnes and Lord Uxbridge were among those who had taken the precaution of having their own carriages brought out.

So seductive was the sense of security that even civilians at that time came to believe that France and not Belgium was expected to be the theatre of war. If anything the Capel family felt more secure than they had at any time since moving to the Low Countries. Lady Caroline Capel did not fancy the idea of spending the summer in Brussels, especially as she was carrying another child, so she decided to move to a country house, a little chateau which she had been lent until the end of August. It had lovely views of the Palace of Lacken, was only two or three miles outside Brussels and was, most importantly for the freeloading Capels, 'free of expence'.

Early in June she made the Chateau de Walcheuse her summer residence and once again military resources were used to help in the move. 'I have had all the Baggage Waggons belonging to the Adjutant General's Office in requisition for the last week to bring our things here,' she wrote proudly to her mother, adding that there was 'nothing so convenient as a Military Friend – They smooth all difficulties, particularly such a one as Sir Edward Barnes.'[15] In fact she was so pleased with their new house that she planned a *'Pick Nick* Dinner Party in the Grounds' and invited 'Lady George Seymour & her daughter – Lady Charlotte Greville – Mr, Mrs & Miss Smyth – General Barnes and his staff – Lord Arthur Hill, Mr Horace Seymour, Colonel Gordon, Major Dawson, and some few more'.[16] She thoughtfully planned to give this little party on Friday 16 June, giving her military guests the weekend to prepare for the invasion of France, if it were to take place the week after.

While Mercer thought that the balloon would go up around 20 June, it is likely that Wellington himself had in mind another, later, date. He could not possibly be thinking of invading France on 20 June; that would have been out of the question, as he was giving a grand ball on 21 June to celebrate the anniversary of his victory at the battle of Vittoria two years earlier.

Nor did the Duke limit his pleasures to just dancing. A notorious ladies' man, as ever he took great pleasure in female company. As has been noted he was often seen in the company of the Duke of Richmond's sixteen-year-old daughter Lady Jane Lennox. For instance, in the midst of his preparations he found the time to take Jane to Enghien to a cricket match and then bring her back to Brussels that night, 'apparently ... for no other purpose than to amuse her'.[7]

Indeed it seems that there was concern that the Duke's love life was beginning to interfere with his military duties. One affair in particular caused concern: Wellington's relationship with a young society woman, Lady Frances Wedderburn-Webster, the aristocratic wife of an affluent man of fashion, James Wedderburn-Webster.

The Wedderburn-Websters were typical of the fashionable civilians attracted to Brussels. She was the daughter of the Earl of Mountnorris, who had arrived in Brussels in poor health the preceding summer and whose coach had broken a spring on the picnic so faultlessly organised by Lord Lynedoch. Lord Mountnorris's other daughter Catherine had caused excitement with her on-off romance and subsequent elopement with Lord John Somerset. Now her sister was about to damage Wellington's reputation, not as a husband – no one really cared too much about that – but as a focused and responsible military leader with his mind on the task of defeating the most charismatic military leader of the age. There were moments when it seemed that Wellington was rather more absorbed in the pursuit of another man's wife.

In Wellington's defence it should be said that Lady Frances was incredibly alluring. Not at all clever, the overriding impression of her portrait of 1812 is that of translucent-skinned, pearl-necklaced stupidity, but possessed of an attraction which had already ensnared her husband's friend Lord Byron. Wellington was either so infatuated or so completely unconcerned about possible scandal that he scarcely bothered to conceal the affair. At one of his balls, 'The Duke himself danced, and always with the same person, a Lady Caroline Webster [Caroline was her second name], to whom he paid so much attention, that Scandal, who is become Goddess here, began to whisper all sorts of stories.'[8] The stories got spicier when James Wedderburn-Webster – by most accounts a crashing bore, tolerated only for his money – went to London at the beginning of May and was absent for the whole summer. Perhaps he felt reasonably sure that he would not be cuckolded, as his wife was by then expecting a child. It seems that pregnancy stopped neither Wellington nor Lady Frances from deepening their relationship.

One staff officer had clear recall of an outdoor tryst where, in a scene straight out of bedroom farce, the two lovers were pursued by Lady Mountnorris, Lady Frances's elderly mother.

> I was sitting one afternoon in the park with an elderly Belgian lady, when a very great man walked past us, and immediately after a carriage drew up at an entrance on the opposite side of the park, and a lady alighted, who was joined by the great man. My friend and I, prompted by curiosity, arose to see the result of the junction, following with our eyes the lady and gentleman until they descended into a hollow, where the trees completely screened them. We then perceived another carriage arrive, from which an old lady descended, whom I recognised as Lady M. N., who went peering about as if looking for some one or something, but was completely baffled by the tactics of the lady and gentleman, and left the park *re infecta*. She was clearly in search of her daughter, Lady F.W., of whom 'busy fame whispered light things'.[19]

It could not and did not stay a secret. The affair was the talk of Brussels that summer and eventually made it into the more scandalous London newspapers, resulting in an embarrassing libel trial, but that was in the future.

With Wellington's mind thus diverted it is easy to see how his example fostered an air of unreal light-heartedness. Wellington was perhaps the cause, or at least the most prominent symptom, of this unreal cocoon in which British expatriate life existed in Belgium during the spring and early summer of 1815. People behaved almost as if their actions had no consequences. Part of this may be ascribed to the *carpe diem* attitude of those about to go into battle snatching their pleasures where they can; and then there was the nature of Brussels itself. It must have been hard for those who found themselves living in a land of plentiful food and cheap drink, where there were parties every night, to believe that they might have to fight and die. The Peninsular campaign had been a genuine war; this had the outward appearance of garrison duty in a fashionable spa town.

The proximity of French forces and the likelihood of armed confrontation increasing with every day did little to rein in the party spirit that prevailed. From their highly social leader to the humblest private with his beer, hollands and tobacco, the British military knew about the coming war, but just could not quite bring itself to believe it.

18

'I thought I should get back, after the great
battle that appeared imminent, in time to mount
guard at St James's'

For all his party-giving, flirting and bravado of the sort he showed with
Creevey while strolling in the park, doubtless wanting to show off a little
to the MP's stepdaughters, Wellington was hard pressed. He might have
been able to front it out during the day, under the sunlight, walking in the
park, raising his hat to the ladies in best Georgette Heyer-approved style;
at night and in the early mornings alone with his thoughts and worries,
before his young and boisterous 'family' of aristocratic A.D.C.s could
crowd around him, it would have been strange indeed if he did not worry
about the situation that faced him.

The French royalists were useless, and although he could rely on Blücher
personally, the troops that the Prussian commanded were, to put it politely,
a mixed bag. Their sober uniforms, lusty hymn-singing and less snobbish
officer corps might have impressed individual Englishmen, but they were
detested by the French-speaking populace who regarded their leader as
little better than a bloodthirsty bandit: 'Blücher by all accounts is a vandal
and is actuated by a most vindictive spirit.'* Moreover there were tensions,
not merely between the Prussians and the local population, but among the
German-speaking forces. At one point Saxon troops attempted to mutiny
and to assassinate Blücher.

Wellington desperately needed experienced officers. Having got rid
of the bumbling Hudson Lowe, he required a new Quartermaster. The
Duke's first choice, George Murray, had recently been appointed
Governor of Canada, so while he waited for Murray he had summoned
the latter's long-time deputy, Sir William Howe De Lancey. De Lancey

had served throughout the Peninsular War, and after six years had returned to Great Britain at the end of 1814 to take up the post of Deputy Quartermaster-General at the Army headquarters in Edinburgh. Handsome, unmarried, his eyes may have had a stern gaze, but there was a romantic side to this man too and in peacetime this side of his character was able to show itself. A distinguished soldier who enjoyed the confidence of the Duke of Wellington, De Lancey was now in his late thirties, and had been knighted for his services in the recent war – his creation as a Knight Commander of the Order of the Bath was gazetted on 3 January 1815. De Lancey became a prominent and impressive figure in Edinburgh social life.

As such he came into the orbit of Sir James and Lady Hall. The Halls' house on George Street and recently completed mansion, Dunglass, on an estate of almost 9,000 acres near the Lammermuir hills close to Dunbar, between the Firth of Forth and Berwick upon Tweed, were open to the social scientific and intellectual elite of Edinburgh. The Halls were examples of that relatively rare specimen of early-nineteenth-century British life: the intellectual aristocrat.

De Lancey liked the Halls and the feeling was reciprocated. December saw him visiting Sir James's country seat, but it was not merely the pursuit of intellectual stimulation that had led him to the North Sea coast in the middle of winter. He had fallen in love with Sir James's daughter Magdalene. Magdalene was 'an amiable, kind, and beautiful young woman'[2] with a childlike delicacy. The courtship was quick and the engagement short. The banns were read during March and the couple were married on 4 April 1815, after which they set off to Dunglass.

At the same time that Sir William and Lady De Lancey were enjoying their first night as husband and wife, Wellington was arriving in Brussels to set in train events that would curtail the newlyweds' Scottish honeymoon. At first the military build-up in Flanders must have seemed very distant from Dunglass with its hills, gorges and eight miles of wind-lashed coastland. However, the situation in the Low Countries and Wellington's frustration with the old-womanish Hudson Lowe would soon make an impact on the young couple's romantic idyll. On 16 April Major-General Sir Henry Torrens wrote to inform Wellington from Horse Guards that 'De Lancey is going out to you immediately'.[3]

Torrens was a little premature in his implication of De Lancey's alacrity. Sir William and his bride of seventeen days arrived in London on 21 April. The contrast with life at Dunglass was stark and he was not at all happy about his appointment, as Torrens's letter to Wellington shows.

De Lancey is in town on his way to go out. He has his scruples as to the indignity of returning to service in the field in the same position only which he so long held; and he has requested of me to withhold the notification of his actual appointment until he communicates with you personally, lest you should imagine that he looks upon the arrangement as one favourable to him. I told him the very handsome and complimentary manner in which you asked for his services, and assured him that nothing could be so gratifying, in my view of the case, to his military and professional feelings, as the desire you expressed to me of having him again with you.[4]

Torrens then went on to outline to Wellington the reasons he had given to De Lancey for not giving him a promotion: namely that Wellington was still waiting for his first choice, Murray, to travel from Canada and there was the delicate matter of easing Hudson Lowe out of position.

All this was hardly satisfactory to De Lancey, and it is clear, by what Torrens leaves unsaid, that De Lancey gave Horse Guards a piece of his mind about the situation. Nevertheless, newly married though he might have been, he was still a soldier, and if his commanding officer wanted him to resume his old job of Deputy Quartermaster-General, standing in for the Quartermaster-General while the first choice was *en route* from Canada, then that is what he would do. Although Torrens wrote that De Lancey was going out immediately on 16 April, it seems that he did not arrive in Brussels until the end of May, and Lowe was only removed from the staff on 2 June. De Lancey quickly reorganised things to Wellington's liking, but on 8 June he was distracted from his work by the arrival of his wife, who settled in the house of the Count de Lannoy on the Impasse du Parc, at the bottom corner of the park on the same side as Wellington.

From their rooms on the third or fourth floor, Lady De Lancey could look out over the park – 'It was amusing enough to see the people parading in the Park'; but her chief interest was her husband. Lady De Lancey was almost unique in not having a social agenda to pursue while in Brussels. 'I saw very little of the town, and still less of the inhabitants,' she says simply.

I wasted no time in visiting or going to Balls, which I did not care for, and therefore I never went out, except for an hour or two to walk with Sir William. The people in general dined at 3, we dined at 6, & walked while others were at dinner, so that literally I never saw any body, except some gentlemen, two or three of whom dined with us every day, Sir William's friends whom he brought to introduce to me.[5]

It was an example of her charming naïveté, that she found it totally natural that her husband, as well as sorting out the logistical side of Wellington's heterogeneous invasion force, found time to spend strolling with her in the park and arranging cosy dinners at the Count de Lannoy's house. 'Fortunately, my husband had scarcely any business to do, and he only went to the office for about an hour every day.'[6] De Lancey had been nothing if not a conscientious officer throughout the Peninsular campaign and his capability obviously recommended him to Wellington, but, able though he was, it seems that his priorities had changed, and instead he found it much more satisfying to spend time with his wife.

Another Knight Commander of the Order of the Bath whose name had appeared in the list of victory honours was that of a gruff unpretentious Welsh squire. Sir Thomas Picton was one of the most distinguished commanders of the Peninsular War, and he was named by Torrens as being 'most urgent for employment' in the same letter that had De Lancey going out immediately. As with De Lancey, it seems that Torrens was overstating the alacrity with which Picton wanted to get out to the Low Countries.

After the campaign in the Peninsula peerages were dished out to military commanders with a freedom characteristic of the time. According to the Duke of Norfolk, 'a greater number of peers had been made in the present reign than had been created in any reign since the Revolution.'[7] It had been confidently predicted that Picton would be one of half a dozen soldiers raised to the peerage as a result of their service in the recent war, and, as it happened, five of the six were rewarded with peerages. Picton, however was given a knighthood, and at the beginning of 1815, with the reorganisation of the Order of the Bath, he was made a Knight of the Grand Cross. It was the highest class in a prestigious order, but while five other generals would sit in the House of Lords and listen to the 'my lord' or 'your lordship' of toadying tradesmen, the best Picton could manage was a seat in the House of Commons, where he served as an MP, and the dignity of being addressed as Sir Thomas. It was not bad for a plainspoken Welshman with yeoman-like ruddy features, once described by Wellington as 'a rough foul-mouthed devil as ever lived',[8] but not as good as a peerage. Picton's problem was that he conspicuously lacked the ballroom polish and easy manner of the noblemen with whom Wellington liked to surround himself.

The snub did not go unnoticed; a letter appeared in *The Times* asking: 'What is the reason that Lieutenant-general Sir Thomas Picton has not been created a peer of parliament, as well as those distinguished officers whose names have appeared in the Gazette?'[9] The letter went on at some length stating why the writer, an anonymous military man, thought Sir

Thomas should have received a greater honour, but two sentences are particularly resonant: 'I shall say nothing as to the rank, fortune, or relative merits of those officers: they are all men of ancient families, good fortunes, and unquestionable characters. But, in the view which I take of the question, those points are quite immaterial.'[10] Such points were far from immaterial to those making the decisions, as Picton's biographer Robert Havard points out. 'That recognition was not based solely on merit may be inferred from the circumstances of the five soldiers honoured, each of whom was well connected'[11] – one the son of an earl, another, the son of a baronet. In the end some military equivocation about the nature of the command that Picton had held – apparently it was not considered to have been a 'distinct command' – was cooked up to explain the snub.

Even though there is little doubt that one of Wellington's favourite vices, snobbery, was at work here, it was not just the rough-edged Picton who felt that the honours dished out after the conclusion of the war in the Peninsula were distributed unfairly. Lord Fitzroy Somerset, scion of the great ducal houses, was seething as he wrote to his brother the Duke of Beaufort:

> I am excessively obliged to you for your congratulations on my app^t. to be K.C.B., but I confess, I am neither satisfied with the Order itself, nor with the manner in which it has been distributed – they have not only nominated every member of the Horse Guards, two of them to the first Class, but also several Officers, belonging to our army, who are without any merit whatever – Two of them indeed are a disgrace to their profession. The Com^r. in Chief has also intimated to us that we are to return to him the Medal and any other badges of distinction which we may received [*sic*], on receiving the Insignia of the Bath. This injunction I propose not to comply with, and I trust others will also refuse it – I conceive the object in desiring one to do so, is to place those who were always on Service, on a par with the gentlemen of the Horse Guards which I have no desire to be, and which I will do my utmost to prevent myself from being – I rather think the Idea originated in General Torrens, who was desirous of being distinguished & that it was caught at by Banbury who had the same Ambition, & who persuaded Lord Bathurst to give into it. I must own I hate the Horse Guards.'[12]

It was this same sense of injustice that afflicted Picton, though it was made worse because of his longing for public recognition. Even Picton's supporters admitted that he 'was greedy of honour',[13] so it was just spiteful to deny him what he, and many others, thought was his due reward. When he was asked why others had been made peers and not him, he answered: 'If the coronet were lying on the crown of a breach, I should have as good a chance as any of them.'[14] Disenchanted with the superficiality of London life and disgusted at the politicking that he felt had deprived him of a deserved honour, Picton retreated to his recently purchased estate at Iscoed, which he had bought for £30,000 and which, come the winter of 1814, he regretted as a venture that was already losing him money and which he determined to sell as soon as so 'great a fool as myself'[15] could be found.

At fifty-seven Picton was an old man and 9 January of the new year brought him further reminder of his mortality when his brother Major-General John Picton died. Living alone in Wales left him in low spirits, even the wines he had sent from London could not console him. 'I don't think wine drinks well by one's self what ever the quality of it may be.'[16]

Thus when the likelihood of war with Napoleon became a certainty, one of Wellington's most able commanders was feeling spurned, embittered and depressed, drinking alone on his miserable Welsh estate. However towards the end of May it became clear that he would indeed be going into service in Flanders and he made all the usual preparations for the imminent campaign. He wrote to his aide-de-camp, Tyler, on 26 May informing him that he would be in London the following week, that he was to alert some other officers, Captains Chambers and Price, and that he should 'look out for some active horses, not above fifteen hands'.[17]

Yet although he made his preparations with the meticulous attention of a seasoned campaigner, he was convinced that this would be a campaign he would not survive, and he told all his friends as much. 'The calmness of his manner when he alluded to the subject made them at first hope that this anticipation might be the result of impaired health,' but Picton believed it to be true and 'expressed this conviction in the most serious manner to the different branches of his family' and arranged 'his affairs with all the exactness and attention of a man who knows that he has but a short time to live'.[18] His thoughts had taken a morbid turn and even his humour was of the blackest sort. One fine evening shortly before his departure he was out walking with friends when they came to a churchyard. Spying a freshly dug grave, Picton urged his friends to come to its edge and look down, while he commented on how neatly the gravedigger had done his job. And then with the words 'Why, I think this would do for me',[19] he leapt in and lay down to try it for size, blithely informing his now disturbed friends that it was a perfect fit.

Nevertheless his grim premonition did not put Picton off doing his duty and by early June he was in London. There has been much speculation about why he set off for Flanders so much later than other generals. It is safe to assume that Picton, though able, lacked aristocratic polish and showed an independence of manner and thought – neither attributes which would have endeared him to Wellington. Perhaps Wellington found Picton tiresome and perhaps he was afflicted with pangs of guilt at the fact that the oldest general in the British Army had not been elevated to the peerage after his service in the Peninsula.

The widely accepted reason for the delay is that Picton wanted to ensure that he would be taking orders directly from the Duke and not from some other officer between the two men in the chain of command. His biographer Havard contends that this 'was not pique at lack of recognition, but the precaution of an old campaigner who was not going to be told what to do by a novice like the Prince of Orange'.[20] It is also possible to detect a desire for revenge in this behaviour. His country may have needed him, but Picton was not going to let Wellington escape from the exquisite embarrassment of being brought face to face, literally, with the necessity of a man like Picton.

Such thoughts may have consoled him as his carriage rolled towards London, and certainly his spirits seemed to rise the further he got from the money-pit that was his Welsh estate and nearer to active service. One of the reasons that his mood might have altered was his introduction to a young Welsh soldier who had seen some service in the Peninsula and was fretting that he might well miss out on the show in the Flanders. Rees Howell Gronow was at the opposite end of his life and military service to Picton; the former was a dainty, diminutive dandy, while Sir Thomas was a bluff 'stern-looking, strong-built man'[21] who dressed plainly in a blue frock coat buttoned to the throat, a black neckcloth that showed virtually no shirt collar, dark trousers, boots and a round hat. The contrast between the two men is interesting. Gronow had been at Eton, where he had known Shelley and received an Ensign's commission in the Guards at the end of 1812. A dandy and socialite, Gronow would eventually be known as a chronicler of nineteenth-century life, recording its fashion, eccentricities, manners and so on in his popular *Reminiscences*. But in the summer of 1815, he was a young man annoyed at being left in London while 'great events' were 'about to take place on the Continent'.[22]

By June he could think and talk about little else, and over dinner one night with his friend Captain Chambers, Tyler and their superior, Picton, conversation turned inevitably to Gronow's chagrin on missing out on the action across the Channel. 'Is the lad really anxious to go out?' asked Picton, plainly intrigued by the dapper youngster. When he was told that

Gronow would like nothing more, he ascertained that all positions on his staff were filled, but added with the black humour that characterised his mood: 'If Tyler is killed, which is not at all unlikely, I do not know why I should not take my young countryman: he may go over with me if he can get leave.'[23]

It was settled. An excited Gronow hastened away to make the appropriate arrangements. His first concern was not that Tyler or his friend Chambers might have to die to create a vacancy, but what he should wear in order to cut a dash in Brussels. Sadly his 'funds were at a low ebb' (later in life he would he would end up in debtors' prison) so he promptly borrowed £200 (about £10,000 in contemporary values) and invested it in a few games at 'a gambling-house in St James's Square', where he won £600 (£30,000). Thus fully funded, he purchased a couple of expensive horses at Tattersalls which he sent to Ostend along with his groom. And then on Saturday 10 June, without even bothering to get leave – 'I thought I should get back, after the great battle that appeared imminent, in time to mount guard at St James's' – he climbed into Chambers's carriage and set off to Ramsgate.[24]

There is some discrepancy in the dates, as Gronow claims that Picton was already in Ramsgate when he arrived, and they embarked for Ostend on Monday, while another source says that Picton left London on 11 June, a Sunday, stopped at the Fountain Tavern in Canterbury for a dinner which was given for him by some locals and which lifted his spirits and embarked the following day from Dover.

According to Gronow's account, which is the more picturesque, Monday night sees Picton in Ostend, which was still just as busy as ever with troops, horses and materiel being landed day and night. (In fact units continued to arrive right up until the time of battle with some troops coming from America, travelling to Brussels and not stopping but marching straight on to battle.) Picton's spirits seemed good enough: he was practising his French by starting a 'flirtation with our pretty waiting-maid'.[25] Another circumstance which must have raised the general's spirits further and played to his vanity was that on the morning of his arrival (13 June according to this source) he 'held a levee to receive the numerous officers who were desirous of paying their respects to their old general'.[26] From there he hurried on to Brussels.

Timings vary slightly, but both accounts see Picton and his suite of officers in Brussels by Thursday, and they were eating at the Hôtel d'Angleterre on the rue de la Madeleine, where Gronow had pulled off the coup of securing rooms, when Picton was informed that Wellington wanted to see him at once. According to Picton's *Memoirs* as assembled by Robinson, 'The Duke of Wellington greeted his old companion in arms with a friendly warmth.'[27]

Gronow however paints a different picture. The Duke was in the park taking a walk in aristocratic company, with his A.D.C. Fitzroy Somerset and the Duke of Richmond. Picton was no doubt in good spirits and probably offered a casual greeting to the Duke and his smart friends. 'Picton's manner was always more familiar than the duke liked in his lieutenants,' observed Gronow:

and on this occasion he approached him in a careless sort of way, just as he might have met an equal. The duke bowed coldly to him, and said, 'I am glad you are come, Sir Thomas; the sooner you get on horseback the better: no time is to be lost. You will take command of the troops in advance. The Prince of Orange knows by this time that you will go to his assistance.' Picton appeared not to like the duke's manner; for when he bowed and left, he muttered a few words, which convinced those who were with him that he was not much pleased with his interview.[28]

Picton was doubtless piqued at what it appears he saw as a snub. He had come out of retirement in Wales, rushed to Brussels so quickly that he was still wearing his civilian clothes because his uniform had not yet caught up with him, and here was Wellington, haughty and aloof, treating him with less warmth than he reserved for junior officers barely out of their teens. The exchange reflects well on neither man, and belies the fiction of cordial relations between Wellington and his Welsh general.

However such differences were soon to be buried. At about half past three on the morning of 15 June the first French troops had crossed the border and started to probe the Allied defences. The brittle glittering carapace of civilised life in Brussels was about to be shattered.

19

'Duchess, you may give your ball with the greatest safety, without fear of interruption'

The giving and attending of balls in Brussels during April, May and June of 1815 was almost mandatory among the smart British set. Even with war imminent Wellington continued to give parties, including a 'grand rout' on 8 June, four invitations for which were allocated to each regiment and distributed by drawing lots. Dancing was reportedly 'kept up to a late hour' and the event was so well attended that 'not one half of the guests could find places at the supper-tables'.[1]

As the domineering Duchess of Richmond, who was led into supper at the Duke's rout by the Prince of Orange, needed to be as near the social fulcrum as possible, it was necessary for her to hold a ball. The expense must have grated on her husband, who had moved to Brussels primarily to save money after his stint as Lord Lieutenant of Ireland. However, if the Duchess was not someone to let pecuniary concerns stand in the way of social advancement, neither was she so stupid as to be blind to the rapid build-up of troops and materiel. She was concerned about giving a large and frivolous party so close to a major military engagement: perhaps she was worried about what her peers might make of her throwing a party on the eve of a battle, or maybe she was concerned that the war might start before she had a chance to give her grand ball.

Whatever the reason, there was one man who could tell her whether it would be timely and appropriate to issue invitations to a ball on the evening of 15 June.

'Duke,' she said to Wellington, 'I do not wish to pry into your secrets, nor do I ask what your intentions may be, I wish to give a ball, and all I ask, is may I give my ball? If you say, "Duchess, don't give your ball," it is quite sufficient,' she said, adding magnanimously 'I ask no reasons.'[2]

Perhaps she thought she was being discreet.

Quite what Wellington thought of the Duchess's question, or of her tact and generosity in not pressing him to reveal his overall strategy and timing, is unknown. However, given the casual, fun-loving façade that he presented to the world, and also the fact that were he to cause the Duchess to cancel her ball the news would certainly have been picked up by Napoleon's spies, there was only one answer he could give. 'Duchess, you may give your ball with the greatest safety, without fear of interruption.'[3] Besides, given that his own ball was still on the calendar for 21 June (the most current rumour for the invasion of France was now 25 June, giving guests time to recover from their night out at Wellington's party) it would have been churlish to deny the Duchess her dance.

Nevertheless the Duchess had some lingering doubts, and perhaps even a trace of guilt. An embassy secretary who wrote to Sir Charles Stuart on 13 June told him: 'The Duchess of Richmond has stated that the Padrone [Wellington] wished to give his Ball on the anniversary of the Battle of Vittoria.'[4] It could be that the Duchess was just showing off that she was in the know regarding Wellington's plans, or it could be that in an effort to make her own ball seem less irresponsible she was citing Wellington's proposed ball for a few days after hers as mitigation.

She was still uncomfortable about the event, as she confided to a family friend, Captain Verner, when giving him invitations to distribute to various cavalry officers he would meet while drilling on the plains of Grammont. He was happy to help, but on giving him the invitations the Duchess felt it necessary to make some sort of apology for her actions, or at least let Verner know that they were officially sanctioned at the highest level. 'It might appear extraordinary me giving a ball at such a time, when all the papers as well as private communications announced that the French Army had marched to the frontier, and when it was not known the moment our Army might be ordered out to meet them.'[5] The Duchess then went on to recount her meeting with Wellington and his assurance that she could give her ball.

It is another interesting example of how closely entwined the upper echelons of expatriate society were with British officialdom, in that the smallest details of the Duchess's social arrangements were the subject of diplomatic correspondence. 'All the cards of invitation for the Duchess of

Richmond's ball are written and arrangements made for their distribution,' continues the embassy secretary in his letter of 13 June.

the Mayor's man is to be charged with the Bruxellois, our running footman with the 'civil' English and with the Corps Diplomatique, and a Sergeant (who carried the Duke's) is to undertake the delivery of the military cards. Prince Frederick and the Hereditary Prince will come if possible, *sans nuire au bien du service*. The Duke of Brunswick and his Owls will be there to take care of Lady John Campbell, the Duchess of Beaufort, the d'Arenbergs, the d'Ursels, d'Oultremonts, Pozzo, of course, and all the rest of *la haute société*, not to mention captains, lieutenants, and Ensigns![6]

And as well as allowing his running footman to act as postman for the Duchess, the British ambassador lent her his plate and put his servants at her disposal for the ball.[7] Just as when the Capels arrived in Brussels and had the Army baggage train to help with their luggage, and then called on them again to help move house, so it seems that even with war looming, part of the duty of the British Army and civil service was to assist the English aristocracy with their domestic arrangements.

While he may have given the Duchess the go-ahead, in private Wellington was less sanguine. For instance when Lady Georgiana Lennox approached him on behalf of a group of young officers who wanted to 'organise a party of pleasure in the neighbourhood, either to Tournay or Lille', the Duke's reply was instant: 'No; better let that drop.'[8]

Wellington continued his outward display of confidence and on the whole it seems to have been very convincing. As late as 13 June, Spencer Madan, who as tutor to the Duke of Richmond's children would have seen and heard much concerning Wellington's behaviour, was able to write to his father:

Tho' I have given some pretty good reasons for supposing that hostilities will soon commence, yet no one wd. suppose it judging by the Duke of Wn. He appears to be thinking of anything else in the world, gives a ball every week, attends every party and partakes of every amusement that offers.

The trouble was that there were so many balls and so many rumours about when hostilities would commence that the effect was of the boy who cried wolf: the threat of war had been imminent for so long that it had lost its power to alarm. As Surgeon John Haddy James recalls, 'no apprehensions appeared to be entertained of an immediate attack, and although it was known that Bonaparte was with the French Army, no difficulty was experienced in officers obtaining leave of absence.'⁹ As it happens James had obtained leave to go and do some sightseeing in Brussels but he had put his visit off until after 15 June because that day Lord Edward Somerset was to review his brigade and then he was to dine with the Second Life Guards: Brussels could wait. It seemed that nothing bellicose would get in the way of plans for a day trip.

So even though the French had already started their invasion on the morning of 15 June, the day began much as any other had that summer. While the smart social set of both officers and civilians was preparing for the Duchess's ball, the two brigades of Guards quartered at Enghien were looking forward to a cricket match.

When remembering the events of that day much later in the century the Duke of Richmond's daughter, Lady Georgiana, who was nineteen at the time, recalled:

> There were such constant rumours of the troops moving for two months before Waterloo, that when they were renewed some days before the 15th we did not attach much importance to them; and on the afternoon of the 15th Lord Hill called upon us, when we were all sitting in the garden, and disclaimed any knowledge of a move.¹⁰

But while the young daughters of the Richmonds were chatting with Lord Hill, the town of Charleroi had been in French hands since noon.

The first impressions of Charlotte Eaton, who arrived in Brussels that day, were of a carefree resort town. The park, she said, was:

> crowded with officers in every variety of military uniform, with elegant women, and with lively parties and gay groups of British and Belgic people, loitering, walking, talking, and sitting under the trees! There could not be a more animated, a more holiday scene; everything looked gay and festive, and everything spoke of hope, confidence, and busy expectation.¹¹

And why should there not have been that air of busy expectation? After all, the Duchess of Richmond's ball was beginning in a couple of hours.

Although one account says that the ball was 'of course attended by "Everybody" at Bruxelles',¹² – 'Everybody' meaning the usual tight circle of high society expats, well-connected officers and a few important locals – this was not entirely true. As the number of those issued with invitations was 228,* and of those not all attended, many prominent members of the

---

* On p.69 of his detailed analysis of the evening, *The Duchess of Richmond's Ball*, David Miller writes: 'it appears that 228 people were invited, plus ten members of the Richmond household, making a total of 238.'

community spent their evening in another way. For instance, Creevey was not invited. Although his stepdaughters made it to the ball, Creevey stayed at home.

The Duchess of Richmond's ball was the main social event that Thursday, and there were plenty of dinners arranged for guests who would want to get together and eat before going on. One such dinner was given by General d'Alava, the Spanish ambassador and representative at the Allied HQ. Alava was a trusted confidant of Wellington and knew how to enjoy himself. It seems that many of Wellington's staff were on a three-line-whip to attend this evening, as it was the first time that Sir William De Lancey had been persuaded to leave the cosy apartment he shared with his wife and where they held intimate little dinner parties; the following evening the companionable Sir Augustus Frazer was to join the De Lanceys for dinner.

Lady De Lancey's *Journal* records most poignantly the scene played out between this tender young woman and her husband, who could plainly not bear to be apart from his wife of a few weeks:

> Sir William had to dine at the Spanish Ambassador's, the first invitation he had accepted, he was unwilling to go, and delayed and still delayed, till at last when near 6 o'clock, I fastened all his medals and crosses on his coat, helped him put it on, and he went off. I watched at the window till he was out of sight, and then I continued to muse upon my happy fate. I thought over all that had passed, and how grateful I felt, I had no wish but that this might continue; I saw my husband loved and respected by every one. My life gliding on, like a gay dream.[13]

As she gazed from her upper-storey window overlooking the park on that summer evening, she was perhaps the most contented woman in Brussels. She did not really mind that her husband went off to an important dinner, as he looked so handsome wearing his medals. Besides, their quiet life would resume the following day and she had already sent out invitation cards to a small private dinner of the type they enjoyed, to be held the following evening. De Lancey knew differently; his vacillation and unwillingness to leave can probably be put down to the alarming news that had been trickling in to headquarters as he left to go home to change for dinner. What neither his wife nor he could possibly know was that within a week he would be dead.

It was about this time that rumours started circulating around Brussels. Kincaid was walking in the park at around seven o'clock when he met one of the Duke's staff; 'he asked me, *en passant*, whether my pack-saddles were all ready? I told him that they were nearly so, and added, "I suppose they won't be wanted, at all events, before tomorrow?" To which he replied, in the act of leaving me, "If you have any preparation to make, I would recommend you not to delay so long.""[14] Kincaid took the hint and returned to his quarters to prepare to move.

Two inexorable forces were now in motion: the French invasion and the Duchess's ball. It was too late to stop either one: as Kincaid and others were preparing to leave Brussels, others were still on their way into town.

Not all the guests at the ball were quartered in Brussels; there were those coming in from out of town, who would want to change and dine before the ball. For instance, having distributed invitations for the Duchess, Verner took a cabriolet into town with his friend Captain O'Grady: 'we went in our usual uniform, taking with us evening dress for the Ball. We put up at an Hôtel de Swède in the lower town, which was at no great distance from the Duke of Richmond's residence, and having dined and dressed, we proceeded to the ball.'[15]

There have been a number of essays and studies written about the ball. These range from the first-hand account of Lady Georgiana de Ros, née Lennox, who was there, to the almost forensic study of David Miller, who goes as far as preparing several tables of statistics analysing everything from the spread of guests among different units (it seems that the Duchess shared Wellington's unfavourable opinion of those under the command of the Master-General of the Ordnance – only two officers out of a total of 128 in these corps were invited) to the number and percentage of guests subsequently wounded or killed.

Yet for all the interest in anything to do with Waterloo, it is remarkable that for many years it was believed that the Duchess of Richmond's ball had been held in some imposing building: either the Hôtel de Ville or the Maison du Roi. Given the significance assumed by the ball in retrospect, it was presumably thought that such an important event was held in a building commensurate with its subsequent stature, a fallacy promulgated by such heavily embroidered accounts of the ball appearing in Byron's *Childe Harold* and Thackeray's *Vanity Fair*. Rather refreshingly, Lady Georgiana de Ros described the lines in the third Canto of *Childe Harold* that referred to 'that high hall' as 'all nonsense'.[16]

The Hôtel de Ville was very quickly accepted as the venue. When he visited Brussels in 1816, only a year after the ball, Byron 'was shown over an apartment in the Hôtel de Ville which answers precisely to his description. It is a high hall of great architectural dignity.'[17] Quite how this came about is unsure. Nevertheless, this view persisted until the late nineteenth century, when Sir William Fraser, Bart, descendant of an officer who had fought at Waterloo, discovered that the house occupied by the Duke and Duchess of Richmond, which their daughter thought had been demolished, was in fact a hospital run by a religious order, a use which persisted until long into the following century: in 1975 *Country Life* described the house as being 'encased by a modern clinic'.[18]

More importantly still, Sir William discovered what he thought was the original location of the ball, a 'long barn-like room'[19] nearby, but separated from the house occupied by the Richmond household by subsequent development of the area. His discovery initiated a lively correspondence in *The Times* and other newspapers; it remained the accepted version for some time, encouraging souvenir hunters to visit and prise out nails from the beams or carry off splinters of wood.

However in 1936 C.C.R. Murphy established to his satisfaction as well as that of 'historians, antiquarians, and all those investigators who have made a serious study of the case'[20] that the ball was held in 'a large room on the ground floor on the left of the entrance to the Duke of Richmond's villa; . . . and that it had been used as a coach-builder's depot'.[21]

The Duchess's daughter, Lady Georgiana de Ros, said that her 'mother's now famous ball took place in a large room on the ground floor on the left of the entrance, connected with the rest of the house by an ante-room. It had been used by the coach-builder, from whom the house was hired, to put carriages in.'[22] According to the Duchess's son, Lord William Pitt Lennox, the venue was not the house itself, but 'some sort of old barn at the back or behind'.[23] But then Lord William told someone else that the ball took place in 'a room *adjacent* to his father's house'.[24] On the whole it seems safe to assume that the ball took place in one of the annexes shown in the 1778 engraving and subsequently demolished in 1827 to make way for houses on the newly built rue des Cendres.

The truth is that it was just yet another party on the giddy social merry-go-round of Brussels, an important party, but one of many. Had Napoleon chosen to invade a day earlier, a party given by Lady Conyngham and attended by the Duke, which according to Creevey had been buzzing with rumours of the French invasion, might have easily taken on the romantic and quasi-mythical status that history has accorded the Duchess of Richmond's ball.

Rather less romantic was the pejorative sobriquet of the 'Wash House' given to the Richmonds' Brussels residence by the Duke of Wellington, a pun on the address of rue de la Blanchisserie. He thought it tremendously funny; the socially ambitious Duchess must have seethed inwardly.

What also riled the Duchess was that the Duke's guarantee, that the Corsican ruffian would not upset her carefully planned ball, looked likely to prove worthless. By the late afternoon, as people started to sit down to dinner (supper would be served later in the evening at the ball), it started to become clear that a major attack had been launched, although details were still sketchy. 'The Duke dined at home on the day of the Duchess of Richmond's ball,' James Thornton, Wellington's cook, later recalled; 'the first course was not over when the Prince of Orange came and desired to see the Duke immediately. They were closeted together for some time, when Sir Colin gave us orders to be prepared to start at a moment's notice, the second course on that day was not served up.'[25]

Perhaps not quite believing the impending clash of arms, officers were remarkably phlegmatic. Charlotte Eaton recalled looking out of her rooms at the Hôtel de Flandres (secured, as befits a well-connected civilian, by a military man, Sir Neil Campbell) and seeing a travelling companion, a Major Wylie. Wylie darted into the hotel and bounded up the stairs to bring her the news that he had just left the Duke of Wellington's table; pudding had just been brought out when a courier arrived to bring the news that Blücher had been attacked by Napoleon that afternoon.*

> 'However, after all, this may end in nothing,' said Major Wylie, after a pause; 'we *may* have to march to-morrow morning, or we may not march these three weeks: but the Duke expects another dispatch from Blücher, and that will settle the business': and so saying, Major Wylie went away to dress for a ball. Yes, a Ball! [so writes Eaton in astonishment] for the Duke of Wellington, and his aides-de-camp, and half of the British officers, though they expected to go to a battle to-morrow, were going to a ball tonight, at the Duchess of Richmond's.[26]

The prospect of an impending battle was not going to stop the many officers, at least those judged sufficiently socially acceptable to be invited by the Duchess, from attending the Richmonds' ball. Although some of them thought they would spend the time more profitably preparing themselves for war and getting some rest, they were in a minority. Kincaid recalls that 'as a grand ball was to take place the same night at the Duchess of Richmond's, the order for the assembling of the troops was accompanied

---

*This account of dinner at the Duke of Wellington's table is at variance with the account given above by James Thornton, who says that a second course was not served. Perhaps the 'Duke's table' is a euphemism indicating another dinner, alternatively one or the other is mistaken. Nevertheless the interruption of dinner by someone bringing news of the attack was a common experience among officers that night in Brussels.

by a permission for any officer who chose, to remain for the ball, provided that he joined his regiment early in the morning. Several of ours took advantage of it.'[27]

After dinner people started making their way out to the ball, and the crush of horses and carriages quite congested the Brussels suburb where the Wash House, the Duchess and the borrowed footmen waited. Supper, served on the loaned plate, was to be had above the dance floor, presumably in galleries which had once overlooked the toiling coachbuilders. Just as the British Embassy had helped out with servants and the dinner service, so too was the entertainment being lent for the evening, this time by the Army.

'She gave a bal to the Higher Rank of officers and wished for [a] Few soldiers from each Scottish Regt. to Dance the Highland Fling &c &c,' recalled Private James Gunn, going on to describe the citizens of Brussels as 'verry kind and willing to please the Duches'.[28] Given the excitement with which locals had greeted the arrival of the kilted regiments and considering how popular they had made themselves with the families upon which they were billeted, some form of Scottish entertainment would have seemed very appropriate.

Thus it was that 'a party of n.c. officers were also invited to show Her Grace's British and foreign friends a specimen of Highland dancing'.[29] For the Duchess there was a family link; her father was the Duke of Gordon, and the regiment from which the dancing sergeants were drawn was known as the Gordon Highlanders. Moreover, in spite of the momentous events unfolding half a day's march out of Brussels, the dancers made an impression on those present. 'The proud march of this little party into the hall, preceded by their pipers, formed a fitting prelude to the deeds that were about to distinguish their garb in the red field of battle'[30] was the stirring, melodramatic way in which one account describes their arrival in the ballroom. And almost three-quarters of a century later, Lady Louisa Tighe (née Lennox) recalled them with sadness:

> I well remember the Gordon Highlanders dancing reels at the ball; my mother thought it would interest the foreigners to see them, which it did. I remember hearing that some of the poor men who danced in our house were killed at Waterloo. There was quite a crowd to look at the Scotch dancers.[31]

Outside the ballroom events had developed at speed. The first inkling that Lady De Lancey had that not everything was as it should be came at around 7 p.m. by her reckoning, when her daydreaming at the window was interrupted by an A.D.C. who rode through the gateway into the courtyard of their house.

> He sent to enquire where Sir William was dining. I wrote down the name; and soon after I saw him gallop off in that direction. I did not like this appearance, but I tried not to be afraid. A few minutes after, I saw Sir William on the same horse gallop past to the Duke's, which was a few doors beyond ours. He dismounted and ran into the house – left the horse in the middle of the street. I must confess my courage failed me now, and the succeeding two hours formed a contrast to the happy forenoon.[32]

Her husband returned at around 9 p.m. and attempted to reassure her, while simultaneously telling her to prepare to leave for Antwerp at six o'clock the next morning. De Lancey then left for his office to write orders mobilising the Army, and any officers he could find were ordered to help in the writing of routes for deployment. For instance Lieutenant Basil Jackson was enjoying an early evening stroll in the park when a soldier came up and summoned him to the Q.M.G.'s office, where he spent two or three hours writing out orders, 'which were expedited by means of hussars, men selected for their steadiness'[33] who were given a time at which they should reach their destination and instructed to return with the 'cover of the despatch, on which the officer receiving it had to state the exact time of its delivery'.[34] Having completed this task Jackson was then instructed to ride to Ninove to deliver a letter.

De Lancey's office had set about its work briskly. Word of mobilisation spread quickly, reaching many officers while they were eating dinner or enjoying a postprandial drink. 'That day I dined with Sir James Kempt,' * recalled Harry Ross-Lewin:

> Coffee and a young aide-de-camp from the Duke of Wellington came in together. This officer was the bearer of a note from the Duke, and while Sir James was reading it, said: 'Old Blücher has been hard at it; a Prussian officer has just come to the Beau, all covered with sweat and dirt, and says they have had much fighting.' Our host then rose, and, addressing the regimental officers at the table, said: 'Gentlemen, you will proceed without delay to your respective regiments, and let them get under arms imme-diately.'[35]

Yet even now, with the French within hours of the city, there were those

---

* Major-General Sir James Kempt, commander of the 8th British Brigade and part of the division under the command of the recently arrived Picton.

who found it hard to believe that their dream-like existence in Brussels was to be threatened. On the way back to rejoin his regiment, Ross-Lewin encountered some officers at the door of a coffee house and passed on Kempt's order. They were incredulous.

> They seemed at first to think that I was jesting, being hardly able to credit the tidings of so near and so unexpected an approach of the French. In a few minutes, however, the most incredulous would have been thoroughly undeceived, for then drums began to beat, bugles to sound, and Highland pipes to squeal in all quarters of the city.[36]

'I have this moment returned from dining with Hawker to celebrate his promotion to a lieutenant-colonelcy. He lives in a very large and comfortable house at the village of Lenniche St. Quentin,' wrote Frazer at ten o'clock on the evening of 15 June.

> We were a jolly party of a dozen, the cheer was excellent, but the roads detestable. On returning I find Ross here, he has dined at General Kempt's, and has learned in the course of the evening that the enemy has moved upon Mons, and that in consequence we are to move during the night. Sir George Wood has just been here to say the same thing. He was one of the party at Hawker's, and has gone to headquarters to learn the news.

Frazer was equanimous in the face of the alert. A seasoned soldier, he felt there was 'nothing new in looking the enemy in the face' and waited for news from HQ, although he doubted they would move. He turned his mind to the invitation to dine with the De Lanceys the following day – 'this will be a pleasanter way of passing the day than marching to Mons.' But as he was writing the letter more news kept coming in and by half past eleven he was sure he would not be dining with the De Lanceys the following evening. 'The Duke has gone to a ball at the Duchess of Richmond's, but all is ready to move at daybreak.'[37]

At the same time as Frazer was writing to his wife, Thomas Creevey, who was waiting up for his stepdaughters to return from the Duchess of Richmond's ball, suddenly 'heard a great knocking at houses in my street – la Rue du Musée – just out of the Place Royale, and I presently found out the troops were in motion, and by 12 o'clock they all marched off the Place Royale up the Rue Namur'.[38]

De Lancey returned to his quarters overlooking the park at midnight but, fuelled by strong green tea made by his wife, did not sleep and visited the Duke of Wellington twice. On the first occasion he found him poring over a map with Baron von Müffling, the Prussian in full dress uniform, 'the Duke ... in his chemise and slippers, preparing to dress for the Duchess of Richmond's ball'.[39]

The Duke was the social star of Brussels and it is interesting that, despite the certainty of a major engagement being just hours off, he chose to put in an appearance at the Richmonds' ball. He felt that his appearance at the ball would in some way calm public anxiety. 'Let us show ourselves at the Duchess's Ball,' he said to Müffling, 'it will reassure people.'[40] It was to be the last time he would assume his Brussels mask of elaborate insouciance, although this time his performance as the man who cared more for flirting than fighting, and was more concerned with balls than with battles, was brief and not entirely convincing.

The Duchess must have been grateful, and Wellington did his gallant best to assume the carefree mask that had characterised his mien since arriving in Brussels. However by now, with the reveille being sounded and the tramp of marching soldiers echoing through the streets, even the least well-informed of the Duchess of Richmond's guests could hardly miss the fact that the Army was on the move. Moreover it was plain that while Wellington might have been physically present, his mind was racing with thoughts and concerns about the coming fray.

Upon his arrival Lady Georgiana left the dancing and went to him directly to question him about the rumours she had heard. There was no hint of his usual unconcerned cheerfulness in the Duke's reply. 'He said very gravely, "Yes, they are true; we are off to-morrow."'[41] However it seems that the Duke stayed to eat something: Lady Georgiana recalls sitting next to him and being given a miniature that the Duke had had painted of himself by a Belgian artist – a token of his affection for her. It was probably after supper that she left the dance to help her brother, who occupied a small house in the grounds, pack his things. Lady Dalrymple Hamilton, who sat next to Wellington on a sofa, said he seemed preoccupied – unsurprisingly given the circumstances – and their small talk was frequently interrupted by terse asides with the headstrong Prince of Orange and the Duke of Brunswick, commander of the death's-head-wearing soldiers who had so amused the Capels.

According to Lady Georgiana the 'terrible news was circulated directly, and while some of the officers hurried away' it seems that others, perhaps unable to take in the news, simply could not tear themselves away from the dancing; however 'others remained at the ball, and actually had not time to change their clothes, but fought in evening costume'.[42]

As ever with accounts of this period, timings are inconsistent. For instance Lady De Lancey places her husband in Wellington's dressing room at around midnight, while Digby Mackworth's journal says that it was 'about 11 o'clock'; just as the 'dancing was yet going with great spirit, we learned from the Duke that the Prussians had suffered severely that same evening'.[43] Given the hazy notion of timing – watches of the era were inaccurate and exertions such as dancing 'with great spirit' would only have compounded their capacity for error – it is probably safer to assume it was some time later in the evening, perhaps shortly after midnight.

It was around this time that Captains Verner and O'Grady arrived after their dinner in the lower town at the Hôtel de Swède.

> Just as we entered the State room, and before we had time to go into the Ball room [incidentally, Verner's recollection supports the theory of the ball having been held in the coachworks annexe], we were met by Lord George Lennox, who, knowing me intimately from having been brother Aide de Camp with his father said, 'Verner, the Prussians have [been] attacked and defeated, and I am going to order the Duke's horses, who is going off immediately.'

Verner then turned to O'Grady and said, 'Let us go into the room, to have it to say we were in the ball-room.'[44]

If indeed this conversation is recalled accurately it marks the beginning of the mythology surrounding the Duchess of Richmond's ball.

By the time that they arrived, the ball was breaking up and men were already hurrying to rejoin their regiments, but it was not quite over, and these two men grasped that they were present at an event of historical significance. Pressing their way against the tide of departing guests they made their way into the room in time to hear Lord Uxbridge announce: 'You gentlemen who have engaged partners, had better finish your dance, and get to your quarters as soon as you can.'[45] Having seen the room, this was their cue to leave. 'Standish, this is no time for dancing, let us try and secure a cabriolet without loss of time, and be off as soon as we can.'[46]

Lady Georgiana remembered it as 'a dreadful evening, taking leave of friends and acquaintances, many never to be seen again'.[47] She said goodbye to the Duke of Brunswick in the ante-room where Verner had met Lord George, where he assured the young lady that the Brunswickers would 'distinguish themselves after "the honour" done them'[48] when she accompanied the Duke of Wellington to their review. Rather less solemn was the high-spirited, dashing James, Lord Hay, the cynosure of his comrades, who had baited the bourgeoisie of Brussels with his illicit rides in the park. Lady Georgiana became quite 'provoked' with him 'for his delight at the idea of going into action, and of all the honours he was to gain'.[49]

According to Mackworth, the Duchess's reaction to this sudden departure *en masse* was less appropriate than her daughter's. By his account she was almost hysterical: 'in vain did the *afflicted* Duchess of Richmond, placing herself at the entrance of the ball room, pray and entreat that we would not "go before supper";* that we would wait "one little hour more" and "not spoil her ball".'[50] Mackworth's occasionally florid hyperbolic style notwithstanding – 'ungentle hard-hearted cavaliers, we resisted all and departed'[51] – the Duchess's actions, while in keeping with her fearsome reputation as a social tartar, seem extraordinary. The suggestion that she would go as far as to bar the exit and implore her guests to stay speaks eloquently of her egotistical approach to life: perhaps she genuinely believed that Napoleon would have the good manners to wait for her party to finish before commencing his attack.

As the ballroom emptied the officers shouldered their way as gallantly as possible past the anguished figure of the Duchess, who saw her carefully planned social edifice collapsing in front of her. Wellington, who had received further news of the seriousness of the situation during the evening, asked his old friend the Duke of Richmond whether he had a map of the area, and they retired to his study on the ground floor, where Wellington made his famous remark that Napoleon had 'humbugged' him and then underlined Waterloo with his thumbnail, announcing that he would stop the French there. The Duke of Richmond subsequently marked the map in pencil, but that map went missing in later years.† Humbugged or not, Wellington made sure he got some rest before setting off and by the time De Lancey visited him at two o'clock, he was sound asleep.

Wellington was one of the few men to get a couple of hours' rest in his own bed that night, as all over the country the news spread, often carried by those riding from the ball. Riding back from Ninove, Jackson 'fell in with several officers of rank, making for their troops, having hurried from the Duchess of Richmond's ball; and I, knowing all the arrangements for the army generally, was able to tell them what roads to take in order to intercept their divisions'.[52]

It is interesting to speculate how many of those officers rushing through the dark Belgian countryside to rejoin units that were already on the move regretted their attendance at the Duchess of Richmond's Ball. William

* Some of the guests at least had already eaten supper.
† There is some suggestion that the account of one Duke's thumbnail marking another Duke's map is apocryphal, but it has been accepted by many as integral to the Waterloo story and the provenance of the story is recorded in Lady Longford's *The Years of the Sword*, p.421.

Hay had received an invitation, but turned it down, a decision with which he had cause to be pleased. 'I did not care to move far from home on rest days, and refused a very pressing invitation to attend the ball given by his Grace the Duke of Richmond.'[53] He recalls his servant coming into his room to put out his uniform at 3 a.m., when upon being informed that his Colonel had just that minute returned from Brussels, 'I jumped out of bed and over to Colonel Ponsonby's quarters. His first exclamation was, "You were lucky not to go the ball, I am quite knocked up, the French are coming on in great numbers, and yesterday attacked and drove the Prussians back!"' He then instructed Hay to give orders for three days' rations to be drawn and for the regiment to prepare to march, and added that he would like a little time to recover from his exertions in the ballroom. 'I should like to be left quiet, as long as possible, to get some rest.'[54]

In the nearly empty ballroom a few 'energetic and heartless young ladies'[55] went on dancing while so many of their beaux were riding through the night to rejoin their regiments; men prepared to fight and die facing the fabled Napoleon, in defence of the recently invented and unhappily conjoined Kingdom of the United Netherlands, with the aim of restoring the decadent Bourbon dynasty to a throne from which their subjects had twice forced them.

20

'We marched from Brussels on the 16th of June, at the sun-rising, in high spirits, our band playing'[1]

'I can give you no account of the enemy or what they are about. I expected ere this we should at least have had a peep at them.'[2] So wrote Private Wheeler in a letter of 13 June. Napoleon's advance two days later was just as unexpected in the ranks as it was in the salons and drawing rooms.

The boy groom Edward Heeley had been in Brussels as part of the suite of Sir George Scovell since 4 June and had been billeted at an Army butcher's where 'the slaughtering was going on day and night without any interruption'.[3] It was a far cry from the gentility of the De Lanceys' apartments looking over the park and the Richmonds' house with its pleasant grounds and ballroom, its borrowed footmen, shimmering silver and Highland dancers; the place was constantly full of soldiers who would collect the butchered carcasses long before they were cold and 'take their meat to the Cathedral steps to divide it, it being very near, and very convenient for the job'.[4] Yet despite the incessant activity of the slaughter-house, young Heeley was happy enough, exercising the horses in the morning and relieving the tedium of keeping watch, so that the horses in his care were not lamed by the cattle awaiting slaughter, by swigging a drink of milk mixed with a ration of spirits.

Heeley recalls the town as 'very gay and bustling, all day long soldiers were parading, music playing'.[5] He too makes note of the balls 'every night' and the existence of 'plenty of amusement for those who wanted it'.[6]

It appeared more like troops assembling to be reviewed than to fight, for no one seemed to think of fighting, though towards the 13th or 14th it was

148

said they were going to prepare for hostilities on the 25th and soldiers were to be seen in various parts with their swords taking them to be ground, and linen drapers shops were full of them, purchasing cloth to make themselves bandages, but in a general way things were going on as if nothing was the matter.

Heeley's verdict was simple: 'In short, everybody in Brussels seemed happy. But a damper was put on the gaiety on the afternoon of the 15th. Thousands of people assembled on the ramparts nearest to Waterloo, listening to a rumbling noise in the air. Some said it was distant thunder, others said it was cannonading.' However, after some concern, 'towards evening the noise died away and seemed to be quite forgotten'. Heeley's editor thinks it unlikely that the sound of the fighting at Charleroi would have carried to Brussels; but if Heeley's recollection is accurate the speed with which it was forgotten and the general air of gaiety resumed is entirely characteristic of the deluded sense of frivolity that enveloped Brussels. Thereafter Heeley does not notice anything particularly out of the ordinary until towards midnight, when a 'little silent sort of confusion began, every one enquiring what was the matter, and beginning to recollect the noise they had heard in the afternoon'.[7]

Private Dixon Vallance of the 79th Regiment of Foot was billeted along with three others on the landlord of a public house, when on the evening of 15 June, they received orders to hold themselves:

> in readiness to march from Brussels on the shortest of notice, as the French army was reported to be advancing on the road to Brussels. On receiving this order, we lost no time in getting everything packed up and ready. Having two shirts with the woman who used to wash for me, I hurried away to get them from her; but, unfortunately she had them steeping in water, and I had just to get them wrung, and packed them up as they were. When we had got all our things ready, we lay down on our beds with our clothes and accoutrements on – not to sleep, however, but impatiently waiting for the sound of the bugles to rouse us to arms.[8]

They did not have long to wait. The little silent confusion mentioned by Heeley soon became large and loud.

> Drums, trumpets, bugles, all kicking up the finest discord that ever was heard. The inhabitants all rose from their beds and the soldiers were collecting in the streets, such shouting, swearing, crying, arms rattling, dragoons and officers galloping about, in short I should think the confusion at Babel was a fool to it.[9]

Similar scenes were replicated wherever large bodies of Allied troops were garrisoned. Capel and two of his daughters had gone to the Richmonds' ball, but the heavily pregnant Lady Caroline had stayed in her new country house, the Chateau de Walcheuse – after all, she was planning her '*Pick Nick* Dinner Party in the Grounds'[10] for the Friday after the Duchess's ball on the Thursday. Her social schedule was rudely disrupted at three o'clock in the morning by a loud drumroll and some hearty hymn-singing. The Brunswickers were marching to war. Her '*Pick Nick*' would have to be postponed.

All across the Belgic provinces the din must have been unbearable: horses, gun carriages and heavy wagons clattering through the streets; the tramp of marching soldiers, the bellowing of orders; and the noise of drums and trumpets.

Back in Brussels at the pub where Dixon Vallance and his comrades were billeted, the noise brought the landlord running to their room.

> Our host kindly treated each of us to a flowing bumper of gin and a loaf of bread, and, as is the custom of the place when friends part, he kissed and shook hands with each of us. Having got our host's blessing and good wishes we returned him our best wishes for his kindness and civility and hurried on to the place of muster in the large square of Brussels, at the Place Royal. When our regiment was mustered, we got provisions given out to us, and our allowance of gin.[11]

There are accounts that even though there were orders to draw three days' rations, much of these were left behind. Their packs were heavy already, and many men, often new recruits, were disinclined to add to their burden. Seduced by the soft life in Brussels, perhaps they doubted that they would really need very much in the way of rations in this land of plenty. Only old soldiers knew otherwise.

'The worst part of the business was to see the officers' and soldiers' wives hanging about them, almost broken hearted and wanting to go with them,' recalled Heeley, 'but that could not be allowed.'[12] Many noted the signs of distress as families and lovers were parted. Charlotte Eaton, who had only arrived in Brussels the day before and had hardly had any sleep at all, was particularly touched by 'one poor fellow' who:

> immediately under our windows, turned back again and again, to bid his wife farewell, and take his baby once more in his arms; and I saw him hastily brush away a tear with the sleeve of his coat, as he gave her back the child for the last time, wrung her hand, and ran off to join his company, which was drawn up on the other side of the Place Royale.[13]

Most men bade an anguished farewell to their families and marched away, but to imply, as Heeley did, that all wives and children refrained from accompanying their husbands and fathers would be inaccurate. Eaton, who spent the early hours of 16 June standing at the window of her room in the Hôtel de Flandre watching the troops forming up and marching out of the city, clearly remembers that 'many of the soldiers' wives marched out with their husbands to the field, and I saw one young English lady mounted on horseback, slowly riding out of town along with an officer, who, no doubt, was her husband'.[14]

The confusion and distress were heightened by another factor. Although the mobilisation had only just begun, the first rumour was already circulating. 'What caused the confusion to be worse than it need have been, was that everybody thought the French were close at the gates.'[15]

In the midst of this turmoil the more seasoned soldiers of those regiments that had formed in the centre of Brussels did their best to get some rest. According to one observer, 'many a soldier laid himself down on a truss of straw, and soundly slept, with his hands still grasping his firelock'.[16] However not every soldier who chose to nod off was allowed to do so in peace, as Kincaid of the Rifle Brigade reveals:

> Waiting for the arrival of the other regiments, we endeavoured to snatch an hour's repose on the pavement; but we were every instant disturbed, by ladies as well as gentlemen; some stumbling over us in the dark – some shaking us out of our sleep, to be told the news – and not a few, conceiving their immediate safety depending upon our standing in place of lying.

These interruptions seemed to get on Kincaid's nerves, particularly as he gave the same answer to every concerned enquiry:

> All those who applied for the benefit of my advice, I recommended to go home to bed, to keep themselves perfectly cool, and to rest assured that, if their departure from the city became necessary (which I very much doubted), they would have at least one whole day to prepare for it, as we were leaving some beef and potatoes behind us, for which, I was sure, we would fight, rather than abandon![17]

Throughout the night the commotion continued. However as the first glimmerings of dawn lightened the night sky, a sense of order began to be felt as infantry regiments formed up in the Place Royale and prepared to march. Having returned from his second visit to the now sleeping

Wellington, Sir William walked with Lady De Lancey to the window and leant out of the cosy little apartment where they had been so happy in recent days, to watch the troops assemble in the park and march off. 'It was a clear refreshing morning,' recalled Lady De Lancey, 'and the scene very solemn and melancholy. The fifes played alone, and the regiments one after another marched past, and I saw them melt away through the great gate at the end of the Square. Shall I ever forget the tunes played by the shrill fifes and the buglehorns which disturbed that night!'[18] Lady De Lancey had grasped the serious nature of the situation, but there were those who still had to wake up to the reality of the predicament as dawn came on 16 June and the Allied forces marched out of Brussels.

> All things arranged, we passed the gates of Brussels, and descended the wood of Soignies, that leads to the little village of Waterloo. It was the 16th – a beautiful summer morning – the sun slowly rising above the horizon and peeping through the trees, while our men were as merry as crickets, laughing and joking with each other, and at times pondered in their minds what all this fuss, as they called it, could be about: for even the old soldiers could not believe the enemy were so near.[19]

So recalled Edward Costello of the men he led out that morning. Even though they knew they were marching to war and some had only hours to live, the enchantment of that summer in Brussels was powerful enough to render reality unbelievable. There were those who seemed to view the French invasion as little more than an opportunity for an excursion. Mercer was overtaken by a cabriolet travelling at a brisk pace.

> In it was seated an officer of the Guards, coat open and snuff-box in hand. I could not but admire the perfect nonchalance with which my man was thus hurrying forward to join in a bloody combat – much, perhaps, in the same manner, though certainly not in the same costume, as he might drive to Epsom or Ascot Heath.[20]

Costello's men stopped for a while; the newer recruits to sleep and more seasoned soldiers to cook breakfast. At 'about nine o'clock the Duke of Wellington and his staff came riding from Brussels'. With all their insouciance this might have seemed like just another morning's ride, except that they were heading somewhere seldom mentioned that summer: 'to the front'.[21]

21

'It was not until their defenders were summoned
to the field, that they were fully sensible of
their changed circumstances'

As the troops marched out of Brussels, their departure coincided with the arrival of traffic bearing goods for market, and one observer was amused 'by the unexpected appearance of a long train of market carts, loaded with cabbages, green peas, cauliflowers, early potatoes, old women, and strawberries, peaceably jogging along, one after another, to market'.[1] Apparently the contrast between these gawping sunburned rustics and the warlike appearance of the Allied troops was comical. However it was a momentary interlude of levity.

> Before seven in the morning, the streets, which had been so lately thronged with armed men and with busy crowds, were empty and silent. The great square of the Place Royale no longer resounded with the tumult and preparations for war. The army were gone, and Brussels seemed a perfect desert. The mourners they had left behind were shut up in their solitary chambers, and the faces of the few who were slowly wandering about the streets were marked with deepest anxiety and melancholy.[2]

For more than a year the streets of Brussels had been filled with colourful uniforms and echoed to the sounds of martial music and the noise of carousing soldiers. Now, as dawn gave way to the full light of day, they had simply vanished. Those civilians who had somehow slept through the noise during the night were, for the first time in over a year, waking up to a day with virtually no British soldiers.

It took some time for the difference to register, and there was a stunned atmosphere, as Heeley, left behind to look after Scovell's horses and equipment and ready to move at a moment's notice, recalled – 'It was quite astonishing to see by this time how quiet the inhabitants had become' – although Heeley ascribes this calm to the efficacy of the few officers posted in town. 'Our officers who were left in charge of the town had completely pacified them, assuring them that Wellington was certain to beat the enemy, but everybody was naturally on the alert.'[3]

The only reminder of what, a few hours earlier, had seemed like the permanent military presence in a garrison town, was heavy military wagons guarded by 'a few sentinels'[4] and the occasional officer riding out of town to join his regiment. Sir Thomas Picton, who had arrived only the day before, was spotted riding through the streets 'in true soldier-like style, with his reconnoitring glass slung across his shoulders',[5] occasionally reining in his charger to greet friends. The Duke of Wellington took his breakfast alone, as usual, at 6 a.m., and then at around eight o'clock he rode out of town with his aides-de-camp. Now, more than ever, it was important that he maintained his mask of sangfroid. He was observed to be in high sprits and was heard to say that he expected to return in time for dinner.

Whether this hollow boast offered any reassurance to the now nearly defenceless domestic and expatriate civilians is uncertain. Certainly De Lancey was not swallowing his chief's line; at six o'clock that morning he had sent his wife to Antwerp with a letter instructing a Captain Mitchell in the Quartermaster-General's department to look after her. On her arrival she spent an hour resting in the back room of an inn, before moving with her maid to comfortable lodgings, from which she could hear no noise from the street. Obviously her husband had grasped the seriousness of the situation and had planned ahead for this eventuality, ensuring that his wife was out of town before the last soldiers had left for the front.

As far as many others were concerned, however, either events had moved so quickly as to overtake any plans they had made, or, quite simply, in the giddy social atmosphere of pre-invasion Brussels the idea of leaving this very jolly city had simply not been entertained. For instance Fanny Burney recalled the sound of a bugle early in the evening of the 15th, causing her to look from her window, but she thought little of it:

I saw a few soldiers, & thought them collecting for some change of sentinels: but about 3 in the morning I was awakened by a *Hub bub* in the street, that made me rise, & run hastily again to the window: it was not light, & a sound of a few voices, in passing stragglers, made me once more conclude there was nothing material, & go quietly to Bed again. But at six o'clock *Friday the 16th* the same sounds called me forth to examine the neighbourhood, & enquire of the maid, who was arranging the sallon [*sic*], what was the matter.'[6]

As for the Richmonds, they stayed put: 'we had post-horses in the stables,' recalled Lady Georgiana Lennox, 'but the Duke had promised to send word if we were to leave.'[7]

Kincaid of the Rifle Brigade offers an astute psychological insight into the thinking of the large expatriate civilian population left, almost defenceless, in Brussels. 'Brussels was, at that time, thronged with British temporary residents; who, no doubt, in the course of the two last days, must have heard, through their military acquaintance, of the immediate prospect of hostilities.' In this it seems that Kincaid was not totally correct, as even the young Lennoxes professed themselves to be unaware of any military move, on the very afternoon that Blücher was under attack at Charleroi. However his theory as to the mass willing suspension of disbelief is interesting.

But accustomed, on their own ground, to hear of those things as a piece of news in which they were not personally concerned; and never dreaming of danger, in streets crowded with the gay uniforms of their countrymen; it was not until their defenders were summoned to the field, that they were fully sensible of their changed circumstances; and the suddenness of the danger multiplying its horrors, many of them were now seen running about in the wildest state of distraction.[8]

However the lure of Brussels was too strong for all soldiers to resist, and Charlotte Eaton had barely sat down to eat her breakfast when she was surprised by the appearance of her friend Major Llewellyn. 'He had ridden a few miles out of Brussels with the regiment, and then galloped back with Sir Philip Belson, who also wished to return.'[9] Their reunion was overshadowed by events but still a source of pleasure, and even now there was still a sense that military and civilians colluded with each other in creating the fantasy that nothing would happen ... at least that day. 'No expectation was entertained of any engagement taking place to-day. Sir Philip Belson and Major Llewellyn, therefore, felt quite at their ease; "being certain," they said, "of overtaking the regiment *at a place called Waterloo*, where the men were to stop to cook."'[10] They stayed for a few hours and when they managed to tear themselves away it was only just in time. As they left the Place Royale they clearly had no idea that within two hours they would be in the thick of the fighting.

For those left behind the atmosphere was one of curiosity and frustration at the lack of information. Creevey, who had stayed up until half past two waiting for his stepdaughters to return from the Duchess of Richmond's ball, complained that 'we were without any news the best part of the day',[11] and for much of the day the civilian population, many of whom were still not expecting any military engagement that day, 'wandered restlessly about the streets'.[12] If they thought of anything other than the impending battle, it was to note the contrast between the scenes of Brussels less than twenty-four hours earlier.

While crossing the park between 4 and 5 p.m. to go to dinner with Mr Greathed, Creevey thought he heard the sound of cannon fire. Charlotte Eaton too was told that cannonading could be heard in the park.* 'At first I was utterly incredulous; I could not, would not believe it; but, hurrying to the Parc, we were too soon, too incontestably convinced of the dreadful truth, by ourselves hearing the awful and almost incessant thunder of the guns apparently very near to us.'[13] By the time he got to Greathed's, Creevey found 'everybody on the rampart listening to it'.[14] The sound 'came through the air like a quantity of heavy muffled balls tumbling down a long wooden stairs – or perhaps more like a rolling ball, and causing it now and then to hop about on the head of a big drum.'[15] Throughout the evening the ramparts remained crowded with people listening as 'the sound became perfectly distinct and regular'.[16] It was even audible in Antwerp, where Lady De Lancey heard 'a rolling [sound] like the sea at a distance'.[17]

Going to bed was of course out of the question, and while Creevey stayed on at Greathed's, Charlotte Eaton tarried until late in the park, noting the contrast between the scene she now witnessed and the park a mere twenty-four hours earlier. 'Then it was filled with female faces sparkling with mirth and gaiety; now terror, and anxiety, and grief were marked upon every countenance we met.'[18]

During the early evening it was the lack of information that was most frustrating and alarming: people had ridden or taken carriages out of the city following the direction that the troops had taken that morning, but had come back 'in perfect ignorance of the real circumstances of the

---

* Some sources including Heeley and Jackson state that the cannonading could be heard from earlier in the afternoon; Jackson says around 2 p.m. (Jackson, p.16).

case'. [19] This ignorance of course powered the rumour mill. Eaton recalled how she variously heard that the French had been repulsed leaving 20,000 dead; that the 180,000 French had cut the British to pieces and were advancing on Brussels. She met one Englishman who told her that 'old Blücher had given the rascals a complete beating'; and ten paces later she encountered a man who advised them to flee the city at once as the French had won a complete victory and the Allied forces were retreating in total confusion. As an Englishwoman, Eaton quite naturally viewed these 'idle tales and unfounded rumours' as 'unworthy of a moment's attention'. However she feared that the 'poor Belgians', being made of less stern stuff, would be more susceptible to the inevitable scaremongering. [20]

Towards the end of the day, the situation became a little clearer. It was at about five o'clock that the first wounded trickled into Brussels, and immediately 'thousands rushed to the gates to make enquiries'. [21] The initial sight of the wounded men limping into Brussels brought home the reality of war to civilians. One observer witnessed the melancholy sight of 'a Belgic soldier dying at the door of his own home, and surrounded by his relatives, who were weeping over him'. [22] Indeed, many who had been wounded in the battle had died on the way back to the city.

Those who survived and were conscious were pestered immediately with questions as to the fate of loved ones, their regiments and the course of the battle. This last question was invariably met with variations on the response that it was 'very bad, worse than anything in Spain'. [23] Occasionally wagonloads of wounded would arrive in the city in a terrible state. Given the limited number of wagons and carts available, only the most severe cases were loaded into transport. Men with shattered or missing limbs passed out; others, screaming in agony, were crammed onto anything that moved, from farmers' carts to gun carriages, and sent off jolting on the twenty-five-mile road to Brussels under the heat of the sun, with every bump on the road sending spasms of pain shooting through their mutilated bodies.

The citizens of Brussels responded nobly to the situation. The hospital soon filled up and those who had been billeted in Brussels returned to places they had left only a few hours previously, while others were taken in by well-meaning citizens. A great many others took baskets of food and kegs of brandy or wine out of the city to meet the walking wounded. Soon the centre of Brussels looked like an open-air hospital, with wounded men lying groaning on the cobbles.

Such was the closeness of the fighting that officers were able to come and go from Brussels. In one of her letters to her mother from her house in the country outside Brussels, Caroline Capel comments on the strange effect of the proximity of ballroom and battlefield: 'to have one's friends walk out of one's Drawing Room into Action, which has literally been the case on this occasion, is a sensation far beyond description.'[24] The juxtaposition of the slaughter at what would become known as the battle of Quatre Bras, and the gentility of smart society in Brussels, separated by barely twenty-five miles, must have proved strange for those officers returning from the front.

At night, 'Colonel Hamilton* rode into Brussells [*sic*] to do some things for General Barnes, and to see us,' wrote Creevey, who was delighted to see his military informant again and pumped him for information until he returned to headquarters at midnight. 'We found from him that the firing had been the battle of Quatre-Bras,' wrote Creevey of his debriefing of Hamilton. 'He was full of praise of our troops, who had fought under every disadvantage of having marched 16 miles from Brussells, and having neither cavalry nor artillery up in time to protect them.'[25]

Meanwhile Charlotte Eaton encountered Sir Neil Campbell at her hotel. Campbell had met Sir George Scovell, for whom young Heeley worked as a groom, and who had been sent into Brussels with orders from the field at about half past five. She heard how 'every regiment, as it arrived, instantly formed and fought' under the conditions described to Creevey, 'and, though the enemy outnumbered them far beyond all computation, they had not yielded an inch of ground, and they were still fighting in the fullest confidence of success'. Even though they were at a disadvantage Scovell had apparently said that 'there can be no doubt of their repulsing the French'[26] once the cavalry had come up, and that the struggle would be continued the following day. According to Heeley, Scovell was back in Brussels at 11 p.m., 'much fresher than we had any reason to expect, but the poor horse was dreadfully knocked up'.[27] Earlier in the day on his journey into Brussels during the late afternoon, his horse had been described as 'white with foam'. After a good supper Scovell went to bed for two hours, giving instructions to have a horse and his baggage ready at two o'clock.

Nor was the darkness to offer much rest to the civilian inhabitants.

---

*Elsewhere at this time Hamilton is referred to as a major but he later became a lieutenant-colonel.

Charlotte Eaton describes a night of constant disturbance as people were wakened from their beds by excitable servants shouting that the French were at the gates of the city. Hotel guests rushed from their bedrooms in their nightdresses, bundles of clothes tucked under their arms, and careered down into the courtyard to try and commandeer a carriage to get them out of town. Indeed the excitable maid shouting '*les français sont ici*' seems to be a stock character of civilian memoirs of this period.

Gradually a picture of the conflict was unfolding for those in Brussels with contacts in the Army. The engagement had taken place at a strategically important cross-roads, running north from Charleroi to Brussels and east to west between the Prussians and the forces commanded by Wellington. There were some Allied troops holding the position already, and as British units arrived they were thrown into the fierce struggle at once. So hard was the fighting that the Duke of Wellington himself came close to being captured near the beginning of the battle, while he was rallying troops that were giving way while under attack from French cavalry.

All situations under fire are confusing, but Quatre Bras particularly so. 'The battle of Quatre Bras was so confused that it is difficult to establish an exact sequence of events, or to detail the exact number of troops in action at any particular moment,'[28] writes one eminent military historian. The tall crops which had been a source of wonder earlier that summer also played their part, hiding troops from each other and the enemy. About the only thing that was not confused was the intensity of the fighting. As one combatant put it, 'A more bloody or obstinately contested thing had seldom or never been seen.'[29] At first the Allies were outnumbered at least two (one source says three)[30] to one, but throughout the day their numerical inferiority declined as more troops came up, and after a bitterly fought and often chaotic battle, the Allies succeeded in holding off the French.

This success was in great part due to Picton's arrival in the mid-afternoon, when he showed that his curmudgeonly qualities of non-conformity and obstinacy, while not much use when it came to obtaining honours and an entrée into high society, came in very handy on the battlefield. At one point, with enemy in front and behind, he looked like being defeated:

> but the gallant old Picton, who had been trained in a different school, did not choose to confine himself to rules in those matters; despising the force in his rear, he advanced, charged, and routed those in his front,

which created such a panic among the others, that they galloped back through the intervals in his division with no other object but their own safety.[31]

So fierce was the fighting and so vigorous Picton's part in it that at one point he seemed more like his old self and confided to his A.D.C. Tyler: 'I shall begin to think that I cannot be killed after this.'[32] But he did not escape completely unscathed, sustaining two broken ribs and suffering internal bleeding, caused in all likelihood by a glancing blow from some grapeshot.

Otherwise the cost at Quatre Bras was high, so high that by the time hostilities ended at nightfall, many Allied troops were not sure in whose favour the engagement had ended. The most illustrious casualty of the day was also one of the earliest: the Duke of Brunswick, who had been at the Duchess of Richmond's ball the preceding evening, received a fatal wound in the stomach while rallying one of his units under French fire and he was carried from the field. One report said that he took seven bullets. His body was brought through Brussels in his carriage and taken to Antwerp, where, as coincidence would have it, it was laid out in an inn, in same back room where Lady De Lancey had rested on her arrival in the town that morning.

Also among the first to fall was dashing James, Lord Hay, the man worshipped by his fellows and flirted with by the ladies. His attraction was doubtless enhanced by the blasé way in which he joked blackly about any fighting he might be involved in. 'Remember I shall fall in the first action,' he had said half laughingly to Maria Capel, 'and I shall fall on Miss Muzzy [his horse named after Maria]; if I have time to speak I shall send her to you, and you must always keep her.'[33] He may have adopted an elegantly flippant pose about the coming battle, but to his friend William Pitt Lennox he had confided his fears that he would not survive the first encounter with the French:

> The day before the battle of Quatre Bras, Hay, who was in love with a young lady, entrusted his secret to me. He said that he felt a pre-sentiment that he should not escape the first action with the enemy, and giving me a gold chain for the object of his affection, and a sword and a sash for myself, we parted. We met at my mother's ball on the 15th June. I shook him warmly by the hand; in less than twelve hours he was buried near the spot where he had fallen.[34]

It seems that the attributes which had made him such a success in

Brussels, his noticeable clothes and his flamboyant horsemanship, had been Lord Hay's undoing on the battlefield. 'Mounted on a splendid charger, called Abelard' – apparently eschewing his favourite mare Miss Muzzy – 'and decked out in a fancy uniform, he was shot, early in the action, by some straggler belonging to the enemy, who evidently took him for a superior officer.'[35]

Another ladies' man to fall at Quatre Bras was Battersby, whose seduction of the pretty wife of a Grenadier had led to her murder by her jealous husband.

22

'On Saturday morning the attention of us and
the Bruxellois was taken up with the wounded
who arrived by hundreds'[1]

'The wounded began to arrive early this morning, and before 11 o'clock a
many had come in, but not so many as the previous day,'[2] Heeley recorded.
However the military situation belied the fragile optimism encouraged by
the drop in the number of casualties coming through Namur Gate. After
their hard-won victory of the previous day the British were retreating
towards Brussels.

It was true that while the Allies had succeeded in fighting Ney to a
standstill at Quatre Bras, the Prussians had been bested (but not destroyed)
by Bonaparte at Ligny. Despatching 33,000 troops in pursuit of the retreating Prussians, Napoleon turned to Quatre Bras. However, Wellington had
anticipated this move. Having spent the night at Genappe and enjoyed a
good dinner with wine sent up from Brussels, which was served at a table
'with covers laid for at least twenty persons',[3] he was up early the following
morning dressed in his customary blue frock coat, short blue cloak, leather
breeches and Hessian boots, and went with his ADCs to Quatre Bras,
where the troops were taking a rather less elegant breakfast of rum and
beef.

Private Dixon Vallance, who had left Brussels in such a hurry the
previous day that he was obliged to pack his shirts wet from the washerwoman, was among those who had survived. Having taken his rum – 'I
never got [a] drink that I was so much the better of as at that time'[4] – he
cast about for something in which to fry his beef, and his eye alighted on
the 'heaps' of dead French cuirassiers, who had fallen in front of squares of
British infantry. The British soldiers were very curious about the cuirassiers'

breastplates, which rose to a ridge down the middle of the chest – the polished brass ones worn by officers were a source of much comment. There had been much debate as to whether they were proof against musket balls, and there are stories of soldiers shooting at breastplates to test this theory.

Vallance had no need of such proof as he had seen what British lead could do to French brass. 'After we examined their false preservers we selected a number of the best of them for our purpose and used them as pans for frying our messes of beef in for our breakfasts. They suited our purpose well only we lost a little bit of gravy by the holes which our bullets had made in them.'[5] Vallance and his comrades then amused themselves by telling passers-by that they were eating their fallen foes' remains.

However they did not have long to enjoy their beef or their jokes. Wellington had sent for information about the course of the battle at Ligny, read the newspaper while waiting and then, placing the paper over his face, took a nap.[6] Once he received confirmation of the defeat of the Prussians at Ligny, he gave the order for a withdrawal to Waterloo. Predictably Picton, who had fought so bravely the previous day, gave a 'surly acknowledgement of the order',[7] his mood not improved by the aching wound strapped up beneath his civilian clothes (he was still waiting for his luggage to catch up with him).

Napoleon meanwhile got off to a slow start and did not reach Quatre Bras until the afternoon of the 17th, allowing the British and their Allies time to withdraw.

However it was not long before the British cavalry, under the flamboyant Uxbridge, had a chance to test themselves against Ney's men. The British cavalry had come up the night before, and the noise of them arriving at Genappe had robbed those lucky enough to find billets of their rest. By morning they had reason to be grateful: as the Allied infantry retreated they were protected from harrying French lancers by the cavalry.

There was a rumour, doubtless due to his propensity to recklessness on the field, that he 'had positive orders not to have an affair of Cavalry'.[8] But Uxbridge was up for a scrap. The two opposing sets of cavalry clashed at Genappe and, keen to give Wellington the chance to withdraw in good order, Uxbridge threw himself and his men at the French lancers who were on the village high street. The British went to their work, to use the delightfully euphemistic adverb of one observer, 'cordially',[9] and it was certainly a most bloody and obstinate clash of horses and men.

As it was taking place, the weather, which had become 'insufferably hot and close',[10] broke; heavy rain began to fall and the gunfire was echoed by loud peals of thunder. The downpour rapidly turned the ground slippery and treacherous, which together with the obdurate nature of the French lancers meant that in the midst of the hard-fought engagement many of the Life Guards were unhorsed, muddying their splendid uniforms. The Life Guards had not seen active service for years and were more used to parading in Hyde Park, where the rule was that if a trooper came off his horse in muddy conditions and got his uniform dirty he would leave the field to tidy up his appearance before returning to the parade. So ingrained was this habit that now, in a hotly contested cavalry engagement, whenever a trooper got his uniform dirty he would calmly lead his horse to the rear to smarten up, before returning to the fray.

Even by the standards of conspicuous male elegance of the day this was too much for many soldiers who could not help laughing at this dandified body of men. 'I thought at first they had been all wounded,' recalled Kincaid who watched the engagement as he withdrew from Quatre Bras, 'but, on finding how the case stood, I could not help telling them that theirs was now the situation to verify the old proverb, "The uglier the better soldier."'[11]

The sartorial propriety of the Life Guards aside, this brutal clash offered up another marvel for those watching: the sight of Uxbridge in action. The reality of armed combat worked like a drug on the British cavalry commander; while Wellington's behaviour during this campaign was to be characterised by a fearless yet understated omnipresence, always turning up where the fighting was thickest to rally faltering troops, Uxbridge was noted for fits of gallantry so outstanding as to be almost lunatic, as he would hurl himself heedlessly into whatever fight happened to be going on at the time. As has been mentioned before, his reason seemed to leave him in the heat of battle, and he has been described as behaving more like an enthusiastic young cornet than the seasoned, gifted and conscientious commander that he was. He got Mercer into a scrape, instructing the artillery officer to follow with two guns.

'What he intended doing, God Knows, but I obeyed,'[12] says Mercer, whose perplexity only deepened as Uxbridge led him down a narrow lane only just a little broader than the gun carriages. 'What he meant to do I was at a loss to conceive,'[13] pondered Mercer, and it is doubtful that even Uxbridge really knew what he had in mind. However the uncertainty cleared in a moment when a group of French cavalry appeared from behind some bushes.

The orderly and methodical Mercer and the hot-headed cavalry commander seemed done for. In later years Mercer seemed unable to believe that the rash and stupid incident had ever occurred.

> The whole transaction appears to me so wild and confused that at times I can hardly believe it to have been more than a confused dream – yet true it was; – the general-in-chief of the cavalry exposing himself amongst the skirmishers of his rear-guard, and literally doing the duty of a cornet![14]

However the dream-like state did not persist for long. With a shout of 'By God! we are all prisoners'[15] Uxbridge dug his spurs into his horse and charged, not towards the French chasseurs and hussars, but towards the bank of one the gardens that lined the lane. His mount scrambled up the incline and forced its way through the hedge, apparently leaving Mercer alone to deal with the situation.

If Uxbridge's action was characteristic of the impetuous side of the cavalry chief's character, then Mercer's was as indicative of his coolness. He gave the order 'Reverse by unlimbering'.[16] It was the only solution, but it involved unfastening and turning round the gun, then pushing it part-way up the bank over which Uxbridge had made his escape and manoeuvring a team of eight horses in a space scarcely wider than the gun carriage itself, while a violent thunderstorm played above their heads. He gave the order having every confidence that it could not be carried out before the French attacked and then, with more sangfroid than he felt, he ostentatiously turned his back on the French.

Perhaps the cavalry could not believe their eyes and expected a trap. Mercer was allowed to conclude his manoeuvre and return to the main road, where he found Uxbridge hurriedly assembling a group of hussars to extricate the stricken artillerymen: Uxbridge was as honourable as he was impetuous. But they were far from safe, more French cavalry were coming up and another group threatened to cut off their line of retreat, so the order to fall back was given, coinciding with increasingly heavy rain, thunder and lightning: a downpour so heavy that visibility came down to just a few yards, which left everyone drenched but effectively hid the retreating British from the pursuing French.

The retreat through Genappe was marked by considerable contact with the enemy, with the 7th Hussars charging straight at French lancers who blocked the street with a wall of lances and then beat them back and pursued them, only to be routed in turn by the 1st Life Guards. It was a bloody day but it had its almost comic moments. The surreal nature of the fighting is captured again by Mercer in his account of directing a rocket troop. Rockets were fired from a triangular stand, and when this had been erected in the midst of skirmishers the first rocket headed straight down Genappe high street and exploded under a gun carriage, scattering French artillerymen. However not one of the other rockets fired that day behaved in the same way. Some went up, some sideways, and some promptly turned on the British, with one of them singling Mercer out as its target 'following me like a squib' until its shell exploded, putting him 'in more danger than all the fire of the enemy throughout the day'.[7]

The sudden deluge was the beginning of several hours of absolutely filthy weather that figure prominently in all accounts of the battle. Within minutes every man was drenched, and almost all of them would remain so, many spending the night in the open and not really fully drying out until the following day. The misery of such a situation cannot be overestimated: the dread of imminent battle; the absence of food (inexperienced soldiers had left much of their three days' rations in Brussels); the lack of shelter; and the penetrating chill of heavy, sodden, woollen uniforms.

One theory for the cause of the downpour is that it was brought on by the battle at Quatre Bras. Apparently thunderstorms and heavy rain were known to be a side-effect of the heated air rising from battles fought using black powder.[18] And as one observer riding towards Quatre Bras the previous day had noted, the conflict was creating its own microclimate:

> The distant battle was announced by another sign. It was an afternoon of clear blue sky, but in the south there were some clouds. These in one part assumed the form of a pyramid, whose base was a line, straight as if drawn with a ruler. It was the canopy which the combatants had formed for themselves.[19]

Whatever the cause the rain was sudden and torrential. Modern computer modelling has recreated the weather front of that distant weekend and as Andrew Roberts records in his superb account of the battle, the rain has been described as 'apocalyptic'.[20] It lasted until the morning of the following day.

After contact with the pursuing French had been broken off, the Allied forces encamped for the night at Mont St Jean. However, just before the fighting ended Mercer, who had been involved in an artillery battle near La Belle Alliance, which would achieve such significance the following day, noticed that:

> a man of no very prepossessing appearance came rambling amongst our guns, and entered into conversation with me on the occurrences of the

day. He was dressed in a shabby, old, drab greatcoat and a rusty round hat. I took him at the time for some amateur from Brussels (of whom we had heard there were several hovering about).

After the sort of day he had had, the last thing Mercer needed to deal with was a curious civilian sightseer, who had made the short journey out from Brussels to check on the progress of the battle. He admits to have been 'somewhat short in answering him',[21] causing him to leave as rapidly as he arrived. A little later, Mercer learned that the sightseeing civilian was in fact General Sir Thomas Picton, whose uniform had still not caught up with him – it was a bizarre end to a bizarre day.

The rumour of wandering amateurs from Brussels shows just how close the withdrawal from Quatre Bras had brought the battle. The action was now about ten miles closer to Brussels than it had been at the beginning of the day and only the Forest of Soignes separated what had been the gaiety of Brussels from the serious business of fighting Napoleon.

The city was anxious and in turmoil, but having been taken by surprise, there were signs that the town's officials were reacting to the situation. On Saturday morning bulletins issued in the name of Baron van Capellen, the Brussels-based Governor-General of the Belgian provinces, began to appear, giving an authorised, reassuring and accurate assessment of the situation. The mayor made an appeal for bedding and supplies to meet the needs of the wounded in the Grand Place, among whom the womenfolk of Brussels moved distributing sympathy and refreshments.

A few of the well-connected expats like Creevey, who had heard of the outcome at Quatre Bras from their sources in the British military, woke up feeling a little less worried.

On Saturday the 17th I remember feeling free from much alarm. I reasoned with myself that as our troops had kept their ground under all the unequal circumstances of the day before, surely when all the Guards and other troops had arrived from Ath and Enghien, with all the cavalry, artillery, &c., they would be too strong for the French even venturing to attack again.[22]

To begin with the events of the day seemed to support Creevey's optimism. The thundering of the artillery which had been heard so distinctly the preceding day and held its listeners rapt in the park and on the ramparts did not provide such an ominous aural backdrop in the early part of Saturday. The mid-morning bulletin brought an official report of the victory at Quatre Bras. However at about 4 p.m., roughly the time that Mercer was being chased down the main street in Genappe by a rogue rocket, Creevey was paid a visit by his friend Marquis Juarenais, 'who I always found knew more than anybody else'.[23] Juarenais had alarming news. 'Your army is in retreat upon Brussels, and the French in pursuit.'[24]

The Marquis's unpalatable news was soon corroborated by the sight of military baggage and horses coming down the rue de Namur, filling up the park and the surrounding streets, of which Creevey's was one. Creevey nervously noted that 'every thing came *down* the Rue de Namur, nothing went up'.[25] By the early evening, the news was out and van Capellen issued a statement that tried to make the best of Blücher's defeat and Wellington's necessary withdrawal to within a dozen miles of the city to maintain his lines of communication with the Prussians.

> According to news which arrived from Headquarters at 6.00 pm, His Serene Highness Prince Blücher, with a view to uniting his army corps with that of General Bülow, has brought his headquarters at [*sic*] Wavre. This movement of the Prussian army corps has determined Field Marshal the Duke of Wellington to concentrate his forces and to establish his headquarters at Waterloo, so as to be constantly ready to carry out his junction with the Prussian armies.
>
> The enemy has made no move since yesterday and his positions are the same. Our troops, only a part of which has been engaged up to now, are in the best dispositions. His Royal Highness the Prince of Orange and His Royal Highness Prince Frederick enjoy the best of health.[26]

However reassuring it was to learn that the Prince of Orange remained in good health, the effect of this news on morale in the city was catastrophic, its impact all the greater because optimists had believed that the lessening of the cannonading and the reduction in the numbers of wounded had augured an upturn in the Allied situation. Although there had been rumours of a Prussian defeat, 'unwilling to believe bad news, we had hoped it would prove false'.[27]

No one was fooled by van Capellen's euphemistic style; the Allies were in retreat and it seemed that the battle for Brussels was imminent. Heeley reports that 'towards the evening the cannonading was very loud and we could not help thinking they were getting very close to Brussels, which caused a great fright to a many [*sic*] of the inhabitants'.[28] In Antwerp stories were circulating that the French had already captured Brussels.[29]

On Saturday evening panic gripped almost all the civilian population and even money could not secure transport out of the apparently stricken city. 'So great was the alarm in Brussels on Saturday evening, that one hundred napoleons were offered in vain for a pair of horses to go to

Antwerp, a distance of nearly thirty miles; and numbers set off on foot, and embarked in boats upon the canal.'[30]

But some were fortunate to have got out earlier in the day, and among them was Charlotte Eaton. After a disturbed night, the relative calm of the morning had given her the opportunity to find a coachman willing to venture outside the city walls. Her account of the refugee-filled road to Antwerp on that sultry day is filled with crying women and infants; carriages jostling for position; camps of displaced peasants by the wayside; ditches filled with overturned carts and broken wheels; droves of cattle blundering about and blocking the roads; a tide of civilians and walking wounded moving slowly one way while soldiers forced their way upstream towards Brussels and the battle. Nor were the waterways any less clogged. 'The canal, by the side of which the road is carried, was covered with boats, and trackschuyts, and côches d'eau, and vessels of every description, and presented a scene of tumult and confusion scarcely inferior to that upon land.'[31]

As is the case in such situations there were incidents of generosity and selfishness. As she drove past the Palace of Lacken, near which Lady Caroline Capel was now waiting in her chateau ready to flee at a few minutes' notice, Eaton boarded some wounded on her carriage, and was appalled that others did not do the same. 'I saw – I am sorry to say – one young English gentleman, who was travelling quite alone in his own carriage, sternly order down two of these unfortunate wounded men from his carriage.'[32] Many of these pitiful-looking soldiers shambling towards Antwerp had sustained their injuries at the battle of Ligny where the Prussians had been mauled by the French; however they were the lucky ones. The wounded of the Franco-Prussian clashes of 15 and 16 June who were unable to move, were to remain without medical attention on the field for almost a week.

By the time the news of the Allied retreat upon Brussels was making its way round the city, and the heavens were opening over the Allies *en route* to Mont St Jean, Eaton was in sight of Antwerp.

> At a distance, we saw the lofty spire of the cathedral of Antwerp, without *then* admiring its beauty, or even being conscious that it was beautiful. We looked, we felt, indeed, like moving automatons. Our persons were there, but our minds were absent. Every step we took only seemed to increase our solicitude for all we left behind.[33]

And as she made her way into the city, passing 'three walls of immense strength and thickness, surrounded by three broad, deep ditches or moats',[34] the rain started. With difficulty she found two very small rooms at the Grand Laboureur, in the Place de la Maire, the same inn at which Lady De Lancey had been lodged; 'one of the apartments in our hotel was occupied by the corpse of the Duke of Brunswick, which had arrived about two o'clock. It had been already embalmed, and was now placed in its first coffin.'[35] Shortly after midnight, with the rain lashing the windows of her room, she heard a sharp tattoo of hammering as the dead Duke's coffin was nailed down, while tapers burned at the foot and head of the coffin and two officers in the suitably funereal garb of their Corps stood guard.

23

'He mounted his horse and took leave of us in a very kind manner, expecting never to see us again'

That Saturday night the mood in Brussels was just as sombre. It was barely forty-eight hours since the Duchess of Richmond's ball, yet the gaiety had long since evaporated and even the stout British pugnacity and talismanic belief in the powers of the Duke of Wellington was wavering as the rain poured in sheets from the sky. 'I will never forget the unearthly howlings and hollow murmurs of the wind,' recalled one soldier. 'It seemed as if myriads of demons were hovering around us, and were exulting over the death-doomed victims whose thread of earthly existence was drawing near an end.'[1]

Those officers who made it out of the rain and into the warm dry drawing rooms of Brussels for a few hours that night were far from optimistic. Creevey went to talk to the Cavalry who were bivouacked in the park; they 'looked gloomy and told me things were looking but badly when they came away'.[2] After nightfall, Hamilton returned and fed Creevey further gloomy reports straight from the HQ of General Barnes (who had been engaged as a guest at Lady Caroline's *Pick Nick* when war rudely interrupted): 'he was graver than usual, left us with his opinion that a most infernal battle for Bruxelles would be fought the next day, and as you may well suppose, we all thought his life was certain of being lost in it.'[3] Having imparted a feeling of gloom, Hamilton returned to headquarters by midnight.

On his way out of town he may well have passed Scovell, who rode into Brussels between 11 p.m. and midnight composed but similarly sombre. 'Ah, tomorrow will be a dreadful day,' he said as he dismounted at his lodgings, 'for the Duke is determined to decide the matter on the position he has taken today. Many thousands will fall.'[4] He clearly expected himself to be among the slain. He ordered his black horse, which he had left the night before, to be ready at 2 a.m., but before he departed, he left detailed instructions to be followed in the event of defeat, his death, or both.

> He made arrangements with the landlord to secrete our heavy luggage in case of a retreat, and wrote directions for us in case he was killed. He enclosed them in his desk with orders to break the desk open if he was killed, and after giving us all strict charge to keep steady, and mind what we were about, he mounted his horse and took leave of us in a very kind manner, expecting never to see us again.[5]

From the highest to the lowest the sense of fear and impending death was oppressive and omnipresent. As Scovell was making his grim preparations, the orderly who was to ride out with him sat sharing a tumbler of spirits with Heeley and his father. 'I feel sure it's all up with me,' he grumbled over his glass of grog, 'for I dreamt my comrade was scraping the blood off me as I lay in a ditch.'[6] Such premonitions form as much a part of the memoirs of fighting men as the panicking maidservants do in the recollections of non-combatants.

The orderly drained his glass. Scovell turned the key in the lock of his desk. They mounted their horses and some time after two o'clock in the morning rode out towards their positions around Mont St Jean, leaving Heeley 'in a more serious mood than hitherto'.[7]

The early hours of Sunday morning were nerve-racking for everyone. For all the unperturbed, almost glacial calm that he had exhibited during the day, which he had begun with an ostentatious nap under a newspaper, Wellington too was in a rather more serious mood than hitherto. He had doubts about the outcome of the battle the following day, and in the early hours it would have been unnatural had those concerns not come crowding into his mind. The scattered Prussians under the irascible Blücher and the untrusting Anglophobic Gneisenau; the untested, recently raised units; the soldiers still arriving from America; the questionable loyalty of the non-British troops under his command; that delicate instrument, the British cavalry, commanded by the battle-crazed Uxbridge; the idiotic Prince of Orange; the abrasive Picton; and his own 'family' of brave, enthusiastic and gilded, but oh so very young, A.D.C.s. – these were just some of the problems facing him on his own side before he even considered what Napoleon, a former ruler of Europe, a military genius and also a desperate man willing to sacrifice tens of thousands of fanatically patriotic soldiers in pursuit of his destiny, would do. Could he really pull it off? With such an infamous Army?

There is evidence to think that just before dawn on Sunday 18 June 1815, the Duke of Wellington experienced, if not a crisis of confidence, then at least a serious attack of nerves. At three o'clock his thoughts turned to that illicit afternoon in the park, and he wrote to Lady Frances Wedderburn-Webster. Even then, hours away from the most important military engagement of his career, a clash of arms that would determine the future of Europe for the next century, the events of the coming day that would maybe see his death, perhaps bring about the fall of the British government, possibly even the collapse of the Alliance forged in Vienna, his mind wondered to the bewitching Lady Frances.

He roused himself from his thoughts and wrote to his lover

My Dear Lady Frances

As I am sending a messenger to Bruxelles, I write to you one line to tell you that I think you ought to make your preparations, as should Lord Mountnorris, to remove from Bruxelles to Antwerp in case such a measure should be necessary.

We fought a desperate battle on Friday, in which I was successful, though I had but very few troops. The Prussians were very roughly handled, and retired in the night, which obliged me to do the same to this place yesterday. The course of the operations may oblige me to uncover Bruxelles for a moment, and may expose that town to the enemy; for which reason I recommend that you and your family should be prepared to move to Antwerp at a moment's notice.

I will give you the earliest intimation of any danger that may come to my knowledge: at present I know of none.

Believe me, &c

Wellington.

Even at so crucial a moment the Duke did not forget his manners. He added a postscript:

Present my best compliments to Lord and Lady Mountnorris.[8]

Perhaps in order to bolster his spirits he also sent a message to his cook, who was woken at 4 a.m. and told that he or his assistant was to go to Waterloo as 'the Duke wished to have a hot dinner on that day'.[9] The cook hurried off to the market.

At about the same time, just as the sun was beginning to rise, Lieutenant Ingilby of the Royal Horse Artillery left his bivouac and struck out for

Brussels. At last the rain had stopped. He was not deserting, rather he was acting on orders to establish a line of retreat through the Forest of Soignes. With his forces fighting with their backs up against the wood, Wellington planned that, if necessary, the Army could melt through the trees. However, for the Army to retreat in any order, roads capable of accommodating guns, limbers, teams of horses and cavalry had to be found, and this was Ingilby's job.

He found the forest, once the venue for *fêtes champêtres* and attempts at foxhunting, now acting as a *de facto* refugee camp for seemingly innumerable country folk and their 'women and children, cattle, pigs, sheep, and whatever valuables they could carry off'.[10]

As well as peasants fleeing in front of the fighting, the forest and its surroundings were witnessing large build-ups of troops where units that had marched from as far afield as Ghent had stopped for the night. Among these was Harry Smith, veteran of the American war, who until a couple of days earlier had been doing ceremonial duties at the court of King Louis.

He had passed through Brussels the day before and had run into the gridlock and confusion on the edges of the forest.

> We were directed by a subsequent order to halt at the village of Epinay, on the Brussels side of the forest of Soignies, a report having reached his Grace that the enemy's cavalry were threatening our communication with Brussels (as we understood, at least). The whole afternoon we were in a continued state of excitement. Once some rascals of the Cumberland Hussars, a new Corps of Hanoverians (not of the style of our noble and gallant old comrades, the 1st Hussars), came galloping in, declaring they were pursued by Frenchmen. Our bugles were blowing in all directions, and our troops running to their alarm-posts in front of the village. I went to report to Sir John Lambert, who was just sitting quietly down to dinner with my wife and his A.D.C. He says very coolly, 'Let the troops——; this is all nonsense; there is not a French soldier in the rear of his Grace, depend on it, and sit down to dinner.' I set off, though, and galloped to the front, where a long line of baggage was leisurely retiring. This was a sufficient indication that the alarm was false, and I dismissed the troops and started for the *débris* of a magnificent turbot which the General's butler had brought out of Brussels.[11]

The contrast was marked between the noisy, crowded forest, where Ingilby also encountered a body of Prussian soldiers, and the eerie calm of Brussels. He found the streets 'wholly deserted, except by the wounded that were straggling in from the Cavalry affair of yesterday and at Quatre

Bras the day before; many were lying and seated about the steps of the houses as if unable to proceed further in search of a hospital.'[12] Ingilby did what any other soldier who had been out all night in the wet would have done, and went immediately to the Hôtel d'Angleterre for breakfast, where he was pressed for news by an Englishman, Admiral Sir Pulteney Malcolm. Having finished his morning meal, he took a 'cold fowl'[13] for his troop, who like so many had had little or nothing to eat for a day or two.

Compared with most of his comrades, Ingilby's start to the day was the very height of luxury. The conditions in which they had spent the night had been horrible, barely anyone had kept dry. The Highlanders had made brightly coloured tents with their tartans; the artillery had erected makeshift shelters using their gun carriages; the cavalry slept leaning on or lying under the heads of their horses, which were constantly bothered by the thunder; and one imaginative individual had covered his coat with the heavy claylike soil and crawled under that. Some spent the night amidst the tall crops which had attracted such attention earlier in the summer. Here the ground was so sodden that when Private Dixon Vallance and his comrades tried to dance and leap about to keep warm, they got stuck in the mud and had to pull each other out.

Otherwise, wherever they could get a fire going in the deluge, men stood or sat hunched in the rain trying to smoke their pipes or cook a few illicitly acquired farm animals or feed their fires using whatever came to hand including, in one instance, a long-case clock which, placed on a fire built by a dragoon, acted as a chimney while it burnt. The incident of the clock stuck in one officer's mind. When he returned to the battlefield with some friends over forty years later he related this story and 'was importuned by a Belgian peasant for compensation, on the ground that the clock belonged to his family!' [14]

Mercer thought himself splendidly well off when he found himself sheltering under a hedge with a brother officer who had an umbrella (about which he had been teased earlier in the day) and together they lit a fire and a couple of cigars. 'Dear weed! What comfort, what consolation dost thou not impart to the wretched,' rhapsodised Mercer, 'with thee a hovel becomes a palace. What stock of patience is there not enveloped in one of thy brown leaves!'[15] In addition to his stock of patience Mercer's stock of food was increased by a Hanoverian who shared his fire for a while and by way of thanks left a 'poor, half-starved chicken', which went straight into a cooking pot, whereupon, 'after various betrayals of impatience, the miserable chicken was at last snatched from the kettle ere it was half-boiled, pulled to pieces, and speedily devoured'.[16]

Mercer got barely a mouthful of scrawny chicken, but he was lucky. Often the men were too numb with tiredness, cold and hunger to feel much else – one detachment, having made a forced march for dozens of miles to make it to the battlefield, lay down on the reverse of a slope (a favourite tactic of Wellington's to protect his troops from artillery fire) and slept through the first four hours of the battle. It may sound strange, but one man even recalls taking a nap in the middle of battle, when he was ordered to lie down to avoid artillery fire: 'I took advantage of this circumstance to obtain an hour's sleep, as comfortably as I ever did in my life, though there were at that time upwards of three hundred cannon in full play.'[17]

As day broke, the men roused themselves shivering with the cold and wet and attempted to dry their clothes either by fires or by hanging them in trees and on bushes. The rain had certainly altered the appearance of some troops, for instance the scarlet tunics of the dragoons had run into their white belts. However the mood improved a little when alcohol was distributed; although there were some instances of drunkenness, it seems that spirits were taken more to drive out the cold and chill of a night under the downpour than to instil courage. And while the men had their oats and grog, Guards officers had their servants bring a rather more substantial breakfast from Brussels. Passing through the bivouacked 1st Foot Guards, Gronow, who had spent the night guarding French prisoners in a Waterloo farmyard, was greeted with shouts of 'Take a glass of wine and a bit of ham? It will perhaps be your last breakfast.'[18] Eventually he joined Captain Burges and Colonel Stuart under 'a sort of gipsy-tent' constructed of 'blankets, a serjeant's halberd and a couple of muskets'[19] for a spot of cold pie and champagne.

Of course not every member of the British Army had passed the night in the open. The commanding officers had found lodgings in the hamlet of Waterloo, the officers' names written in chalk on or above the doorways of the houses, but while they may have been dry, not all were comfortable. Picton for instance, who had given a good impression of a civilian sightseer in public, suffered terribly in the privacy of his billet from the broken ribs and internal bleeding sustained at Quatre Bras and spent the night groaning with pain: however he swore his A.D.C.s to secrecy about his injuries.

Frazer of the artillery, meanwhile, snatched four hours' sleep in Brussels. Almost like a modern office worker, he was one of the officers who seemed to have settled into a routine of commuting to and from the fighting. His letter of 17 June, at 11 p.m., reads like the comment of a frayed office worker who has been working late. 'Just arrived from the front tired, jaded, dirty, and going to bed.' But writing again four hours later he professed himself

The Duke of Wellington set the military and social tone by surrounding himself with ADCs and staff officers of almost exclusively noble descent: (left to right) the Prince of Orange, the Duke of Brunswick, the Duke of Wellington, Lord Hill, Sir Thomas Picton, Prince Blücher and the Marquess of Anglesey.

A Swarm of Bees Hiving in the Imperial Carriage – this image by master satirist George Cruikshank conveys the sense of panic as civilians tried to flee what they thought was a doomed city.

The Battle of Quatre Bras, engraved by Thomas Sutherland.

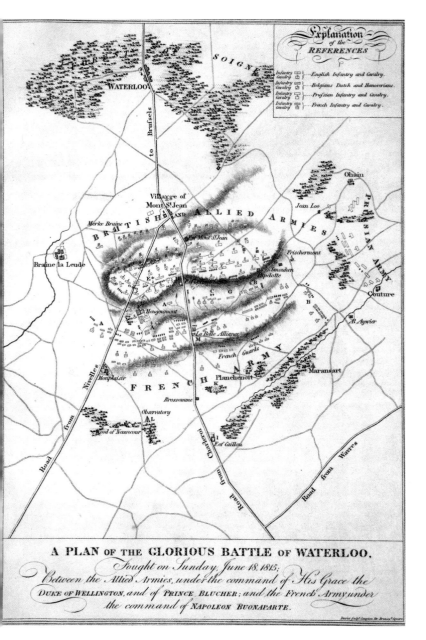

Plan of the battle of Waterloo.

According to one historian, no battle since Waterloo had managed to fit such a large number of men and animals into such a tiny area. The slaughter was appalling.

Although the Duke was often present in thick fighting, 'the finger of Providence was upon me, and I escaped unhurt'.

The village of Waterloo. A brisk trade in souvenirs started soon after the battle, and the looting of the dead and dying was horrific.

Comrades-in-arms, heroes of Waterloo: Thomas Graham, Rowland Hill, Thomas Picton, Henry Paget.

Prize-fighter and heavy drinker Private Shaw was one whose reputation was cleaned up for public consumption during the latter half of the nineteenth century.

Public sculptures to honour Wellington sprung up all over the country. The most controversial was behind his London house: a twenty-foot-high bronze representation of a naked Achilles. This cartoon shows William Wilberforce doing his best to preserve public morals and Achilles' modesty.

Baron Raglan in the last year of his life, forty years after the battle of Waterloo. He was married to Wellington's niece and remained a loyal aide to the Duke until the latter's death, when he succeeded him as commander of the Army. He left an arm at Waterloo and lost his life and reputation in the Crimea.

In old age the Duke became a national monument.

Annual banquets hosted by the Duke of Wellington to celebrate the battle became a fixture on the London calendar.

This high-blown allegorical image of Wellington's apotheosis shows how he was seen as a secular saint at his death.

'quite refreshed after a comfortable night's rest'.[20] His route to 'work' took him along the main Brussels road, which he found 'crowded and choked with carriages of every kind, many of them overturned'.[21] He was in a position to advise that it was cleared, which it was by 9.15 a.m. The broken-down wagons had been burnt by an infantry brigade looking for fuel with which to cook its rations, enabling supplies and ammunition to be brought up.

Daylight also saw the Duke of Wellington in fine spirits. If he had been assailed by doubts in the dark of the night, they were banished by the sun, which according to Gronow 'shone most gloriously'[22] (although others write of a light drizzle persisting for some time), and by the news received during the night that the Prussians had regrouped and that Blücher would be bringing a sizeable force to the battlefield in the middle of the day. Looking across the swaying fields of rye he must have hoped for their speedy arrival, as he saw the wall of humanity arrayed against him, the sunlight catching the breastplates of the cuirassiers.

Gronow caught sight of the Duke that morning dressed, as was customary, not in uniform but in the sort of clothes a gentleman might wear out riding, viz. 'a gray great-coat with a cape, white cravat, leather pantaloons, Hessian boots, and a large cocked hat'.[23] He was riding around his Army with his entourage and 'they all seemed as gay and unconcerned as if they were riding to meet the hounds in some quiet English county'.[24] Given that most of the men were young noblemen had learnt their skill in the saddle pursuing foxes across their fathers' estates, this is hardly surprising; but the description also reinforces the sense of warfare being seen as an extension of the field sports at which a young man of breeding should at least prove competent.

Here and there in accounts of the battle the notion of warfare as an aspect of the lifestyle of the sporting gentleman is reinforced with appropriate similes: grapeshot, the lethal hail of lead fired by cannon instead of a solid ball, has 'a hum like the sound of the flight of a covey of partridges';[25] a wounded man is knocked from his horse with such force that he 'bounded up again into the air like a struck pheasant'.[26] Captain William Hay says of his dog Dash, who accompanied him at the battle, 'with the shooting going on I dare say he fancied himself transported to a field-day on the Lammermoor Hills, where he and I had on other occasions amused ourselves with a different description of sport.'[27] These sporting allusions demonstrate how many of those who participated in the battle approached it and, in modern parlance, processed the event in retrospect.

Among the group of mounted sportsmen taking to the field (albeit for battle rather than hunting), Gronow identifies 'the Duke of Richmond, and his son, Lord William Lennox'.[28] Young Lord William was still recovering from the injuries sustained while falling from his horse during the near-fatal race. Nevertheless he had not wanted to miss out on the action: 'Prevented though I had been from doing service in the great battle, I was not to be kept from getting into it.'[29] Moreover he had heard of the death of his friend, hero and fellow A.D.C. the dashing James, Lord Hay, and felt guilty, experiencing what he called 'a restless anxiety to join my general'.[30]

On Saturday evening he asked his father if he might go to the battle. Richmond answered that he must follow the medical advice he had been given and then added, perhaps with an indulgent smile of paternal pride: 'If however, you like to ride with me to-morrow morning to the field, where the army will bivouac to-night, there can be no objection to your doing so, and we shall then be better able to judge of your strength and powers on horseback.'[31] Lord William was thrilled, and his youthful excitement is still palpable in his memoirs which were published almost half a century later, by which time he was well into his sixties. Early the following morning he mounted his first charger and headed out to Waterloo with his father.

According to the tutor, Madan, the Duke of Richmond had lost some of his confidence and wanted the Duke of Wellington's advice on what to do with his family:

> On Sunday morning the Duke of Richmond, who I must say has been a little too confident considering his large family, finding that Wellington was so near, and the rest of the English residents here gone or going, gave orders that we shd. be ready to start at a quarter of an hours [*sic*] notice, and rode himself to the Duke of W. to ask his opinion. In consequence the carriages were packed and horses quite ready to be put to.[32]

As the Richmond household bustled with the activity of preparing for flight, the Duke of Richmond and his son enjoyed 'a very delightful ride through the forest of Soigny'.[33] They met Uxbridge, who was just mounting his charger, and on catching sight of the father and son, greeted them as if they had arrived just in time for dinner, a performance at the theatre, or a day's sport. 'You're just come in time,' said Uxbridge by way of welcome, 'for we shall have a smartish affair today.'[34] Together with the cavalry commander they rode onto the field and paid a visit to General Maitland who, while 'cheerful and calm', had 'a look about him that told how intensely he felt the loss of his aide-de-camp, and other officers, who had fallen, or been severely wounded'.[35] As Maitland and the officers of his brigade were all friends of Lord William and his father, the atmosphere was pretty much that of a hunt meet or similar out-of-doors social event typical of a weekend at an English country house.

Next stop on their pre-battle social schedule was a visit to Wellington, who shook Richmond by the hand and said 'William ought not to be here', before returning to his preparation. Again the atmosphere among Wellington's entourage would have been immensely clubbable. For a start Lord George Lennox, Richmond's son, was among their number, and time must have flown in such pleasant company, because before the Duke of Richmond could return to the Wash House with news from the Duke, the battle had begun.

It is of course entirely possible that as a soldier who had been thwarted in his attempts to secure a position in the Army, Richmond had decided that he would be damned if he was going to miss out on what looked like being a decisive engagement, especially as he had sons who were serving in the Army. Besides, it was an excuse to get out of the house and out from under the feet of the mercurial and domineering Duchess, who for once was not in control of either herself or rapidly changing events. 'At home,' wrote Madan, 'the poor D.ss harassed by the thoughts of the Duke being absent of her 10 children with her and her 3 sons in the action was a pitiable object.'[36] Napoleon had already scored one major victory: reducing the once proud and imperious queen of British Brussels to nothing more than a frightened woman fearing for the safety of her husband, her children and herself.

24

'The French are in town'

The tension in Brussels that morning must have been unbearable. Like the Richmonds, any British who were left weighed up their options every few minutes. The equivocation was evident in a letter written by Fanny Burney, who vowed to set out for Antwerp at 5 a.m. 'if Danger here approaches' only to add a line later: 'If better prospects arise, I remain at Brussells.'[1]

Burney's letter highlights the scarcity of reliable information on which to make a decision to stay or go. In such an atmosphere any information to do with the disposition of troops was eagerly seized upon and analysed, in the hope that it would illuminate the scene. From late morning the wagons that had been stationed in Brussels began to move out of town, Creevey watching their departure with keen concern. 'I never felt more anxiety than to see the route they took; for had they taken the Antwerp or Ostend road, I should have concluded we were not to keep our ground. They all went up the Rue de Namur *towards the army*.'[2]

At about half past eleven the thunder of the cannon commenced and the citizens of Brussels received the most audible notice that the battle for their city had begun in earnest. Frye noted with wry amusement that many were preparing for the imminent arrival of the French. 'All the caricatures and satires against Napoleon have disappeared from the windows and stalls.'[3] Panic began to be felt and the blandishments of the authorities were powerless to assuage the worried populace: 'the proclamation of the Baron de Capellen to the inhabitants, wherein he exhorts them to be tranquil and assures them that Bureaux of Government have not yet quitted

Bruxelles, only serves to increase the confusion and consternation.'[4]

Churches emptied, late breakfasts were abandoned as people tried to find out what news they could. 'For the present awful moment,' wrote Fanny Burney, 'all the people at Brussels LIVE in the streets or at the windows – the whole population is in constant view.'[5]

However, some got exasperated and tired of looking out of their windows, wandering around the streets or standing on the ramparts listening to the cannon fire; they wanted more information. One such man was of course the terminally curious Creevey. An information addict and a hardened gossip, being in the know was crucial for Creevey: he prided himself on being the best-informed and the first with the news. It was torture for him to be ignorant of the world-shaping events taking place just a few miles away, and he ventured out of the Porte Namur in search of information.

> I walked about two miles out of the town towards the army, and a most
> curious, busy scene it was, with every kind of thing upon the road, the
> Sunday population of Brussells being all out in the suburbs out of the
> Porte Namur, sitting about tables drinking beer and smoking and making
> merry, as if races or other sports were going on, instead of the great pitched
> battle which was then fighting.[6]

Moreover there were estimated to be around eighty prominent citizens who supported Napoleon, and plans were being made for a victory banquet to honour the French.

Not everyone shared the mounting confidence of the fifth columnists or the cheerful unconcern of the beer-swilling Bruxellois enjoying their tobacco under the summer sun while the cannon boomed in the near distance. Fanny Burney, together with the Boyd family, tried to get away to Anvers in a barge, and they were about to embark when the vessel was requisitioned by the military and filled with wounded officers who were to be transported to Antwerp. The hospital and medical facilities of Brussels were already overstretched, and those wounded that could be moved were being shipped out of town.

Meanwhile in her chateau a couple of miles outside Brussels the pregnant Lady Caroline Capel fretted, equally unable to escape. She had passed a terrible night. The storm had unsettled her and the courtyard had filled up with wounded who had been drenched during the night and of whom she was doing her best to take care.

On Sunday morning her husband had left her to go to Brussels with the rather optimistic aim of 'trying every means to get a conveyance for us in case Lord W was defeated'.[7] A few days earlier their free country house had seemed a pleasant sylvan retreat from bustling Brussels, but now Lady Caroline, imagining the countryside crawling with French skirmishers, saw its secluded setting as a potential hazard. 'In this situation,' she wrote, 'a House in a Wood, without any neighbours or means of assistance in the case of a party of French stragglers coming up, was not to be borne.'[8] All sorts of worries would have been racing though her mind. In the event of a breakdown in military discipline, even the wounded and deserting Allied troops could have turned violent. Already there were rumours of gangs of marauders:

> chiefly cowardly rascals who had abandoned their colours, and were prowl-ing for plunder; these were mostly the scum of Blücher's army – not true Prussians, I trust, though clad in Prussian uniforms; they stole several horses left by British officers who were in the field, besides committing other depredations.[9]

When Capel returned it was of course without any transport. 'Not a Horse to be had,' lamented Lady Caroline. 'The Mayor had put them all in requisition for the Military – 1 man had paid 10 guineas for a pair of Horses to go the first stage to Antwerp.' Even at this time the exorbitant cost does not lose its power to shock the money-conscious Lady Caroline: 'the same difficulty in obtaining a barge; by the greatest interest and acquaintance with the Mayor he got the promise of an order for one, for which we were to pay 20 guineas' – how that must have hurt! '25 was all we could procure any where for all the Banks were shut up.'[10] However, given the experience of Burney and the Boyds, it was highly unlikely the Capels would ever board their boat, let alone reach it. Instead, if the situation deteriorated, they resolved to make for Brussels, hoping at least to be safer in the city.

At the time the Capels were formulating their plan to get to what they saw as the relative safety of Brussels, Creevey had just got in from his stroll among the city's beer-drinking bourgeoisie. He had gone to dress for dinner – standards must be maintained, especially in times of crisis – when his stepdaughter Elizabeth came running into his room. 'For God's sake, Mr Creevey,' she shrieked, 'come into the drawing-room to my mother immediately. *The French are in the town.*'[11]

Creevey ordered the blinds to be drawn and the door closed at once. He then went to the drawing room to be with his wife when the invaders arrived. But, Creevey being Creevey, after ten minutes his curiosity got the better of him and he went out of the house.

I found the alarm had been occasioned by the flight of a German regiment of cavalry, the Cumberland Hussars, who had quitted the field of battle, galloping through the forest of Soignes, entering the Porte Namur, and going full speed down the Rue de Namur and thro' the Place Royale, crying out the French were at their heels. The confusion and mischief occasioned by these fellows on the road were incredible.[12]

Poor Edward Heeley had the misfortune to be caught right in the middle of this alarming incident. He and his father had been on the way to the commissary to collect some hay and grain for the horses. On the way his father had bumped into a hussar with whom he was friendly and stopped off for a glass of wine, telling his son, who was astride a mule, to go on and he would catch up. He had not gone far when he was faced with a mass of hard-riding cavalry pelting down the road, shouting 'Franceuse, Franceuse, the French, the French'.[13] Rather than head towards this imposing body of horsemen, his mule did the sensible thing and turned round. Within seconds young Heeley, on his mule, was a part of this high-speed cavalcade of cowards. The mule, now completely out of Heeley's control and moving at 'full gallop', further demonstrated its intelligence when it took a turning that led to its stable. 'Such a scene of confusion had now began [sic] as baffles all description.'[14]

The confusion was further exacerbated by women riding in pursuit of their husbands, of whom Heeley gives a compelling account:

They were well mounted, riding astride on men's saddles, they had on boots and trousers like dragoons, and wore a gown over all, with small round bonnets on their heads. I think they belonged to the Brunswickers and German Legions – for I saw no caricatures of this sort amongst the British, and these women were amongst the first retreating party who entered Brussels screaming all the way as they came. They rode well, for their horses' feet made the fire fly out of the pavement. I never shall forget them, for they galloped on straight forward and if the D . . . l had been in the way, they would have went over him.[15]

The immediate effect was seen in carriages damaged and overturned, among them that of General Barnes, as this tide of wild horsemen and women surged through the town, with the result that 'people in all directions were closing their doors and pulling down their signs'.[16]

'As soon as I got to the stable, I bridled the horses all ready for a start. My father was running about the town looking for me for a long time before he returned to the stable. As soon as he came I wanted to mount and be off to Antwerp.'[17] Heeley was not alone in his wish to get as far away from the city as quickly as possible. This last shock had been the final scare for many and hundreds if not thousands took to the road, servants of soldiers fighting at Waterloo simply abandoning their masters' belongings and fleeing. It was a scene of pandemonium which only increased on the road to Antwerp as even greater numbers of panic-stricken civilians and deserting military personnel, believing that all was lost, swelled the throng of those fleeing already.

Juana, Spanish-born wife of Harry Smith, was already *en route* to Antwerp when the wave of panic and fear caught up with her a few miles outside Brussels. As she had met and married her husband while he had been campaigning in Spain she was no stranger to wartime conditions, and had spent the night with him in the encampment on the Brussels side of the Forest of Soignes. She was loath to leave her husband, but she dutifully followed his advice and when the troops moved forward she rode back into Brussels to await the outcome of the battle. Upon her arrival she found her servant and her luggage in the Place Royale.

However it was not long before an order came down to move the Army's baggage out of the city and in the direction of Antwerp. After the heavy rain the road was in worse condition than it had been the preceding day when Charlotte Eaton had made the journey, and with the baggage and camp followers of a force of tens of thousands, not to mention the carts loaded with wounded, it was certainly no less crowded. Going was slow, but by about five o'clock Juana had crossed a canal and made it to the village where the baggage train was ordered to halt.

On reaching the village I dismounted, the baggage was unloaded, and West was endeavouring to get something for me to eat in the inn. It was about five o'clock. Suddenly an alarm was given that the enemy was upon us. West brought my mare to the door as quickly as I could run downstairs, but from the noise, confusion, and everything, my horse was perfectly frantic. West succeeded in tossing me up, but my little pug, Vitty, was still below. I said, 'Now, West, give me my dog'; when, as he put her into my lap, I dropped my reins. West, knowing I always gathered up my reins before I jumped up, let go, and off flew the mare with such speed that, with the dog in my lap, it was all I could do for some time to keep my seat. I had the snaffle rein in my hand, but I could not restrain her; the curb rein was flying loose, and I couldn't stoop to get hold of it. She flew with me through the streets of Malines, across a bridge over the river, the road full of horses and baggage, still flying away, away, until I was perfectly out of breath. I saw a waggon upset lying immediately before me across the road, and I knew that if I could not turn her on one side, I must inevitably be knocked to pieces. The mare would not answer my snaffle rein, and I felt her charge the waggon as at a fence to leap it. The height was beyond the spring of my horse. As the animal endeavoured to leap, the loose curb rein caught. This brought her at once to a halt, and I was precipitated on her head, pug and all. I had come at this rate eight miles, over a road covered with mud and dirt. The mare was as much out of breath as I was. I managed to get back into the saddle, and felt that now was my only chance to get hold of the curb. I succeeded in doing so, and we were then on terms of equality.

Having righted my habit, I looked back and saw some five or six men on horseback, whom of course I construed into French Dragoons, although, if I had considered a moment, I should have known that no Dragoon could have come the pace *I* did; but I was so exhausted, I exclaimed, 'Well, if I am to be taken, I had better at once surrender.' The first horseman proved to be one of my servants, riding one of the Newmarket horses, having taken the animal from West against his orders. The others were a Commissary, an officer of the Hanoverian Rifles, and an officer, I regret to say, of our own Hussars. I addressed myself to the Hussar, who appeared the oldest of the party. 'Pray, sir, is there any danger?' (I had forgotten almost all the little English I knew in my excitement.) 'Danger, mum! When I left Brussels the French were in pursuit down the hill.' 'Oh, sir, what shall I do?' 'Come on to Antwerp with me.' He never pulled up. During the whole conversation we were full gallop. One of the party says, 'You deserve no pity. You may well be fatigued carrying that dog. Throw it down.' I was very angry, and said I should deserve no pity if I did.

Our pace soon brought us to Antwerp, where the Hussar was very civil, and tried to get me a room in one of the hotels. This he soon found was impossible, as all the English visitors at Brussels had fled there. We must now go to the Hôtel de Ville and try for a billet. Whilst standing there, the officer having gone inside, I was an object of curious attention. I was wet from head to foot with the black mud of the high-road. On my face the mud had dried, and a flood of tears chasing each other through it down my cheeks must have given me an odd appearance indeed. While standing on horseback there, an officer of the English garrison, whom I did not know (he must have learnt my name from my servant) addressed me by name. 'Mrs. Smith, you are in such a terrible plight, and such is the difficulty of your getting in anywhere, if you will come with me, I will conduct you to Colonel Craufurd, the Commandant of the Citadel; his wife and daughters are most kind and amiable people, and readily, I know, would they contribute with happiness anything to your comfort.' My situation was not one to stand on delicacy. I therefore promptly accepted this offer, leaving my kind Hussar in the Hôtel de Ville. When I arrived, nothing could exceed the kindness of all, which was as striking at the moment as it seems to me now. I was stripped from a weight of mud which, with my long riding-habit, I could hardly move under. A shower of hot water again showed my features, and I was put in the clothes of good Mrs. Craufurd, a very tall woman; and in these comfortable dry clothes I was nearly as much lost as in the case of mud I had been washed out of.[18]

Juana Smith might have felt herself safe, but reports that the French were in Brussels gained currency in Antwerp. Panic soon began to spread and those in command began to believe that with Brussels fallen, Antwerp would soon be attacked. Tomkinson traces the path such rumours took and mentions one cavalry officer, perhaps the very one who helped Juana Smith, who:

galloped to Malines, and on his arrival there he stated, that as he left the upper town in Brussels, he SAW the enemy's troops in the lower part of the town. Some person with the baggage advised him to inform the commandant of Antwerp, and possibly through his report the gates of Antwerp were shut. They were closed for a short time.[19]

But even shutting the stout gates for the shortest of periods would have stoked the fear and confusion, pushing those who already believed that they were fleeing for their lives to greater acts of desperation: 'in one instance a batman was seen throwing his master's baggage into the canal going to Antwerp.'[20] Those inside the city, fearing that Antwerp was now unsafe and not far enough from the French, started out for Holland.

Meanwhile those left in Brussels awaited the arrival of the French. 'All the baggage of our Army and all the military Bureaux have received orders to repair and are now on their march to Antwerp, and the road thither is so covered and blocked up by wagons that the retreat of our Army will be much impeded thereby,' noted Frye gloomily, adding with grim humour: 'Probably my next letter may be dated from a French prison.'[21]

Eventually it was established that alarm caused by the fleeing cavalry was false, and as soon as this was established order was restored, but for an hour and a half chaos had convulsed the city, sending shockwaves pulsing up the road to Antwerp. Speculation was then rife about what had caused this chaos. Some blamed Napoleonic supporters in Brussels. Another theory was that some Belgian regiments had been mistaken for French soldiers. A third suggestion was that the camp followers and supporting paraphernalia had been crowding the rear echelons of the Army as it was being pressed by the French, which given the busy scenes earlier in the day in the forest of Soignes was highly likely, and that the baggage etc. had been ordered to keep back, this sparking rumours of an imminent retreat. After that, all it took was a few shouts to the effect that the French were coming and the English were beaten to fan the flames of fear into a conflagration of chaos.

Even though this panic proved ill-founded, the atmosphere was tense. In retrospect the Duke of Wellington called the battle 'the nearest run thing you ever saw in your life',[22] and until Monday morning the outcome would remain unclear. With every passing hour the mood in Brussels changed. After the mad Hussars had charged through town claiming that the French were on their tails, the French really did march down the rue Namur . . . as prisoners. Creevey, whose pre-prandial preparations had been interrupted, left his dinner and made haste to the Place Royale to see them file past, their escorts carrying captured colours and eagles. He had barely returned to his house and resumed his dinner when he heard more shouting, announcing the arrival of 'another larger body of prisoners'.[23] By the time Creevey finished his dinner he was at his most optimistic since the start of the fighting. Meanwhile, over at the Wash House, the Duke of Richmond had returned and 'reported that all looked favourable',[24] but insisted that his family still be ready to flee at fifteen minutes' notice.

However it soon became clear that the situation on the battlefield had changed since the Duke of Richmond had left it. More wounded poured in, either 'giving shocking accounts of the action'[25] or just frightening the civilians with the extent and severity of their wounds. Everyone kept asking them 'Are the Prussians come?',[26] anxious for news that Blücher's long-awaited arrival on the field had taken place, and each received a shake of the head.

After his dinner Creevey was hanging out of the window when he spotted a fellow British MP, Mr Legh, of Lyme, who had been one of the civilian spectators at the battle all day. Delighted to have found someone who could share his enthusiasm for the way things were going, and in the hope of acquiring yet fresher information and gossip, Creevey 'rejoiced with him upon things looking so well'.[27] However, Legh surprised Creevey by being anything but optimistic. From what he said things were at best 'in the most ticklish state possible'[28] and 'looked as bad as possible; in short, that he thought so badly of it that he should not send his horses to the stable, but keep them at his door in case of accidents'.[29]

As Legh's horse trotted away, Creevey was left thunderstruck. He had to go at once to the oracular Marquis Juarenais's house in the park, in the hope that he would have more recent and better news. Just as he was rounding the corner of the Hôtel Bellevue he encountered a Life Guard who had just come into town and told him that when he had left the battlefield the British were retreating. Looking over his shoulder to check that he would not be heard, he said: 'Why, sir, I don't like the appearance of things at all. The French are getting on in such a manner that I don't see what's to stop them.'[30] Quickening his pace, Creevey arrived at Juarenais's house and was shown into the drawing room, where the first thing he saw was a wounded officer of Foot Guards, in great pain as a corporal picked fragments of his epaulette out of a nasty wound, while Madame de Juarenais held smelling salts under his nose. Demonstrating impeccable manners, the officer apologised for the trouble he was putting his hostess to and assured her he would not be staying long; he had to get on, as the French would be in Brussels that night. Just after that he passed out.

Creevey did not even bother to press the well-informed Marquis for any information, but went out of the drawing room onto the balcony overlooking the park, where he saw General Barnes's chaise, which had survived its encounter with the deserting hussars and was now being pulled at speed by four horses from the General's house in the park towards the Porte Namur and onwards towards the battlefield. Quick as he could Creevey was down the stairs and over at Barnes's, where he heard that the General was badly wounded, that his A.D.C. Captain the Hon. E.S. Erskine had lost an arm, and that Creevey's own Major Hamilton had been wounded, albeit not severely.

Creevey returned home between eight and nine o'clock thoroughly dispirited, but did not let on to his wife or her daughters. Worse was to come. Later that night, between ten and eleven, Hamilton walked in, come from the battle on foot, leading the wounded Barnes on his horse, and brought bad news: 'his impression was that when they left the field the battle was lost, that the Prussians had not come, and that all was over or nearly so.'[31] Hamilton said that he would find carriages to take them out of town; however, as usual, the frail and ailing Mrs Creevey refused to be moved, doubtless much to the relief of Creevey, who could not possibly have borne being taken away from a scene of such excitement.

The night was a tense one in the Creevey household. The Misses Ord did not undress but lay down fully clothed on their beds. The same was true of Fanny Burney who, with the Boyds, was going to make another attempt to break out of Brussels at first light; but she was too highly wrought to sleep and instead wrote to a friend saying how she had been busy making 'Chapie' (lint for bandages) and how the Boyds had gone to look at the prisoners.

Creevey however slept until 4 a.m., when he went to the window and saw not the French coming down the rue de Namur, but Allied traffic moving up. A good sign. He dressed and 'loitered about till near six',[32] which he thought a perfectly reasonable time to go and call on his friend the Marquis Juarenais. When he got there the large gate into the courtyard was still locked, the Marquis still in bed asleep and his wife wandering around in a state of undress. Nevertheless the excitable Creevey was brought into his bedroom, where he heard that the French had been defeated. This time it was copper-bottomed information. General Sir Charles Alten had been brought in seriously wounded late at night, but had left strict orders that he was to be brought news of the outcome as soon as possible, and had heard of the victory at three o'clock in the morning.

Barely pausing for breath, Creevey was out to spread the news – 'my news'[33] as he called it proprietorially. His first stop was nearby, at Barnes's house, where he had the satisfaction of being the first to tell General Barnes and the man who was usually his informant, Major Hamilton. In his recollection of events, he is plainly delighted at being first with the news: 'when I told him the battle was won (which he did not know before), and how I knew it, he said: – "There, Hamilton, did not I say it was either so or a drawn battle, as the French ought to have been here before now if they had won."'[34]

And then Creevey returned home triumphantly bearing what he thought was an early report of the victory. He would have been disappointed to learn that he was far from being the first to hear of the victory. According to Spencer Madan, word had reached the Wash House in the form of a note from an A.D.C. to the Duke of Wellington some time before midnight. Fanny Burney heard the news at dawn from a British officer, just when she was setting off; she says that there had been no official news since three o'clock on the morning of the 19th (the same time that Alten was notified) and from her letter it is plain that the extent of the Allied victory was not yet clear. 'Brussells is saved!' she wrote, '– though the *War* is only beginning.'[35] Even the groom Heeley claims that the news was widely known in Brussels on the night of the battle (although had this been the case it is conceivable that some sort of impromptu celebrations would have been audible). And by the time Creevey was regaling his family with details over the breakfast table, the news had already reached Antwerp, where there were scenes of jubilation.

A little later that morning the Duke of Wellington returned to Brussels, having been prevented from sleeping or writing his despatch by the groans of the wounded and dying at his field headquarters. A crowd soon gathered outside his house overlooking the park. Creevey was, of course, among them, and his sense of self-esteem soared when the Duke, taking a break from writing his despatch, walked to the window, looked down, recognised Creevey and with a crook of his finger beckoned him to come upstairs.

Creevey did not need to be asked twice. This was his chance for a ringside view of history as it was being written. He passed through the jostling crowd and having entered the house, was confronted by Lord Arthur Hill, the fattest young man in the British Army, who had survived Waterloo, even though his size made him a tempting target for French snipers. After exchanging the customary pleasantries, Hill told Creevey he could not go up as the great man was in the middle of composing his despatch. Anyone else would have been humbled by this observation and observed that yes indeed he should be allowed some peace. Not Creevey: 'as I had been invited, I of course proceeded'[36] and barging past the chubby A.D.C. he mounted the stairs. Posterity should be grateful to the pushy Creevey, for he left an intimate and insightful account of the Duke and the state of his emotions on the morning he awoke to find that he had changed the course of history.

As ever when two English gentlemen meet, whatever the circumstances, they shook hands. As was usual the Duke was the very model of restraint, but he spoke differently, his words shorn of the contrived insouciance that Creevey had detected in him in the weeks before the battle, his manner much changed from the offhand, almost flippant man who had parried enquiries about the outcome of the war as they had walked with Creevey's stepdaughters that afternoon in the park.

He made a variety of observations in his short, natural, blunt way, but with the greatest gravity all the time, and without the least approach to anything like triumph or joy. – 'It has been a damned serious business,' he said. 'Blücher and I have lost 30,000 men. It has been a damned nice thing – the nearest run thing you ever saw in your life. Blücher lost 14,000 on Friday night, and got so damnably licked I could not find him on

Saturday morning; so I was obliged to fall back to keep up my communications with him.'[37]

The Duke seemed to be in a state of some shock: the mask of imperturbability had dropped. All through the battle he had remained as calm
as if reviewing troops in Hyde Park. Not just his courage, but his remarkable
steadiness of nerve and refusal to allow even the most vestigial flicker of
emotion to become apparent, are conveyed time and time again in the
accounts of those who saw him during the battle. Now however, with the
tumult of the battle swapped for the tranquillity of a Brussels drawing
room, he seemed dazed, unsure as to quite how he had managed to pull off
such a victory, and grateful for the presence and company of an intelligent,
sensitive and non-military man with whom he could be Wellington the
man rather than Wellington the commanding officer.

> Then, as he walked about, he praised greatly those Guards who kept the
> farm (meaning Hugomont [*sic*]) against the repeated attacks of the French;
> and then he praised all our troops, uttering repeated expressions of aston-
> ishment at our men's courage. He repeated so often its being *so nice a
> thing – so nearly run a thing*, that I asked him if the French had fought
> better than he had ever seen them do before. – 'No,' he said 'they have
> always fought the same since I first saw them at Vimeira.' Then he said: –
> 'By God! I don't think it would have been done if I had not been there.'[38]

It is almost as if the realisation of the importance of his personal presence
on the field, as distinct from his skill as a soldier in deploying and directing
the forces at his disposal, had just struck him. Certainly Creevey, who was
by no means a fan of the Duke's subsequent record as a politician, viewing
him as a caricature reactionary, is at pains to point out that there was not
a hint of self-aggrandisement in his words: 'There was nothing like vanity
in the observation in the way he made it. I considered it only as meaning
that the battle was so hardly and equally fought that nothing but confidence
of our army in himself as their general could have brought them thro'.'[39]

It is interesting to speculate if this was the first time that Wellington
truly realised the esteem, even the affection, with which he was regarded.
Later in life his cynicism would again get the better of him when it came
to human relations, but for now he seemed to marvel, entirely ingenuously,
at the fact that the belief of others in him had been the deciding factor of
a truly dreadful battle. And his normally unemotional nature made this
realisation all the more profound.

Before he left the Duke, Creevey asked if the French were in a position to make another stand and the Duke, his brisk self again when asked for his professional assessment of a military situation, answered that he thought it impossible for them to be in a position to offer serious resistance before the Allies reached Paris. And with that Creevey was down the stairs and back in the rue du Musée, busy at his writing desk scribbling an account of this unique meeting to his friends back in England, which was sent by the same courier who carried the Duke's despatch.

But if Creevey thought he was the first civilian to offer his congratulations to the Duke of Wellington, he was to be disappointed. That particular honour had been snatched by that canny social predator the Duchess of Richmond. She had been waiting at Wellington's house since before eight o'clock in the morning for news of a wounded nephew, 'and was at the door when the Duke arrived, being the first to wish him joy'.[40]

It is also worth noting that one of the first things Wellington did, before even settling down to write his report, was to pen a letter to 'My Dear Lady Frances' in which, under the pretext of informing her that it was safe for her father to remain in Brussels, he described his victory and his loss, ending with the momentous line: 'The finger of Providence was upon me, and I escaped unhurt.'[41]

25

⤙⤚

'The whole of the horse Guards stood behind us. For my part I thought they were at Knightsbridge barracks or prancing on St James's Street.'

As far as anyone can tell the battle of Waterloo began at around half past eleven, although estimates vary between 11 a.m. and 11.50 a.m. The sun had risen to reveal the two Armies, Wellington's of approximately 73,200[*] looking south towards a French force of 77,500;[2][†] each Army on a ridge of ground, facing the other across a gently undulating plain covered in the high crops that characterised the Flanders countryside that summer. At times the two forces were separated by little more than a couple of hundred yards.

In between the two huge Armies there were two buildings: the chateau of Hougoumont which, although well forward of the main Allied position, was held by British Foot Guards and other Allied troops; and the walled farmhouse of La Haye Sainte, which would be defended by the King's German Legion. Wellington had stationed crack units in each position with orders to hold them at all costs. They would provide an immediate impediment to any French advance, leaving Napoleon's troops vulnerable to enfilading fire from these strong points.

Given that sunrise was early and the battle did not begin until almost noon, there was plenty of time for Wellington's men to be dazzled and awed by the sight of the French Army arranging itself on the opposing

---

[*] Wellington held an additional 17,000 (approx.) troops in reserve near Hal, presumably to cover a retreat to Ostend.

[†] A further 30,000 (approx.) troops were supposed to be harrying the Prussians and preventing them from regrouping.

ridge and to listen to the cries of 'Vive l'Empereur' as Napoleon rode the length of his front line. It is interesting to note that although the opportunity presented itself for a shot to be taken at Napoleon, Wellington vetoed it on the grounds that it was not the business of Commanders-in-Chief to be shooting at each other.

As they watched their opponents form up, the more pensive and philosophical British troops pondered the situation. Private Dixon Vallance had spent the night dancing in the mud to try to keep warm and had occupied his morning cleaning his gun and getting dry ammunition: the rain had been so heavy that 'most of our powder and balls were mixed together like a mass of dough'.[3] He found it 'strange that two of the most powerful and civilised nations, ranked foremost in every department of knowledge, science and art, found no other way of settling their differences, than the old and barbarous method of going to war and killing each other.'[4]

'It is an awful situation to be in, to stand with a sharp edged instrument at one's side, waiting for the signal to drag it out of its peaceful innocent house to snap the thread of existence of those we never saw, never spoke to, never offended,' wrote Wheatley.

On the opposite ascent stand hundreds of young men like myself, whose feelings are probably more acute, whose principles are more upright, whose acquaintance would delight and conversation improve me, yet with all my soul I wished them dead as the earth they tramped on and anticipated their total annihilation. 'Tis inconceptible how one's ideas should be so diametrically reversed from what is equitable and correct.[5]

The least sensitive, most battle-hardened soldier could not fail to be moved. Even 'the oldest veteran must have been struck with the solemnity of the scene'[6] was Wheatley's verdict. Moreover before the powder and shot tore through the assembled men, rendering human beings into mangled masses of gore and splintered bone, the sight of two huge Armies in the splendid polychromatic uniforms of the day possessed a nobility and beauty that struck many that morning. 'It was singular to perceive the shoals of Cavalry and artillery suddenly in our rere [*sic*] all arranged in excellent order as if by a magic wand,' mused Wheatley as he gulped down his allowance of rum and descended onto the plain to form a square. Looking back, he saw: 'The whole of the horse Guards stood behind us. For my part I thought they were at Knightsbridge barracks or prancing on St James's Street.'[7] He did not know it but it was the last time on European soil that a British Army would be so picturesquely arranged against a foe.

There have been many theories as to why Napoleon left it until almost noon to start the battle – everything from Imperial haemorrhoids to a lazy over-confidence has been cited – but the most likely answer is that, as a trained artilleryman, Napoleon was waiting for the ground to dry out.

He had slightly more men in the field than Wellington, but enjoyed a vast superiority when it came to artillery: 246[8]* pieces compared to the Allies' 157.[9] The Allies also had a troop of rockets, but given their performance the day before it is difficult to judge to whom they posed a greater threat.

For cannon to function at the peak of their effectiveness, the ground needed to be dry. The effect of round shot on massed infantry was rather like that of a huge and heavy bowling ball moving among human ninepins. A single well-aimed shot could kill or maim a couple of dozen infantry-men, and had a terrible effect on morale: one minute a man would be standing next to you, the next he would be a headless torso. A cannon ball would bounce along the ground as many as five times, and even rolling along the ground with most of its momentum gone, a so-called 'spent' ball posed a danger. Officers warned inexperienced men not to put a foot out to stop it as if it were a football: even at an ostensibly low speed, it could mangle a leg.

However, with the preceding evening's rain, the effectiveness of artillery was substantially reduced; instead of bouncing lethally amidst their human targets, cannon balls would simply splat into the mud. This was not to say that the artillery would not prove deadly, but it is probably true to conclude that many of those who survived Waterloo owed their lives to the downpour that they had endured the previous evening . . . a silver lining well worth the storm clouds of the preceding day. Moreover, every moment that Napoleon delayed went in Wellington's favour as he himself waited for the arrival of the Prussians.

At around 11.30 Napoleon tired of waiting and his lines erupted in a huge artillery bombardment. Anyone who had hoped for a battle of tactical complexity was to be disappointed. Napoleon's plan was far from subtle: smash the centre of the Allied Army, causing it to break in half, and move down the main road to Brussels in time for a slap-up banquet. This kept things even simpler for Wellington: all he had to do was stand in the way. That two such complex men directing large and varied forces should simply slug it out has led to the conflict being likened to two knuckleheaded prizefighters simply milling away at each other.

---

* The French had a further 96 pieces at Wavre and eight at Ligny, making a total of 342 pieces of French artillery in the Netherlands – Adkins p. 53.

At the same time as the French artillery opened up, a French corps attacked Hougoumont. As Wellington would admit to Creevey the following morning, Hougoumont proved crucial to the outcome of the battle: its remarkable and heroic defence against numerically superior French forces tied up many French units which could have proved decisive had they been deployed elsewhere. Although its wood and orchard changed hands during the day, Hougoumont never fell to the French, even after being set ablaze in the middle of the afternoon. At one point a giant Frenchman forced a way in for a small detachment of troops, but they were killed after the gates were closed against those who followed. In later years Wellington stated that the entire battle turned on the closing of those gates.

La Haye Sainte, the other Allied strong point around which the battle eddied and swirled, also held out against attack until about 6.30 p.m., when its defenders ran out of ammunition, at which point it seemed to many on the British side that the battle had been lost.

Barely an hour and a half after the start of the battle, Napoleon caught sight of the very first Prussians arriving on his right flank and detailed a force to deal with them, while having it put about that the men emerging from the woods on his right were in fact Grouchy's men, who had been pursuing the Prussians after their defeat, joining the battle. A little later, doubtless prompted by the signs of Prussians trickling onto the field, there was a full-scale attack on Wellington's left by 16,000 men under the command of the Comte d'Erlon. After getting to the top of the ridge and routing some Netherlands troops, they faced the Fifth Division under Picton which, after firing into the oncoming troops, was ordered to fix bayonets and charge. It was the last order the rough-spoken Welsh general would give. Still dressed in his civilian clothes, he took a musket ball through the right temple.

It was then that Uxbridge stepped, or rather charged, in. This well-timed cavalry charge would sweep through the French, sending d'Erlon's corps reeling back in disarray and leading to the prestigious capture of two Eagles (the standards under which the French rallied). It was a stunning success, but Uxbridge being Uxbridge, in the thick of things leading the Household Brigade, he would not do the sensible thing and regroup.

Wellington may have been fighting a defensive battle with a heterogeneous Army of mixed ability, waiting until the arrival of the Prussians which would give him the numerical edge enabling him to go over to the attack, but the glamorous Uxbridge, in the grip of his favourite intoxicant, battle, had other ideas. He meant to carry the fight to the French lines, and during the charge one enthusiastic cavalry officer shouted out, 'To Paris.' In the end Ponsonby's Union brigade went further than Uxbridge and was so badly mauled by the French that it was effectively out of the battle, and Sir William Ponsonby was lanced to death.

By around four o'clock the French had failed to take a commanding position anywhere on the battlefield and the Prussians were beginning to arrive in some numbers. It was then that Ney ordered a massive cavalry charge, and it is from this point in the battle that the enduring image of waves of French cavalry breaking against impregnable British squares of infantry comes. However to think of the battle falling into a neat chess-board-like pattern is a massive over-simplification.

The infantry square was a defensive manoeuvre that was almost impregnable to cavalry: ranks of men, kneeling, then standing, would form a 'square' (more usually an oblong and sometimes a triangle), bayonets pointing outwards and rear ranks loading and firing, while officers and wounded stood in the middle. However the concentration of troops in a square made it vulnerable to artillery fire: so at Waterloo troops were constantly forming and breaking squares as cavalry charged and retired, charged and retired. If Uxbridge was a maniac in battle, then Ney was his match; but although not a single square broke under cavalry attack for two hours, the artillery fire that raked the field claimed many casualties.

Between six o'clock and half past six, La Haye Sainte fell and the French horse artillery were brought up and started to fire into the Allied left flank. An attempt to retake it failed, but had the benefit of wounding the young Prince of Orange, much to the relief of the men he commanded. This was probably the most critical point of the battle for Wellington, but his line held . . . just.

At half past seven, with the Prussians now engaged on the right flank of the French and fierce fighting taking place around the hamlet of Place-noit on the eastern edge of the battlefield, Napoleon threw in the Imperial Guard and led them up to La Haye Sainte himself. They were mown down and fell back. The blow to French morale compounded the effect of the withering British fire and the advancing Prussians. By half past eight the rout of the French began and only a few isolated French units made a stand. Blücher and Wellington met at La Belle Alliance which had been just behind French lines all day.

The above is a very sketchy account of the battle and gives only the briefest overview. Moreover as an overview, even a very poor one, it gives an artificial sense of the development of events and overall knowledge of proceedings that would not have been available even to the commanders. Any such account of the battle militates against conveying the chaos, fear and ignorance of the state of the battle experienced by most of those who took part in it.

This was not a mobile battle with rapid and reliable communications. The limit of a man's actual knowledge was what he could see with his spyglass, and restricted though this was, it was a privileged position compared with that of the infantrymen locked in their squares who spent much of the day enveloped in clouds of gunsmoke, unable to see further than a few yards. Information only travelled as fast as an A.D.C. on horseback – provided of course that he could avoid getting shot.

It is interesting to note that one of the most extraordinary and most likely apocryphal stories of the day concerns the depletion of Wellington's 'family', which was so severe that he could not find an A.D.C. to take an urgent order. Instead he beckoned to 'a single horseman, rather quaintly attired',[10] asked him who he was and what he was doing on the battlefield.

'I am a traveller for a wholesale button manufactory in Birmingham,' came the surprising answer, 'and was showing my samples in Brussels when I heard the sound of the firing. Having had all my life a strong desire to see a battle, I at once got a horse, and set out for the scene of action; and, after some difficulty, I have reached this spot, whence I expect to have a good view.'[11]

A button salesman at the battle of Waterloo may sound ridiculous, but given the number of fashionable society people in Brussels it is not beyond the bounds of possibility that an enterprising British haberdasher would send a salesman out to pick up some orders. And it is certainly true that civilian spectators were a feature of the battle. Moreover the Duke of Wellington did move about the battlefield a great deal, so he might have met the button man. In the report, the button salesman is credited with delivering a message that turned the course of the battle, and on seeing the order being carried out, Wellington snapped shut his telescope and uttered the deathless words: 'Well done, Buttons!'[12]

Buttons was not the only civilian spectator to play a part in the battle. Just as the Earl of Uxbridge could not hold himself in check when he saw the opportunity for a cavalry charge, nor could the Duke of Richmond, even though his application to serve in the campaign had been denied, resist getting involved and issuing orders. 'The whole of the morning he talked to his friends, and made his remarks as if he was on service, not an amateur,'[13] recalled his son. As well as coming into his own when out of the house and on the battlefield, he was particularly pleased to note that his fifteen-year-old son, prevented by his injuries from being officially attached to General Maitland's staff, nevertheless acquitted himself well on the battlefield, saying proudly: 'I'm glad to see you stand fire so well.'[14]

Richmond was clearly enjoying himself, and when urged to move to a safer position he preferred to remain where he was. He was a totally different man to the morose night owl portrayed in Caroline Capel's letters, or the almost invisible husband to the domineering Duchess. At one point when the French were advancing up the hill, they encountered a regiment of cavalry and were about to turn. 'A person in plain clothes, standing near the hedge' – the Duke of Richmond – 'cried out, "Now's your time,"'[15] to the cavalry, at which they went over the hedge and were soon in among the column of French infantry.

26

'By God, Sir, I've lost my leg!'
'By God, Sir, so you have!'

Often in accounts of the battle given by those who fought at Waterloo, there comes a time when the writer admits that he finds it hard to believe how anyone survived, or wonders if this would be the first battle in which all combatants would be slain (an early version of the Mutually Assured Destruction that was such a key part of the Cold War). The battle seemed to consume human life with a voracity that even long-serving soldiers found remarkable. One man noted that he was the fourteenth individual to be called to the regimental colours that day, his predecessors in this dangerous work having been cut down. One square was noticed to be behaving a little erratically, and after enquiries were made it was discovered that all its officers had been killed.

Many of these accounts were written by seasoned veterans so it imposs-ible to discount them as being the excited exaggeration of raw recruits. It was a genuinely concentrated engagement in terms of the space and time in which it was fought and in its decisive nature. It could be argued that Waterloo was an entire war in one afternoon. Even Wellington was struck by the enormity of the sacrifice.

After meeting Blücher at La Belle Alliance, Wellington's ride back to Waterloo was a slow one, and yet during the 'half to three quarters of an hour'[1] that this took, he was not seen to utter one word to his much-depleted suite of officers. He was 'evidently sombre and dejected'[2] and the sense of loss was with him for some time afterwards. During the battle he had maintained his icy calm even though he had been described as looking paler than usual, but now with the battle gone and the excitement ebbing away he entered a period of profound blackness and depression.

This was of course a long time before the psychological effects of battle had been analysed and codified, even into anything as crude as 'shell-shock'. But Lt Basil Jackson, a staff officer who was among those who returned to Waterloo with Wellington that evening and fell asleep in the corner of the common room of the inn, recorded in some detail a vivid nightmare in which he 'beheld the chief incidents of the battle in distorted forms. There were furious attacks, and triumphant shouts as our battalions were overwhelmed.'[3] His nightmare found him in 'the midst of a vast mass of fugitives, who, strangely enough, belonged to the enemy's Imperial Guard'.[4] His horse shot from under him, he found himself in the grip of a French captain (a wounded man to whom he had given water and help earlier) and just as he was about to be run through by a gleaming blade he was woken by a fellow, British, officer. It is difficult to believe that Jackson was the only man to experience such vivid and haunting nightmares.

In the days before such things were acknowledged and treated there is no knowing how many men suffered from these and other sorts of symptoms following the trauma of such a battle. Indeed, given that Wellington was so mobile, always where the battle was thickest, it stands to reason that he saw a greater quantity and variety of death than any other man on the field that day. Perhaps the pallor indicated an inner revulsion that his almost mechanical sangfroid – his favourite means of dealing with difficult situations – had managed to keep at bay until the battle was over. Unlike Napoleon he was not careless with the lives of his men; unlike Napoleon he did not believe that he was following his destiny; instead he was a man doing his duty. And while his oft-quoted remark that the 'finger of providence' was on him that day and preserved him, he must have paid for it in private for years and years to come.

While he himself survived without so much as a nick, the Duke saw countless others around him fall wounded or dead. He was riding next to Uxbridge and talking to him when grapeshot passed over the neck of Wellington's horse and caught Uxbridge full in the leg – Wellington was so close that he supported Uxbridge in his saddle and stopped him falling. Tradition has it that Uxbridge looked down and remarked as coolly as possible: 'By God, sir, I've lost my leg!' at which Wellington looked away from the telescope and said: 'By God, sir, so you have!'[5] It is difficult to say whether this exchange actually took place, but in its exaggerated 'Dr-Livingstone-I-presume' coolness it sounds a little like a Victorian invention. Nevertheless, given the temperament of both men, it is possible that they spoke like this, even though the leg itself was not actually lost but so injured as to necessitate amputation. Moreover, it was late in the day and Uxbridge was among the last of the British to be hurt. Wellington had seen so many men he knew killed and maimed that he was, if not blasé, at least accustomed to seeing such wounds.

He was near Lord Fitzroy Somerset, whose wife had recently given birth to their first child Charlotte in Brussels, when a French musket ball fired from La Haye Sainte smashed into Somerset's right arm and knocked him off his horse. The arm had to be amputated. He was next to Sir William Howe De Lancey, whom he had called from his honeymoon to replace Hudson Lowe as Quartermaster-General (until Wellington's first choice could be recalled), when a cannon ball, a 'spent' one, knocked him from his horse (it was De Lancey who hit the ground with such force that he 'bounded up again into the air like a struck pheasant').[6] De Lancey was presumed mortally wounded and hauled from the battlefield in a blanket.

No wonder Wellington observed that 'The finger of Providence was upon me, and I escaped unhurt',[7] but as he marvelled at his good fortune he must have wondered if it had been bought at the expense of other men's limbs and lives, men who were his friends. Did he wonder in his quiet moments if he had, unknown to himself, been party to some ghastly Faustian pact? When it came to visiting the wounded and writing letters of condolence to people who were often personal friends, he surely felt a pang of guilt and wondered why he had been spared and others so close to him not.

The letters he wrote to the relatives of casualties who were close to him are freighted with his depression. Among those to whom he wrote the day after the battle was the Duke of Beaufort, to acquaint him with the wound sustained by his brother Fitzroy. 'Indeed the losses I have sustained have quite broken me down; and I have no feeling for the advantages we have acquired.'[8]

Rather than being conventional military platitudes offered to grieving families these letters appear to have been written with feeling and genuine sadness. 'I cannot express to you the regret and sorrow with which I look round me, and contemplate the loss I have sustained, particularly in your Brother,' he wrote to Lord Aberdeen on 19 June.

> The glory resulting from such actions, so dearly bought, is no consolation to me, and I cannot suggest it as any to you and his friends: but I hope it may be expected, that this last one has been so decisive, that no doubt remains that our exertions and individual losses will be rewarded by the

early attainment of our first object. It is then that the glory of the actions in which our friends and Relations have fallen will be some consolation for their loss.[9]

The writing of such letters and the concomitant re-enactment in his mind of the death and wounding of so many friends was grim work, and taking a break from his mournful duty to take a turn in the park with the Duke of Richmond and his daughter Lady Georgiana did little to raise his spirits. 'He looked very sad, and when we shook hands and congratulated him, he said "it is a dearly bought victory. We have lost so many fine fellows." My father asked him to dinner, but he refused.'[10] Watching Wellington speak to Richmond, Lord William Pitt Lennox was struck by a change in his appearance: 'how different were his look and voice, as in hurried tones he talked of the severe losses he had met with – of the deaths of those to whom he had been bound by the strongest ties of friendship and companionship in arms.'[11] Wellington's acute melancholy was remarked on by many. 'The Duke of Wellington never was known to be in such low spirits as he was in consequence of the blood shed at Waterloo,' wrote Lady Caroline Capel, 'which they say exceeded any that ever was shed at any other they remember.'[12]

Even in an age when valour and an almost congenital sense of duty were far less remarkable than they are a couple of centuries later, the level of sacrifice chilled Wellington. A man with a highly developed sense of duty, not least towards the men he commanded, he cannot have failed to feel a sense of guilt, even if he had little or nothing to reproach himself for – he had after all shared the peril if not discomfort of his soldiers and had placed himself in conspicuous danger throughout the battle.

The injuries sustained at Waterloo were terrible, as were the methods of treating them: heavy bleeding was cauterised by plunging the afflicted part of the body in boiling pitch. Bleeding was still widely practised, and often weakened already injured men. Amputation was regarded not so much as a final resort after attempts to save a limb had been exhausted, but as a preventative measure and in this, British practice was significantly different to the French, for reasons which Tomkinson of the cavalry explains:

> The wounded of a British army generally receive more attention than those of other nations. The French system is to run great risks with a man's life in hopes of saving a limb, from knowing that a soldier without a leg or arm is incapable of service, and probably a burthen to the State. With us, the practice is possibly too much in favour of hasty amputation.

There have been instances of officers saving their limbs, from not allowing the surgeon to operate, choosing rather to run the risk of losing their life than being cut [it is unsure whether Tomkinson intended a pun] out of their profession.[13]

Occasionally a soldier would refuse amputation, preferring to risk further complications than lose a limb. For instance Captain Garland of the 73rd had his thigh broken by a musket ball and amputation was judged to be imperative. However, he preferred to keep the limb and so complicated and difficult were his treatment, recuperation and rehabilitation, during which four inches of the damaged bone were removed, that he was the last injured officer to leave Brussels.

However, the majority submitted to the medical wisdom of the day. When Fitzroy Somerset was hit in the arm and it was amputated, he greeted the grisly operation with a stoicism and Spartan fortitude that seems remarkable. He was so silent during the amputation that someone nearby only realised that an operation had taken place when Somerset raised his voice to say: 'Hallo! don't carry away that arm till I've taken off my ring' – one given to him by his wife.[14] Another amputee is also recorded as having asked for the return of his arm, so that he could shake hands with it before it was disposed of.

However the most senior and celebrated amputee was Uxbridge. He was carried from the battle and returned to his headquarters in Waterloo, where the surgeons elected to amputate. 'Well gentlemen,' responded Uxbridge with characteristic phlegm, 'I thought so myself. I have put myself in your hands and, if it is to be taken off, the sooner it is done the better.'

Either before or very shortly after the operation he wrote a brief letter to his wife:

Dearest Cha,
Be bold, prepare for misfortune; I have lost my right leg. A miracle might have saved it but for the sake of you and my dear children I have taken the better chance of preserving my life.
God Bless you all.[15]

While preparations were being made, Uxbridge chatted about the battle with those of his staff who were present, and during the operation he neither moved nor complained. According to one who witnessed the surgery:

He said once perfectly calmly that he thought the instrument was not very sharp. When it was over, his nerves did not appear the least shaken and the surgeons said his pulse was not altered. He said, smiling, 'I have had a pretty long run, I have been a beau these forty-seven years and it would not be fair to cut the young men out any longer' and then asked us if we did not admire his vanity.[16]

However it seems that Uxbridge shared some of Tomkinson's concerns about over-eager amputation. Later, when Sir Hussey Vivian came to see how he was, he said: 'Vivian, take a look at that leg, and tell me what you think of it. Some time hence, perhaps, I may be inclined to imagine it might have been saved, and I should like your opinion on it.'[17] Sir Hussey inspected the severed limb and reassured his chief that it was indeed beyond saving.

While it may have been beyond saving, the leg took on a life of its own as a visitor attraction: instead of being disposed of among the mass of mangled limbs, it was interred with much solemnity by the owner of the house in which the operation was carried out, and a plaque put up to mark the leg's final resting place, placing it firmly on the Waterloo tourist trail. As the cult of Waterloo grew, even a bloodstain on a chair in the room where the leg was cut off became a venerated relic and when, in later life, Uxbridge, by then the Marquis of Anglesey, returned to the house with two of his sons, he found the table on which the operation had been conducted, and was so pleased that he ate his dinner at it.

Post-battle amputation was a ritual in the British Army during the Napoleonic wars. Costello, who had a finger removed at the socket, recalls: 'I remained in Brussels three days, and had ample means here, as in several other places, such as Salamanca, &c., for witnessing the cutting off of legs and arms.'[18] In his experience the French were less robust than the British in the way they took their medical treatment. In particular he recalled one veteran of the 1st Royal Dragoons who chewed tobacco throughout the amputation of an arm and held the injured limb during the operation.

Near to him was a Frenchman, bellowing lustily, while a surgeon was probing for a ball near the shoulder. This seemed to annoy the Englishman more than anything else, and so much so, that as soon as his arm was amputated, he struck the Frenchman a smart blow across the breech with the severed limb, holding it at the wrist, saying, 'Here, take that, and stuff it down your throat, and stop your damned bellowing!'[19]

Drastic though it might have been, the policy of prompt amputation ensured that many wounded men survived, although the quality of life 'enjoyed' by the more seriously injured can only be imagined. Harry Smith went to see a wounded friend who had already lost one arm in the Peninsula, and like Lord Fitzroy Somerset, had had his elbow shattered by a musket ball at Waterloo.

> The ball had dreadfully broken the elbow of the sound arm, and had passed right through the fleshy part of his back, while the broken bone of the arm previously shattered at Foz d'Aruz was still exfoliating, and very painful even after a lapse of years. I got hold of a surgeon, and his arm was immediately amputated. When dressed, he lay upon the stump, as this was less painful than the old exfoliating wound, and on his back he could not lie. He recovered, but was never afterwards able to feed himself or put on his hat, and died, Heaven help him, suddenly of dysentery.[20]

Tales of men losing both arms were not unusual, and worse still was the story of a nineteen-year-old driver in the German artillery who lost his arms and legs to become a 'branchless trunk'.[21]

However, these men were fortunate to receive prompt attention; many of the wounded lay on the battlefield for the better part of a week. It was not until 23 June that all the carriages in Brussels were requisitioned to go to the battlefield and collect the remaining wounded. Even so, there are accounts of casualties lying on the battlefield for almost as long as a fortnight.

Brussels was full: what hospital facilities there were were overwhelmed, and many wounded officers were returned to the houses in which they had been billeted, where some of them died while waiting for medical attention. The wounded of other ranks lay in the streets. The citizens of Brussels did their best, distributing food and drink, while hotels like the Hôtel d'Hollande laid straw in their courtyards to make the wounded more comfortable.

It may seem remarkable that many thousands of wounded men were left in the open for so long, at the mercy of the elements and looters, some of whom did not scruple to kill or maim the living in search of plunder. The story of a woman who cut off a wounded Prussian officer's fingers to steal his rings was far from out of the ordinary and there is an account of 'several patrols of Prussians shooting their own and the French wounded soldiers, who were beyond recovery'.[22]

But it must be remembered that the Allied Army was in pursuit of the remnants of the French Army. Although the outcome of the battle appeared to be conclusive, the extent of the victory had yet to become clear, and if the success was not followed through, the reputation of Napoleon was such that the Allied commanders might reasonably have feared him staging some form of desperate and dazzling counter-attack. Therefore only a limited number of personnel could be spared for the task of caring for the wounded, and this limited number seemed all the more pusillanimous when viewed in the context of the horrific new league of slaughter and maiming that characterised Waterloo.

'I had been over many a field of battle, but with the exception of one spot at New Orleans, and the breach of Badajos, I had never seen anything to be compared with what I saw,' recalled Harry Smith.

> At Waterloo the *whole* field from right to left was a mass of dead bodies. In one spot, to the right of La Haye Sainte, the French Cuirassiers were literally piled on each other; many soldiers not wounded lying under their horses; others, fearfully wounded, occasionally with their horses struggling upon their wounded bodies. The sight was sickening, and I had no means or power to assist them.[23]

The lines where French attacks had been halted suddenly by annihilating British fire were marked by rows of dead bodies, fallen in formation.

The density of corpses and wounded can only be imagined and it comes across in the smallest of details. For example William Hay, who was sent back to look for stragglers and wounded, said that 'on gaining the road it was with difficulty my horse could pick his way or keep his footing as it was literally paved with steel, the cuirasses were so numerous, shining and glittering, in the midday sun of June, making it quite dazzling to the eyesight'.[24] The field was littered with arms, armour and materiel which had been abandoned, and the morning after the battle, looking for somewhere to sit to enjoy his breakfast, Mercer simply stacked a load of cuirasses until they made a comfortable seat.

The scale of the problem was such that those who went to the battlefield could do little more than give sips of brandy from their flasks to the wounded lying thick on the ground, as they searched for their own loved ones. The gruesome and melancholy nature of this work can only be imagined as, with news of the victory spreading among the civilian population, soldiers' wives dashed to the battlefield to try to find their husbands.

While many officers' wives had moved to Antwerp for safety, the spouses of private soldiers and non-commissioned officers had often spent the battle only a little distance from the fighting, sometimes rushing onto the battlefield to rescue their wounded husbands, and sustaining injuries themselves. The most famous was the pregnant wife of a sergeant who was wounded trying to get her husband to safety. He lost his arms but survived, and miraculously she gave birth to a daughter to whom the Duke of York was godfather ... sadly she died a year or so after her birth.

Juana Smith, who had made her mad dash to Antwerp, was keen to set off to the battlefield in search of her husband.

> Seeing some of our Rifle soldiers, with an eagerness which may be imagined, I asked after my husband, when to my horror they told me that Brigade-Major Smith of the 95th was killed. It was now my turn to ask the 'Brass Mare' to gallop, and in a state approaching desperation I urged her to the utmost speed for the field of battle to seek my husband's corpse. The road from Brussels to the field almost maddened me, with wounded men and horses, and corpses borne forward to Brussels for interment, expecting as I was every moment to see that of my husband, knowing how he was beloved by officers and soldiers. The road was nearly choked which was to lead me to the completion, as I hoped, of my life; to die on the body of the only thing I had on earth to love.

Nearing the battlefield:

> I saw signs of newly dug graves, and then I imagined to myself, 'O God, he has been buried, and I shall never again behold him!' How can I describe my suspense, the horror of my sensations, my growing despair, the scene of carnage around me? From a distance I saw a figure lying; I shrieked, 'Oh, there he is!' I galloped on. 'No, it is not he! Find him I will, but whither shall I turn?'

Plainly hysterical, Juana Smith had the good fortune to meet 'a dear and mutual friend, Charlie Gore, A.D.C. to Sir James Kempt', who told her that her husband was 'as well as ever he was in his life; not wounded even, nor either of his brothers'. 'Oh, dear Charlie Gore, why thus deceive me? The soldiers tell me Brigade-Major Smith is killed.' It transpired that it was Smyth, not Smith, who had been killed. 'This sudden transition from my depth of grief and maddening despair was enough to turn my brain, but Almighty God sustained me.'[25] Thus the voluble and emotional Juana Smith's emotionally testing ride to the battlefield ended happily.

Another young wife, very different from the spirited Spanish-born Juana, was also setting out from Antwerp in search of her husband. And while from a totally different background to Juana Smith, the demure Lady De Lancey was experiencing exactly the same violent swings of emotion. On the morning of 19 June she learnt of the end of the battle, heard that her husband was safe and was 'almost in a fever with happiness'.[26] She then heard that he had in fact been desperately wounded, and set off on the difficult journey from Antwerp to Waterloo to find her husband. While *en route* she heard that he had in fact died.

Still she pressed on. 'When within ten miles of Brussels, the smell of gunpowder was very perceptible,'[27] she recalled, and the closer they got to Waterloo itself, the stronger the stench of death, so that 'the horses screamed at the smell of corruption, which in many places was offensive'.[28] The last stage of the journey from Brussels to Waterloo must have been particularly agonising for her as it took three and half hours to complete, and all the time she was turning over further reports she had received that her husband was both dead and alive. When she did finally arrive at Waterloo, Sir George Scovell, who had survived the battle after a series of near misses, including a cannon ball which passed straight through his cloak when his arm was raised and shaved the rump of his horse, told her that her husband was alive and that surgeons thought he would recover. The surgeons were wrong. She nursed him in a cell-like room in a Waterloo peasant's cottage for six days until he died, then she buried him and left for England on 4 July, three months to the day after she had got married.

During her journey out to Waterloo Lady De Lancey had been assisted by William Hay, who had acted as part bodyguard, part guide. Hay was a retired officer, one of the many English people with friends or relatives in the Army to have made the journey over to join in the social life afforded by Brussels in the summer of 1815. He had served with the 16th Light Dragoons in the Peninsula and had come over to spend time with his regimental friends and also to introduce his young brother, who had recently joined as a cornet. Like a number of more adventurous civilians he had spent much of the 18th of June at the battle as 'an amateur', 'but towards evening, the business becoming too hot for him, prudence dictated the necessity of his taking leave of his brother and making his own way to the rear of the army'.[29]

However, the day after the battle his visit lost all its pleasurable overtones when he found that his brother had gone missing. He searched among piles of dead and wounded but found nothing. Then he heard a rumour that Cornet Hay had been helping a wounded man back to Brussels, and galloped there to follow it up, but a few days later the search for the young man was resumed on the battlefield and in the end, unable to find his brother's body, Hay placed a memorial tablet in the church at Waterloo.

Given the horror of the scene it is hardly surprising that among the thousands of corpses, many horribly disfigured, looted of personal possessions and beginning to decompose in the heat, not all the dead could be identified or the remains of loved ones located. Even if the modern method of identifying corpses using dental records had been available, it would have been of only limited use, as corpses often had their teeth chiselled from their jaws, removed to be used as dentures.

Picking through the dead and dying was a grisly and daunting task, as Gronow's account makes clear.

Early on the morning after the battle of Waterloo, I visited Hougoumont, in order to witness with my own eyes the traces of one of the most hotly-contested spots of the field of battle. I first came upon the orchard, and there discovered heaps of dead men, in various uniforms: those of the Guards in their usual red jackets, the German Legion in green, and the French dressed in blue, mingled together. The dead and the wounded positively covered the whole area of the orchard; not less than two thousand men had there fallen. The apple-trees presented a singular appearance; shattered branches were seen hanging about their mother trunks in such profusion, that one might almost suppose the stiff-growing and stunted tree had been converted into the willow: every tree was riddled and smashed in a manner which told that the showers of shot had been incessant.[30]

As well as the tens of thousands of dead and wounded men, there were many thousand dead or wounded horses. One observer noted that those horses which were unable to move had eaten away the grass around them, leaving a bald circle.

Once again the proximity of the battlefield to a fashionable city brought about a unique state of affairs. As well as enabling soldiers to leave the ballroom, ride into battle and then, if they survived, ride back into town for some supper, a few hours' rest and a change of horses, it also enabled those civilians brave or foolish enough to want to, to witness the battle, and it meant that within less than twenty-four hours, long before the wounded and dead had been attended to, civilians were back on the battlefield.

Some, such as Lady De Lancey, were distressed relatives; but inevitably the scene of the battle drew the merely curious, many of whom started for the battlefield on hearing the news of the victory: 'we resolved to make up for our former retreat,' wrote one visitor to the Low Countries who had fled to Ostend during the fighting, 'by being among the first to contemplate the scene of action.'[31] On the morning of the 19th, at about the time that Wellington was trying to clear the gruesome and disturbing memories from his mind in order to write a cogent report, coaches of war tourists were already converging on the battlefield. Mercer was sitting down to a late breakfast when he saw a carriage pull up and a party descend; 'it was amusing to see the horror with which they eyed our frightful figures,' he recalled with grim humour, remembering in particular 'a smartly dressed middle-aged man, in a high cocked-hat' who 'approached holding a delicately white perfumed handkerchief to his nose; stepping carefully to avoid the bodies (at which he cast fearful glances *en passant*), to avoid polluting the glossy silken hose that clothed his nether limbs'.[32] The foppish visitor engaged the weary and filthy artillery troop in conversation, keeping the handkerchief under his nose. Mercer's description of the juxtaposition of fashion and slaughter is one image that encapsulates the surreal quality of all that had happened in the preceding days.

The elaborate politeness of the visitor, who leaves in 'a world of bows',[33] adds to the strangeness of the scene, heightens the short geographical but huge emotional gulf between Waterloo and Brussels, and also demonstrates the unease of a civilian visitor drawn ineluctably to the scene of slaughter, yet uncomfortable about his role as a civilian sightseer.

But once arrived, even with their olfactory nerves protected by scented silk and linen, not all sightseers could stand the battlefield. 'This morning I went to visit the field of battle,' wrote Frye on 22 June,

> but on arrival there the sight was too horrible to behold. I felt sick in the stomach and was obliged to return. The multitude of carcases, the heaps of wounded men with mangled limbs unable to move, and perishing from not having their wounds dressed or from hunger, as the Allies were, of course, obliged to take their surgeons and wagons with them, formed a spectacle I shall never forget.[34]

Creevey went to the battlefield on the 20th and surprised himself 'at not being more horrified at the sight of such a mass of dead bodies'.[35] While he was on the way out to the field he was overtaken by the Duke of Wellington who was on his way to visit the wounded on his staff, among them De Lancey. Once they arrived at Waterloo, where the names of staff officers, many of them dead or dying, were still chalked on the door of cottages where they had spent the night before the battle, Creevey was given a tour of the field by the portly Lord Arthur Hill. As they picked their way among the casualties, Hill dispensed brandy and water to the French wounded, apologising to one sergeant of the Imperial Guard for not moving him sooner, but explaining that there were so many Allied wounded to take care of.

The magnitude of the slaughter, especially given the compact size of the battlefield, was simply too much for many to take in. Moreover disposing of the large number of corpses presented a serious risk to public health – 'in the court-yard it is said they have been obliged to burn upwards of a thousand carcases,'[36] wrote Frye of the manner in which Hougoumont was cleared of its dead. For some time an estimated 3,000 corpses lay unburied on the ramparts of Brussels and by the 22nd the 'smell arising from the carcasses [was] insufferable'.[37] The British who had been piling into the city so enthusiastically a week before, now started moving away for fear of pestilence. Mass burials were carried out, but these were sloppy, hurried affairs, with hands and feet left poking out of the ground.

When Charlotte Eaton visited the battlefield almost a month later she was struck by the 'confined space'.[38] The scene she describes is not much changed. She almost faints at the sight of a human skull visible through the earth, and she is paralysed with shock at the sight of a hand almost clean of flesh 'outstretched above the ground, as if it had raised itself from the grave'.[39] She even says that piles of human ashes were still smoking as locals endeavoured to get rid of the dead one way or another.

> The countrymen told us, that so great were the numbers of the slain, that it was impossible entirely to consume them. Pits had been dug, into which they had been thrown, but they were obliged to be raised far above the surface of the ground. These dreadful heaps were covered with piles of wood, which were set on fire, so that underneath the ashes lay numbers of human bodies unconsumed.[40]

Yet appalled as she feels by the scene, she cannot resist taking a few macabre souvenirs: among them a broken sword bought from a peasant and some human ashes wrapped in one of the pieces of paper – letters or pages of discarded novels and bibles – blowing about the battlefield.

dance with you any more except with a wooden leg.' And, after leaving Brussels on the 16th, able-bodied soldiers had marched on to pursue the enemy to Paris.

After the initial chaos and lack of preparation, the wounded were well cared for, with doctors coming from England, and after intense days of yet more amputations many of those who survived the first week or two began to make good progress. Order established itself and the recovering wounded were spread out across the Kingdom of the United Netherlands. Four weeks later straw was being laid on the streets outside hospitals, but this time it was not to accommodate the wounded, instead it was intended to deaden the sound of horses' hooves and carriage wheels.

Uxbridge was recovering rapidly. He spent only a few days in bed, after which he got up every day as normal. His recovery was helped by the presence of his wife Char, who had come over as soon as she had received the letter he had written at the time of the amputation. Before the family friend who had delivered the letter could get a word out, she had screamed: 'He is dead!',[2] so when she was reassured that this was not the case, news of the loss of his leg came almost as a relief. Even though polite society had shunned her since her adultery and subsequent marriage, she still had powerful friends who were not bothered by the taint of scandal – or were so scandal-tainted themselves that it would have been hypocritical to snub her – and she was able to get to her husband's sickbed quickly, because the Prince Regent gave her the use of the royal yacht.

Given the notoriously inaccurate information that wives such as Juana Smith and Lady De Lancey had received, Char's anxiety as she entered the house of the Marquis d'Assche where her husband was recuperating must have been tremendous. However hers was to be one of the happier Waterloo reunions; 'instead of being ushered into his *dark bed room as we all expected*, I came into a large drawing room, and saw the dear little fellow sitting up in an arm chair looking as lively or *more lively than ever* for I never saw him *with whiskers* before & they are beyond!'[3] Typically the 'dear little fellow' disobeyed instructions to keep quiet: he was quite restless and insisted on frequent changes of scene, being carried between one of his four beds. And then there were the visitors: 'he was *to see nobody*, but they *will all* come in – The Dukes of Richmond & Bedford have been in & lots of other people, amongst the rest Lady Caroline, Mr Capel and Georgina.'[4]

However there was one notable absence: it seemed to Char that Wellington could have been more interested in the recovery of his cavalry chief and grateful for what the loyal wife saw as her husband's charismatic leadership on the field. Even if Uxbridge himself was not too bothered by

Wellington's apparent indifference, she seems to have suspected a resumption of the Wellesley family's former hostility.

> He is so generous about the expressions or rather *no expressions* in the Gazette. He says he is sure the Duke means kindly and appreciates him which is enough for *him*, but *not* so for us, however he begs and entreats & [unclear] that none of you will say any thing on the subject – He says the Duke has a cold dry manner about every thing, but that he is perfectly satisfied with his public as well as private conduct – for the first, he declares at [*sic*] his opinion that no other man alive would have gained that victory, & for the latter that he has universally behaved to him with the greatest friendship & most unbounded confidence.[5]

Even when Uxbridge did receive a letter, Char judged it to be too little too late: 'Get* has just had a most kind letter from him – nothing I say can nor do I wish to *justify* him, but at least it palliates.'[6] And she exhibits touching uxorial loyalty when she writes of the cavalry: 'I rather wish they may disgrace themselves the next time they are called upon, especially if Ld. Combermere is sent to them.'[7]

His wife's letters, written as he gained strength, show a touching relationship based not on lust, as the more colourful accounts of the initial stages of their affair would have it – it will be recalled that one observer had wished for 'some huge Paddy to satisfy her lust and outdo Paget' – but apparently on a deep and touching love. It is charming to read of one of the most senior of British Army officers described as 'the dear little fellow & his Cavalry',[8] terms which would not be out of place describing a young child and his toy soldiers. She writes movingly of the happiness she derives from 'looking at his dear face'[9] while he dozes, describing him as 'looking so interesting & so lovely'.[10]

However even at such a time the stigma of their marital arrangement, which attached itself mainly to Char, was inescapable. Uxbridge's sister Lady Caroline Capel would be forced to come into contact with his wife – it was not a meeting that Caroline anticipated with any pleasure. Shortly before they were to meet, news reached Lady Caroline that Uxbridge had been made the Marquis of Anglesey. 'I rejoice that Paget has this honor [*sic*],' she wrote to her mother, 'but I am sorry to have dear Old Uxbridge sunk into a Second Title – & again I rejoice that [Lady Uxbridge†] will no longer bear the same name with your pure, virtuous, precious Self.'[11] For

---

* Presumably a shortened form of Paget and a nickname for Uxbridge.
† i.e. Char.

her part, Char was understandably bitchy about the Capels: 'little Jane is exceptionally pretty,' she wrote but 'the girls are in my opinion any thing but handsome'.[12]

Nevertheless it seems that Uxbridge's sister and wife were civil to each other, with Char even writing of going to visit the Capels at Walcheuse. He appears not to have let much bother him and he became stronger and healthier with each passing day: 'all the surgeons declare they never saw such an instance before, and attribute it all to his calmness & fortitude.'[13] However the sight of her husband hobbling into the park was almost too much for Char:

> it is too cruel to see him! That beautiful creature whom one has been used to see jumping and more active than any body, it is I say too cruel to see him upon crutches! & that without any apparent discontent in him, but he does it all with the same composure that he used to get upon his horse! indeed, indeed it requires all *my fortitude* (which you know is pretty strong) to bear it without his seeing it – I am generally obliged to go away when he requires to be moved, it is so heart breaking, and yet I *know* I ought not to suffer one moments [*sic*] repining after all I have heard – more and more every day – of his *dreadful* gallantry.[14]

However the crutches were not a success, as he wrote to his children: 'I am carried out into the Park every day where I stay several hours to breathe fresh air. I made an attempt to use crutches but it w'd. not do, I am not quite strong enough for them, but I hope in a few days to be able to use them.'[15] Nevertheless the 'dear little fellow' was doing well enough to talk of moving back to England in a few days.

As Uxbridge was clearly out of danger, Char paid a visit to the Fitzroy Somersets.

> I have seen Emily Somerset & her dear little baby, such a pretty little thing – she has been obliged to wean it in the middle of all this bustle and misery – conceive her feelings, who sat in this town & heard all the cannonading of the action in which her husband was! He looks much worse than Get does, and his arm is not near so forward towards recovery – they are coming too to England directly.[16]

Lord Fitzroy was described as 'a great deal thinner than he was',[17] and suffering from such pain that he found himself 'unequal to the exertion' of writing his own letters and instead dictated them to Emily. However he ascribed the pace of his recovery to the method of treatment. 'My wound is going on as well as possible & the increase of pain to be attributed to the mode only of dressing the wound which the Surgeon is anxious to heal and with that view has brought together more closely since Saturday.'[18]

On 28 June he felt strong enough to try to write a letter to his mother. Even though short, barely more than 100 words, the strain of writing this note is plain, as the quality of the script, written with his left hand and considerable effort, deteriorates noticeably over the two pages. He does his best to allay his mother's fears, claiming that he gets 'stronger daily' and that he does 'not suffer more pain than is usual in such cases'. He mentions that he intends to leave Brussels in '8 or 9' days, and estimates that he will be in London on 11 or 12 July, and it is with this news that the seriousness of his wound and the effect it is has had on him becomes evident, as he adds that 'it may be as well for both parties, if we don't meet, till I shall have recovered from the fatigues of the voyage'.[19]

Just as he was thoughtful about the effect his appearance would have on his mother, so he was inclined to be philosophical about his injury:

> Having been at the D. of Wellington's side in every action which he has fought since the year 1808 it certainly would have been gratifying if I could have continued by him to the last, but when I reflect upon the valuable lives that were lost at the Battle of Waterloo, that many indeed of those who have for years been fighting under him were killed on that occasion, I feel that I must not repine at the loss of an arm, but rather that I should thank Providence for the preservation of my life, amid so many dangers.[20]

In early July, before they made the journey back to England, Char and Emily set off to visit the battlefield in Uxbridge's barouche. Char wanted to see where her husband had lost his leg, Emily the place where her husband had parted company with his arm.

> We went to the two houses in Waterloo where their poor limbs were amputated *just opposite each* other, & the dear old woman (a farmer's wife) where Get was taken cried when she talked about him – She said he *was so good*, & bore it so well. She took me into the garden to show me where his poor dear *dear* leg was buried, & she has promised me to plant a tree over the spot.[21]

By this time the dead were buried and the smoking mound of smouldering corpses that Charlotte Eaton noticed a fortnight later was already burning. Although the battlefield was strewn with 'caps, helmets & different bits & scraps of all sorts', anything of value had been carried off, but Char came away with a souvenir.

Lady Fitzroy and I have each got some grape that [we] picked up there, &
one of mine is the exact size that wounded your beloved Papa – it just fits
the hole in his Cossacks which he wore that day – I need not tell you that
I have saved them also, but the poor old farmer I have before mentioned
(where he lived) would keep the boot, & offered two Guineas for it.[22]

A fortnight after the battle, the market in Waterloo souvenirs was already
rising, and by the time that the Misses Capel visited the battlefield, in
August, accompanied by the Duke of Richmond, the boot would be
an important prop in what might be called the 'Uxbridge amputation
experience' ... along with the bloodstained bedding on which he had lain.
The Capel girls also noted that the spot where the leg was buried would
shortly be marked with a stone that was being carved in Brussels. The site
of battle was already on its way to becoming a major tourist attraction.

Almost immediately after her visit to the battlefield Char accompanied
her husband home. They arrived at Ostend on 6 July and found that the
Admiralty had sent a yacht to bring them back.

There was a rumour that Brussels would once again become a centre of
pleasure and parties, as it was suggested that it might play host to the
reconvened Congress. However it was restarted in Vienna. Just as the
wounded were leaving the city, so were the more socially ambitious civilians;
some headed to Spa, others made for France.

With the swift collapse of French resistance and the capture of Napoleon
the social nexus had shifted abruptly from Brussels and relocated to Paris.
The Duke of Wellington and his entourage had trundled out of Brussels
in five carriages:

> the first was the Duke's carriage with four horses, driven by Head coach-
> man, the second was a carriage for the plate, with the Butler and his
> Assistants, driven by the second coachman. The third was a sort of carriage
> for the kitchen furniture, with myself and my assistants, the fourth was
> the old Nelson with the coachman's baggage, the fifth was the Duke's
> curricle, drawn by two horses, and there were two led horses ridden by the
> coachman's lads. These were all independent of the Saddle Horses, the
> Duke rode on horseback all the way.[23]

According to his cook, this motley caravan arrived in Paris 'the first
week in July'[24] and by the end of July Wellington was once more inhabiting
the highly social and doubtless highly sexed persona that he had presented
to the world in Brussels during the summer. On 1 August he gave a grand
ball, attended by Allied leaders and the flabby Louis XVIII, who had

returned puffing and wheezing to his throne after his sabbatical in Ghent. Also present was a heavily pregnant Lady Frances Wedderburn-Webster who was spotted chatting to another Regency femme fatale, Lady Caroline Lamb; each sat either side of the Duke of Wellington. Lady Frances was out of commission for a few days in August to give birth to her child, but soon she was back in the ballrooms, leading the pack of women who chased Wellington until he was joined by his wife in October and things had to be toned down . . . a little.

The poor Duchess of Richmond missed out on this frantic socialising. By the end of July she was still in Brussels in 'a grand fuss to get to Paris' while the Duke was said to be 'very much adverse'.[25] It was not until October that the Duke, Duchess and four of their daughters went to Paris – it can only be imagined how the Duchess bore the wait. And her mood cannot have been improved by the news that her daughter Lady Sarah Lennox had eloped with the Guards' commander in Paris, General Maitland, with whom she had conducted an affair in Brussels. There was more bad news for the Duchess when her daughter Lady Mary announced her intention to marry 'Sir Henry Bradford, an almost pennyless [*sic*] Colonel in the Guards'.[26] As Georgiana Capel wrote mischievously, 'The Duchess's high flown hopes are dashed to the Ground, & will not I fear improve her *gentle* temper.'[27] It was enough to have the Duke of Richmond say 'he had been long enough in Paris and wish'd himself back, and at Brussels'.[28]

Meanwhile back in Brussels at the end of the year some of the indiscretions during the frenzied period of pleasure were still coming to light. Lady Caroline eventually discovered that her gambling-addict husband had managed to run up substantial debts at the covert games organised under the cover of the 'Literary Club'. The Capels stayed in Brussels for another year, long enough to witness the first anniversary celebrations of Waterloo, before moving to continue their nomadic existence on the economical plan in Switzerland.

By that time the Duke of Wellington's relationship with Lady Frances Wedderburn-Webster had passed from being an open secret in high society to being public knowledge. The relationship had leaked into the press and Lady Frances's husband, who only returned to the Continent in August 1815, had apparently confronted Wellington, who convinced him there was nothing in it. However Webster sued the owner of one paper for libel, seeking £50,000 damages for the outrageous slur that his wife had committed adultery with the Duke of Wellington. Given the advanced state of her pregnancy there is some question as to exactly what the level of physical intimacy was, but there is little doubt that the Duke was besotted with this young girl.

The trial was a masterful whitewash. Neither Wellington nor the Wedderburn-Websters were called as witnesses, but the victor of Waterloo was handsomely protected by his friend the Duke of Richmond, who presented Lady Frances as a woman of impeccable virtue, completely incapable of an immoral act, and with whom, he added, he and his Duchess had been quite happy to leave their unmarried daughter ... even after reading the newspaper reports.

In the end the Wedderburn-Websters received £2,000 (comfortably in excess of £100,000 today) in damages: a tidy sum, but only 4 per cent of what they had sought. Later events showed that Lady Frances was incapable of remaining faithful to her husband for long – he even challenged one of her lovers to a duel. She died in 1837, although the scandal still rumbled on, with letters written to her by the Duke surfacing a year after her death and Wellington having to buy them and allegedly burn them, saying: 'I was a damned fool when I wrote those letters.'[29]

EPILOGUE

In addition to being chilly, June 1852 was shaping up to be one of the wettest ever. As the rain poured down on mid-nineteenth-century England, the England of Victoria and her Prince Consort, the England of railways and electoral reform, there must have been many times when the aged Duke of Wellington's mind drifted back to that sodden Saturday thirty-seven years earlier when he had decided to meet Napoleon head on just outside Brussels.

The intervening years had seen the philandering, dandified, successful general, surrounded by his noisy 'family' of aristocratic officers, turned into a national monument. He had served as Prime Minister on two occasions and had officiated at three coronations. Wellington's memories of the events on that distant June weekend, and indeed Wellington himself, had become the property of the nation. He was a living connection to the old days and the old ways; seemingly every bit as permanent as the numerous sculptures raised in his honour.

From the back of Apsley House, his splendid London residence, he could see the most controversial one every day; a twenty-foot-high bronze representation of a naked Achilles made from cannon captured by him, and erected by the 'women of England' to honour 'Arthur Duke of Wellington and his brave companions in arms'. Every year on the anniversary of the battle the Duke could expect another national flurry of recognition. This year the burghers of Edinburgh had honoured Wellington with what one newspaper called 'a colossal bronze equestrian statue', 'the first bronze statue, ever cast in Scotland' and 'one of the most striking objects in that romantic and beautiful city'.[1] Although the bronze of the Duke on his charger giving orders was a few feet shorter than the Achilles, together with its pedestal of good Aberdeen granite, it towered twenty-six feet over the citizens of the Athens of the north.

Almost four decades after his greatest triumph, a grateful nation was still expressing its thanks with public sculptures – and there was of course the sumptuous annual Waterloo banquet. The dining room at Apsley house could only accommodate three dozen diners in comfort: perfect for intimate supper parties, but hardly suitable for an event such as the Waterloo banquet, or at least that was what the Duke must have been thinking when in the late 1820s he decided to add on the stunning Waterloo Gallery.

The effect of all the accumulated trophies and gifts put out on display on the evening of 18 June 1852 in this long, high-ceilinged room was simply dazzling. The single table, at which the eighty-five diners sat, creaked under the weight of towering candelabra and impressive gewgaws such as the Portuguese plateau, a monstrous creation in silver that alone occupied twenty-six feet of the table with its allegorical figures and various other decorative effusions. There were flower-filled vases of Potsdam porcelain (the gift of a grateful, now dead, Prussian king); silver gilt statuettes by the late Count d'Orsay depicting Wellington and Napoleon; and sundry other costly decorative items crammed onto every flat surface. The light that sparkled and danced off this bravura collection of trinkets beamed from chandeliers that had been the gift of the late Alexander Tsar of Russia.

By 1852 the Waterloo banquet was a noted tourist attraction. As the battle receded into history, the banquet gained in importance and totemic significance. Britain was beginning to flex its imperial muscle and Waterloo had become an important part of the national myth. From being a get-together of veterans, the banquet had acquired the status of a state occasion. Special passes allowed visitors to traipse through the house on the morning of the big day to see the room being set up, and during the afternoon, such was the number of sightseers and well-wishers, that a large number of another post-Waterloo invention, the police (in an earlier age, crowd control had been the job of the 'Piccadilly Butchers', the Horse Guards), was deployed. Despite the large crowds there were no disturbances and from half-past six, when the first guests arrived, the air was filled with cheers, mingled with the sound of the full band of the Grenadier Guards who played in the vestibule.

As popular characters such as Major-General Sir Harry Smith of the Rifle Brigade arrived, loud cheers went up, with the most rapturous reception being reserved for the gallant one-legged Marquis of Anglesey, a Field

Marshal since 1846. Anglesey's charisma and vitality remained undimmed, however he was now just as hard of hearing as the Duke of Wellington: the raised voices of the two deaf old men trying to communicate with each other often distracted attention from debates in the House of Lords. As well as the one-legged Anglesey there was the one-armed Major-General Lord Fitzroy Somerset, still loyally serving his old chief – he was now military secretary to the Commander-in-Chief, none other than Wellington, who been reappointed to the post in the 1840s. Other figures, perhaps not so prominent in the public imagination, included Colonel Whinyates, whose rockets had caused as much consternation among the British as their enemies, and Sir George Scovell, the code-breaker and employer of teenage groom Edward Heeley, who was now Governor of the Royal Military College.

At five minutes past seven the Prince Consort arrived with Wellington's nephew the Hon. Rev. Gerald Wellesley, private chaplain to the Queen. And at 7.30 precisely (in contrast to the inexact timekeeping of the Waterloo era, trains in the mid-nineteenth century ran on Greenwich Mean Time and in 1852, an electronic device conveyed G.M.T. by telegraph throughout the country), the Duke and the Prince Consort led the veterans into dinner.

Unlike the ad hoc nature of the refreshments available on the eve of battle, the culinary arrangements for the banquets at Apsley House had become increasingly elaborate. For the banquet of 1852 'all the plate used at the dessert was of gold; the service to the guests was of Dresden china, a present from one of the European potentates'.[3]

After struggling through dozens of dishes, Wellington called upon his guests to fill their glasses, gave the toast: 'the Queen', and the military band in the next room, which had been playing waltzes and snatches of Donizetti during dinner, struck up the National Anthem. The Prince Consort then stood and gave 'The health of the noble Duke our distinguished host' – a toast greeted with loud cheers and which was drunk 'with three times three, the band playing "See the Conquering Hero Comes"'.[4] There then followed toasts to almost every branch of the Army involved on that day from the cavalry (apparently Wellington's opinion of the mounted troops had mellowed with age, and 'he spoke in most complimentary terms of the services of that portion of the army')[5] to the King's German Legion. The recipient of the toast stood and made a speech of thanks amidst much cheering. For old men, they made quite a racket.

The toasts finished, the party moved to the salon for coffee and tea and at a quarter to eleven the Prince Consort's departure signalled the end of the evening. However the octogenarian Wellington was far from finished; having packed off his guests, he called for his carriage and, in spite of the unpleasant weather, went on to receptions given by the Marchioness of Salisbury and the Duchess of Beaufort.

The banquet had been a huge success, as *The Times* noted the following morning: 'On no previous anniversary was there such a throng of visitors.'[6] Indeed it would be the banquet that attracted the largest number of spectators as it was the last to be held: within three months the Duke of Wellington was dead.

The annual Waterloo banquet demonstrated how much Britain had changed and how little the Duke of Wellington had changed with it. Even the style of entertaining, with all the plate on display, smacked of an earlier age: he had had mahogany cases made in which to display his flatware and it has been suggested that he had copied this style from the Prince Regent.[7] *The Times* reported that Wellington had said: 'there was no occasion to remind the public of bygone transactions, but of this he was confinent [*sic*], that should an emergency arise, of which he was happy to say there was no prospect at present, the officers and army, would do their duty as they had done before.'[8]

However, the world in which the British Army would have to do its duty had changed, partly as a result of Waterloo and partly in spite of it. Waterloo had cleared away the remnants of Napoleon's 'Continental System', but the European order that was supposed to replace it, and for which so many thousands had given their lives, had also disappeared in the years between the battle and the final banquet. Revolt in 1830 destroyed the artificial Kingdom of the United Netherlands and there followed the foundation of the Kingdom of Belgium, independent of both the Dutch and French, under the rule of Prince Leopold of Saxe-Coburg-Gotha who was crowned Leopold I. The same year the Bourbon dynasty ceased to rule France and was replaced by the Orléanist King Louis-Philippe, who in turn had been swept off his throne by the revolutionary upheaval that ripped through Continental Europe in 1848, dislodging, among others, Metternich from Vienna. The chief irony was that there was once more a Napoleon on the throne in France, Napoleon III, nephew* of the man who, defeated by Wellington, had died on St Helena in 1821.

Although prepared for unrest, through electoral reform and the repeal of the Corn Laws, Britain's rulers had defused enough of the discontent to

---

*His mother was married to a younger brother of Napoleon I; there is, however, speculation about the identity of his biological father.

survive 1848 unscathed. Now, instead of involving itself too closely in Europe, Britain concentrated on shaping its empire. For instance, the British view of India, where Wellington first distinguished himself militarily half a century earlier, had almost completed its change from the amoral one of a lucrative trading zone, to a colony which the British felt a duty to 'improve', 'educate', and govern. Britain's commercial zeal was no longer naked, having acquired imperialist clothing and morals.

This is not to say that Wellington deliberately ignored change – he was so fascinated by the Great Exhibition, which demonstrated how almost every aspect of life had altered since the Regency, that he had been one of the most frequent visitors. He had also supported Catholic Emancipation in spite of his own views. But the Waterloo generation was, inevitably, out of step with this world, and trapped inside the mythology that had grown up around the last clash with Napoleon.

The problem was that men who had fought and won a battle in a very different age were still in charge of Britain's armed forces halfway through the century. As well as getting rid of Napoleon, Waterloo validated and cemented the power of the British aristocracy: the more impressive the mythology about the battle, the braver and more heretical one would have had to have been to challenge it. Any defender of the *status quo* would only have to point to the victory – which although a close-run thing, had been decisive in its effect – and to the peace, which the Duke had struggled to his feet on the evening of 18 June 1852 to celebrate.

In his wonderful book about nineteenth-century England, *The Victorians*, A.N. Wilson contrasts the dated attitudes of Wellington and his circle with the changes around them. Writing of the 'old belligerent attitude to Europe', which many saw as being 'replaced by international concord based on commerce', Wilson explains that 'to the end of his days he [Wellington] took seriously his duties as warden of the Cinque Ports, the guardian of England against Continental invasion. Long after the threat of a French invasion had become, to say the least, unlikely, he had strengthened fortifications on the south coast.'[9]

Such an attitude is understandable in a man who throughout his twenties, thirties and forties had viewed Revolutionary and then Napoleonic France as dangerous and then downright hostile. And those younger members of his 'family', such as Lord Fitzroy Somerset, had grown up with a view of France as at best unstable. This book is certainly not a military history, but it has been observed elsewhere that the legacy of Waterloo was an Army that was humiliated in the Crimea.

While Wellington may have confidently stated that the Army and officers would do their duty if the need arose, he did not live to see the war against the Russians three years after his death. This time Britain's allies were the Turks and the French, which made Lord Raglan's [Fitzroy Somerset's] habit, picked up during his youth, of calling the French the enemy a little awkward.[10] Some accounts of the Crimea would have been recognisable to those who fought at Waterloo forty years earlier: officers amused themselves by going duck shooting even at the risk of getting killed by Russian snipers, attending race meetings, one of which was mistaken for an impending attack by the Russians, or just wandering around in flashy clothes, one officer cutting an astonishing figure in a red flannel suit.

And of course the pointless valour of the charge of the Light Brigade echoes the behaviour of the cavalry about which Wellington used to complain. Time may have moved on since Waterloo, but many aspects of Wellington's Army remained. Many of the same systems prevailed, such as the tradition of aristocratic patronage about which Morris complained in his account of military service in the Netherlands; and they were not all good for a professional Army.

The war cost the life and reputation of Lord Raglan, but many aspects of the template established by Waterloo were applied to the Crimea. The acts of reckless gallantry were similar in character to the battle of Waterloo and although this time the outcome was very different, they were still viewed in the same way: commemorated on canvas and in verse as noble deeds, almost as intrinsic victorious actions, whatever the military result.

Without Wellington the aristocratic officer caste was shown to be a collection of elderly incompetents, whose personal rivalries, individual ambitions and inability to communicate led to such catastrophes as the charge of the Russian battery at Balaclava by the Light Brigade. This military disaster was presented by Palmerston, then Prime Minister, as a triumph of almost Wellingtonian dimensions and a vindication of the aristocratic principle. Whether or not the invocation was conscious, his speech in the House of Commons bristled with the Waterloo spirit.

Talk to me of the aristocracy of England! Why, look to that glorious charge of the cavalry at Balaklava – look to that charge, where the noblest and wealthiest of the land rode foremost, followed by the heroic men from the lowest classes of the community, each rivalling the other in bravery, neither the peer who led nor the trooper who followed being distinguished the one from the other. In that glorious band there were sons of the gentry of England, leading were the noblest in the land, and following were the representative of the people of this country.[11]

By the end of this encomium 300 members of parliament were on their feet cheering and the Earl of Cardigan, a violent lecher who had led the charge, returned to England a hero.

On the battlefield the sense of war as a surreal form of aristocratic sport was heightened by the invitation, after Balaclava had been pounded to rubble, from the British to the Russian officers to a dinner that would not have disgraced the dining table at Apsley House. Dishes included 'Filets de turbot clouté à la dame Blanche', 'le dindonneau farci à l'anglaise', 'le gannet garni d'ortolans à la Victoria' and 'The Crimean cup à la Marmora'.[12] The Russians were impressed that the British could conjure up such a magnificent banquet in such inhospitable surroundings.

The growing empire needed heroes, and the wars of the nineteenth century supplied them; it is interesting to see which elements of the Waterloo story were highlighted as the nineteenth century wore on.

Lady De Lancey's journal became a sentimental classic. Sir Walter Scott professed 'high admiration of the contents of this heartrending diary'[13] and Charles Dickens said: 'If I live for fifty years, I shall dream of it every now and then, with the most frightful reality.'[14]

Even after the last combatant, a private called Morris Shea, died aged ninety-seven in Canada in 1892, late-nineteenth-century newspapers still had an appetite for Waterloo stories. There remained a handful of people who had been present at Waterloo, albeit as infants, toddlers, or children of soldiers, and their fragmentary memories were treasured by a public that revered the Waterloo mythology that had grown up in the decades since the battle. Such stories kept appearing until the early years of the twentieth century; for instance 'Notes and Queries' published the following snippet on 5 December 1903:

> Elizabeth Watkins, of Norwich, born 31st January 1810 at Beaminster, near Bridport. Her father, one Daniel Gale, was pressed into the King's Service just before Waterloo. Gale's wife and child followed him to Brussels and were in the women's camp near the field of Waterloo. The child remembers cutting up lint – saw many dead, and some stirring incidents of the battle.

During the Victorian era into which many of the combatants survived, and by whose standards many of their recollections were coloured, many of the men, flawed as human beings have a tendency to be, were deified. Wellington became the greatest Englishman ever ... until that post was taken by Sir Winston Churchill. Wellington was elevated by the situations in which he found himself until he became a great but two-dimensional figure, a symbol rather than a person. He reacted to history; he did not make it in the way that Napoleon did. But this does not minimise his achievements nor the remarkable loyalty and confidence his chilly public persona inspired in those whom he led to victory after victory, in India, the Peninsula and then Waterloo. However, these achievements are, if anything, more intriguing when viewed in the context of the rounded figure of the whole man: the snob, the married man who went off to canoodle with Lady Frances Wedderburn-Webster in the park in Brussels and the man who got down on his hands and knees to play with the children at the Duke and Duchess of Richmond's rented 'Wash House'.

Indeed the 'Wash House' is appropriate in that it can also be said to refer to the laundering effect of the Waterloo myth on many reputations. Charismatic, intelligent, popular and valorous as he was, the Earl of Uxbridge was seen by many as a flawed commander. Of his conduct during the brief campaign of June 1815, one observer had this damning verdict: 'I think the result to the Duke must be, that Lord Uxbridge is too young a soldier to be much relied on with a separate command, from a feeling that he will risk too much in a desire to do something.'[15] Instead he was hailed a hero and pushed one rung further up the aristocracy from earl to marquis. The fact that he was an aristocrat and a friend of the Prince of Wales, maimed by a wound sustained at the moment of victory, would have made it difficult for him to be regarded as anything other than a great Englishman. Moreover his personality was one that many warmed to, so questions as to his suitability as a responsible leader were obscured or just dropped.

One of the most interesting examples of the 'Waterloo washes whiter than white' phenomenon is to be found among the non-commissioned officers of the cavalry.

Corporal John Shaw was the pugnacious prizefighter who was adopted as a sort of regimental mascot by the 2nd Life Guards. Although Shaw's is not a name that springs to the lips of anyone asked to name the heroes of Waterloo today, it was, at least according to the Deeds of Daring Library of September 1876, very different during the Victorian era, when 'by those of his own position in life the name of the gallant Guardsman has been at least as much associated with the battle of Waterloo as that of Wellington himself. Indeed, in many popular panoramas of the great battle, it is the Corporal, not the Field Marshal, who is the most conspicuous figure.'[16] Apparently the explanation for this was simply that 'the mass of the nation are incapable of appreciating the marvelous combination of military talent in the Great Duke'.[17] So in effect the Corporal was a working-class hero: while the aristocracy had the Duke of Wellington, the common people had men like the corporal, and by the last quarter of the nineteenth century Corporal Shaw had been sanitised.

The Deeds of Daring Library is stirring in its account of Shaw's prowess: 'He had been foremost among his brave comrades the whole day, and is said to have slain a fabulous number of Frenchmen, receiving, however, numerous sword-cuts in the course of the fight.'[18]

Then comes the description of his death:

In the melée he found himself isolated, and surrounded by *ten* of the enemy's horsemen. Whirling his good blade swiftly around, he for a time keeps his foes at bay. At length his sword breaks in his hand; but Shaw will not give in, he tears his helmet from his head, and tries to use it as a cestus. The Cuirassiers now close in upon him, and the heroic Guardsman is struck to the earth, and they ride off exulting in the thought that they have at length avenged the hecatomb of Frenchmen who have fallen victims to Shaw's slaughtering right hand.[19]

It is all great stuff, full of dash and heroism, and doubtless an inspiring example to all late nineteenth-century working-class men who wanted to join the Army, but rather different from the account given by one who saw Shaw at Waterloo. Thomas Morris recalled having 'Shaw, the fighting man, of the Life Guards' pointed out to him:

we little thought then, that he was about to acquire such celebrity. He drank a considerable portion of the raw spirit; and, under the influence of that, probably, he soon afterwards left his regiment, and running 'a-muck' at the enemy, was cut down by them as a madman.

I admire, as much as any man can do, individual acts of bravery, but Shaw certainly falls very far short of my definition of the term *hero*. The path of duty is the path of safety; and it is quite likely that Shaw, if he had remained with his regiment, might have exercised his skill, courage, and stamina, quite as effectively against the foe, without the certainty of losing his own life; and to rush, in such a way, on to certain death, was, in my opinion, as much an act of suicide, as if he had plunged with this horse from the cliffs of Dover. In 'union there is strength'; but if every man were to follow Shaw's example – quit his regiment – there would be an end to all discipline, and consequently, to all chance of success.[20]

Depending which account you believe, Shaw was either cut to pieces, shot, or died the following day of his wounds . . . expiring rather prosaically on a dunghill.

Sergeant Morris takes a dim view of Shaw's behaviour, while the Deeds of Daring Library dresses it up as the empire-building heroics that were increasingly in demand during the late nineteenth century. But it is precisely the fact that Shaw behaved the way he did, for the reasons he did, that makes Waterloo such an evocative and perennially fascinating conflict. It was an extraordinary time of extraordinary men and women: whether hulking great drink-crazed bruisers like Shaw; elegant and restrained men like Wellington, who eschewed a uniform in favour of the sort of clothes he might wear at a weekend house party; romantic newlyweds like Sir William and Lady De Lancey, or socially ambitious monstrous matriarchs of the calibre of the Duchess of Richmond.

The Duchess's ball and the Duke's battle have inspired poets, novelists and film-makers to create memorable works, but no fiction can compete with the excitement and horror, glamour and squalor of those hectic months while the world held its breath and the British in Brussels danced into battle.

NOTES

PROLOGUE

1 Lennox, *Fifty Years' Biographical Reminiscences*, Vol.I, pp205-206
2 Lennox, *Fifty Years'*, Vol.I, p205
3 Lennox, *Fifty Years'*, Vol.I, pp205-206
4 Lennox, *Fifty Years'*, Vol.I, p206

CHAPTER 1

1 Paget, *The Capel Letters*, p71
2 Madan, *Spencer and Waterloo*, p62
3 *The Capel Letters*, p76
4 *The Capel Letters*, p75
5 Madan, p79
6 Madan quoted in Miller, *The Duchess of Richmond's Ball*, p15
7 *The Capel Letters*, p57
8 Brocklebank 'Home of the Waterloo Ball', in *Country Life*, 11 December 1975
9 Brocklebank 'Home of the Waterloo Ball', in *Country Life*, 11 December 1975
10 Lennox, *Fifty Years'*, Vol.I, p133
11 Stanley, *Before And After Waterloo*, p75
12 *The Capel Letters*, p24
13 *The Capel Letters*, p28
14 *The Capel Letters*, p28
15 *The Capel Letters*, p37
16 Stanley, p82
17 Stanley, p94

18 *The Capel Letters*, p39
19 *The Capel Letters*, p42
20 *The Capel Letters*, p42
21 *The Capel Letters*, p43
22 *The Capel Letters*, p43
23 *The Capel Letters*, p42

CHAPTER 2

1 Jackson, *Notes of A Staff Officer*, p8
2 Jackson, p2
3 Mercer, *Journal of the Waterloo Campaign*, p111
4 Mercer, p111
5 Madan, p52
6 *The Capel Letters*, p153
7 Madan, p52
8 Madan, p52
9 *The Capel Letters*, p75
10 *The Capel Letters*, p75
11 *The Capel Letters*, p91
12 *The Capel Letters*, p72
13 Jackson, p9
14 Jackson, p9
15 *The Capel Letters*, p85
16 Adkin, *The Waterloo Companion*, p98
17 *The Capel Letters*, p89
18 Mackworth, in *Army Quarterly*, Vol.XXXV, p126

19 *The Capel Letters*, pp46-47

20 *The Capel Letters*, p48

21 *The Capel Letters*, p52

22 Badminton Archives, Fm M4/1/16(1)
    John Somerset to D. of Beaufort, 8
    February 1815

23 *The Capel Letters*, p52

24 Stanley, p197

25 Stanley, p198

CHAPTER 3

1 *The Capel Letters*, p70

2 Stanley, p181

3 Norman Davies, *Europe: a History*, p693

4 Morris, *Recollections of Military Service*,
   pp144-145

5 Stanley, p181

6 *The Capel Letters*, p55

7 Lennox, *Fifty Years'*, Vol.I p141

8 Quoted in Adkin, p99

9 *The Capel Letters*, p67

10 *Creevey Selected and Re-edited*, ed. Gore,
    p124

11 Stuart-Wortley, *Highcliffe and The
    Stuarts*, p225

CHAPTER 4

1 Hibbert, *The Wheatley Diaries*, p57

2 *The Wheatley Diaries*, p57

3 *The Wheatley Diaries*, p57

4 Stanhope, *Conversations with
   Wellington*, p10

5 Stanhope, p10

6 Stanhope, p10

7 Lennox, *Drafts on My Memory*, pp199-
   200

8 Lennox, *Drafts on My Memory*, p200

9 Morris, *Recollections*, pp148-149

10 Morris, *Recollections*, p150

CHAPTER 5

1 Lennox, *Fifty Years'*, Vol.I, p221

2 *The Waterloo Companion*, p17

3 *The Waterloo Companion*, p18

4 Badminton Archives, Fm M4/1/11(3)
   FRS to Beaufort, 7 March 1815

5 Badminton Archives, Fm M4/1/11(4)

FRS to Beaufort, 11 March 1815

6 Fanny Burney, *Journals and Letters*,
   Vol.VIII, p71

7 Burney, Vol.VIII, p71

8 Burney, Vol.VIII, p72

9 Macdonald, *Souvenirs du Maréchal
   Macdonald*, quoted in Dallas, *The Final
   Act*, p332

10 Figures from *The Waterloo Companion*,
    p23 and Chandler, *Waterloo, The
    Hundred Days*, p30. Where figures
    differ an estimated or median figure has
    been selected.

11 Figure from *The Waterloo Companion*,
    p22

12 Figures from *The Waterloo Companion*,
    p23 and Chandler, *Waterloo, The
    Hundred Days*, p30. Where figures
    differ an estimated or median figure has
    been selected.

13 *The Memoirs of Prince Talleyrand*, Vol.II,
    p119

CHAPTER 6

1 *The Capel Letters*, p87

2 *The Capel Letters*, p87

3 Stuart-Wortley, p219

4 *The Capel Letters*, p93

5 *The Capel Letters*, p96

6 Creevey, *Life and Times*, ed. Gore, p74

7 Creevey, *Life and Times*, p75

8 Burney, Vol.VIII, p83

9 Somerset Archives, Fm M4/1/11(6)
   FRS to Beaufort 6, April 1815

10 Somerset Archives, Fm M4/1/11(8)
    FRS to Beaufort, 25 April 1815

11 Somerset Archives, Fm M4/1/11(6)
    FRS to Beaufort, 6 April 1815

12 *The Creevey Papers*, ed. Maxwell, p220

13 *The Creevey Papers*, pp220-221

14 *The Creevey Papers*, p221

15 Creevey, *Life and Times*, p75

16 Creevey, *Life and Times*, p75

17 *The Creevey Papers*, pp221-222

18 *The Creevey Papers*, p222

19 *The Capel Letters*, p97

20 *The Capel Letters*, p98

21 Madan, p89
22 Madan, p89
23 *The Capel Letters*, p97
24 *The Letters of Private Wheeler*, p160
25 De Ros, *Personal Recollections of Lady de Ros* in *Murray's Magazine*, Vol.V, p38
26 De Ros in *Murray's Magazine*, p38
27 *The Wheatley Diary*, p58
28 Morris, *Recollections*, p187
29 *The Capel Letters*, p98
30 *The Capel Letters*, p99

CHAPTER 7
1 Stanley, p243
2 Stuart-Wortley, p222
3 Gronow, *The Reminiscences and Recollections of Captain Gronow*, p163
4 *The Capel Letters*, p94
5 Tomkinson, *Diary of a Cavalry Officer*, p273
6 Richardson, *Long Forgotten Days*, p372
7 Tomkinson, p273

CHAPTER 8
1 Mercer, p2
2 Mercer, p2
3 *The Autobiography of Sergeant William Lawrence*, p202
4 Mercer, p2
5 *Lawrence*, p201
6 *The Autobiography of Lieutenant-General Sir Harry Smith Bart GCB*, pp257-258
7 Frederick Mainwaring quoted in Sutherland, *Men of Waterloo*, p75
8 William Hay, *Reminiscences 1805-1815 under Wellington*, p157
9 Hay, pp157-158
10 *The Letters of Private Wheeler*, p159
11 Kincaid, *Adventures in the Rifle Brigade*, pp149-150
12 Black Watch Archives, BWRA 0233, *Memoir of James Gunn*, p.48
13 Mercer, p1
14 Mercer, p2
15 Albemarle, *Fifty Years of My Life*, Vol.II, pp4-5
16 Chandler, introduction to *The Journal*

of Edward Heeley, p95
17 *The Journal of Edward Heeley*, p98
18 *The Journal of Edward Heeley*, pp98-99
19 *The Journal of Edward Heeley*, p99
20 *The Journal of Edward Heeley*, p99
21 James, *Surgeon James's Journal*, p4

CHAPTER 9
1 Costello, *Military Memoirs*, p150
2 Lejeune & Lewis, *The Gentlemen's Clubs of London*, p291
3 Lejeune & Lewis, p13
4 Albemarle, Vol.I, p319
5 Albemarle, Vol.I, p320
6 Frye, *After Waterloo*, p vii
7 Albemarle, Vol.I, pp317-318
8 Albemarle, Vol.I, p319
9 Knollys, *The Life of Shaw*, pp8-9
10 Albemarle, Vol.I, p322
11 Knollys, p8
12 Knollys, p9
13 Knollys, p8
14 Knollys, p10
15 Knollys, p13
16 Knollys, p14

CHAPTER 10
1 Badminton Archives, Fm M4/1/11(6) FRS to Beaufort, 6 April 1815
2 *The Capel Letters*, p100
3 *The Letters of Private Wheeler*, p161
4 *The Letters of Private Wheeler*, p161
5 John Wilson Croker quoted in Hibbert, *Wellington a Personal History*, p11
6 Hibbert, *Wellington: a Personal History*, p57
7 Lennox, *Fifty Years'*, Vol.I, p223
8 *Memoir of Charles Gordon Lennox, fifth Duke of Richmond*, p46
9 James, *The Iron Duke: a Military Biography*, p198
10 *Memoir of Charles Gordon Lennox, fifth Duke of Richmond*, p47
11 *Memoir of Charles Gordon Lennox, fifth Duke of Richmond*, p50
12 Quoted in *Memoir of Charles Gordon Lennox: fifth Duke of Richmond*, p51

13 *Memoir of Charles Gordon Lennox: fifth Duke of Richmond*, p63

14 Stanhope, p13

15 Morris, *Recollections*, pp133-134

16 Morris, *Recollections*, p136

17 Thornton, *Your Most Obedient Servant, Cook to the Duke of Wellington*, p75.

18 Mercer, p91

19 Mercer, p91

20 Mercer, p92

21 Frazer, *Letters of Colonel Sir A. S. Frazer, K.C.B.*, p ix

22 *The Waterloo Companion*, p26

CHAPTER 11

1 Madan, p96

2 *Supp. Despatches of the Duke of Wellington*, Vol.X, pp83-84

3 Madan, p102

4 Badminton Archives, Fm M4/1/16(5) Edward Somerset to Beaufort, 23 May 1815

5 *The Capel Letters*, p99

6 Fitchett, *Wellington's Men*, p354

7 Capt. Jones, 15th Hussars, quoted in Paget, *One Leg*, p119

8 Wellington quoted by James, *The Iron Duke*, p198

9 Gronow, p74

10 Wellington quoted by James, *The Iron Duke*, p198

11 Paget, *One Leg*, p121

12 *One Leg*, pp89-90

13 *One Leg*, p90

14 *One Leg*, p96

15 *One Leg*, p95

16 Lord Graves, Paget's brother-in-law, quoted in *One Leg*, p97

17 Charles Paget to Arthur Paget, 9 March 1800, quoted in *One Leg*, p93

18 Lord Graves, quoted in *One Leg*, p100

19 Lord Graves, 10 March 1800, quoted in *One Leg*, p97

20 *One Leg*, p99

21 Lord Graves, quoted in *One Leg*, p100

22 Lord Enniskillen, another brother-in-law, quoted in *One Leg*, p101

23 Lady Bessborough, late 1811, quoted in *One Leg*, p111

24 Sir William Fraser, *Words on Wellington*, quoted in Hibbert, *Wellington*, p169

25 Mackworth, *Army Quarterly*, p321

26 Frye, p12

27 *The Capel Letters*, p102

CHAPTER 12

1 *The Capel Letters*, p109

2 Smith, *Autobiography*, p263

3 Smith, *Autobiography*, pp263-264

4 *Journal of Lieutenant Woodberry*, p258

5 *The Journal of Edward Heeley*, p100

6 *The Journal of Edward Heeley*, pp99-100

7 *Surgeon James's Journal*, p6

8 *The Wheatley Diary*, p56

9 Mercer, p5

10 Frye, p3

11 Mercer, p8

12 *The Journal of Edward Heeley*, p100

13 *The Journal of Edward Heeley*, p101

14 Mercer, p8

15 Mercer, p9

16 Mercer, p14

17 Mercer, p8

18 Costello, p103

19 Costello, p103

20 Morris, *Recollections*, pp190-193

CHAPTER 13

1 *The Journal of Edward Heeley*, p103

2 Arthur Kennedy quoted in Hunt, *Charging Against Napoleon*, p238

3 Mercer, p20

4 Simmons, *A British Rifle Man*, p358

5 Frazer, p488

6 Eaton, *The Days of Battle*, p7

7 Mercer, p15

8 Frye, p13

9 *Journal of Lieutenant Woodberry*, p261

10 Frye, p13

11 Frye, pp13-14

12 *The Journal of Edward Heeley*, p103

13 *The Capel Letters*, p106

14 *The Journal of Edward Heeley*, p105

15 Stanley, p197

16 *History of the Gordon Highlanders*, Vol.I, p347

17 Frye, p8

18 Mercer, p32

19 Mercer, p81

20 Tomkinson, p275

21 Simmons, p359

22 *Journal of Lieutenant Woodberry*, p269

23 *The Wheatley Diary*, p56

24 Frazer, pp487-488

25 Tomkinson, p276

26 Albemarle, Vol.II, pp12-13

27 Albemarle, Vol.II, pp8-9

28 Albemarle, Vol.II, p9

29 *Letters of Private Wheeler*, p162

30 Arthur Kennedy, quoted in Hunt, *Charging Against Napoleon*, p232

CHAPTER 14

1 Lady De Lancey, abridged version of her account reproduced in Miller, *Lady De Lancey at Waterloo*, p169

2 Burney, Vol.VIII, p131

3 Burney, Vol.VIII, p149

4 *Letters of Private Wheeler*, p162

5 Kincaid, *Adventures*, p152

6 Quoted in Hunt, p235

7 Frazer, p516

8 Mercer, p24

9 Mercer, p37

10 Mercer, p38

11 Mercer, p83

12 *Letters of Private Wheeler*, pp163-164

13 Quoted in Hunt, p235

14 Hunt, p236

15 Quoted in Uffindell, *Wellington's Armies*, p272

16 Woodberry quoted in Hunt, pp238-239

17 Lennox, *50 Years'*, Vol.I, p224

18 Lennox, *50 Years'*, Vol.I, pp224-225

19 Wellington to Lady Sarah Lennox in Lennox, *50 Years'*, p226

20 Lennox, *50 Years'*, Vol.I, p228

21 Albemarle, Vol.II, p13

22 Albemarle, Vol.II, p13

23 *The Capel Letters*, p85

24 Albemarle, Vol.II, p13

25 Lennox, *50 Years'*, Vol.I, pp247-248

CHAPTER 15

1 Quoted in Uffindell, *Wellington's Armies*, p268

2 Hay, *Reminiscences*, p159

3 Order to 18th Hussars quoted in Uffindell, *Wellington's Armies*, p273

4 Uffindell, *Wellington's Armies*, p272

5 Macready quoted in Uffindell, *Wellington's Armies*, p272

6 Frazer, p514

7 Mercer, p116

8 Frazer, p515

9 Frazer, p519

10 Badminton Archives, Fm M4/1/16(6) FRS to Beaufort, 26 May 1815

11 Frazer, p522

12 Mercer, p118

13 Mercer, pp117-118

14 Arthur Kennedy quoted in Hunt, p237

15 Frazer, p522

16 Arthur Kennedy quoted in Hunt, p237

17 *The Capel Letters*, p101

18 *The Capel Letters*, p102

19 Woodberry; *The Battle of Waterloo . . . by 'A Near Observer'* [George Jones], Vol. II, p50; Frazer; and Mercer, respectively

20 Frazer, p521

21 Woodberry in Hunt, p237

22 Woodberry in Hunt, p237

23 Mercer, p119

24 Frazer, p522

25 Frazer, p522

26 Frazer, p522

27 Frazer, p524

CHAPTER 16

1 Mercer, p120

2 Stuart-Wortley, p233

3 Wellington to Earl Bathurst, 28 April 1815 in *Supp. Despatches*, Vol.X, p168

4 Wellington to Earl Bathurst, 28 April 1815 in *Supp. Despatches*, Vol.X, p168

5 *Creevey Selected*, p136

6 Mercer, p119

7 Badminton Archives, Fm M4/1/11(1)

FRS to Beaufort, 14 January 1815

8 Mercer, p29

9 Tomkinson, pp277-278

10 Badminton Archives, Fm M4/1/11(8)
FRS to Beaufort, 25 April 1815

11 Badminton Archives, Fm M4/1/11(6)
FRS to Beaufort, 6 April 1815

12 Newman Smith, *Flying Sketches of the
Battle of Waterloo*, p10

13 *Flying Sketches*, p10

14 Smith, *Autobiography*, p265

15 Badminton Archives, Fm M4/1/11(2)
FRS to Beaufort, 8 February 1815

16 Eaton, p6

17 Mercer, p38

18 Frye, p5

CHAPTER 17

1 *Creevey Selected*, p136

2 *Creevey Selected*, p134

3 *Creevey Selected*, p135

4 *Creevey Selected*, p135

5 *Creevey Selected*, p136

6 Jules Michelet quoted in Dallas, p327

7 *Creevey Selected*, p135

8 *Creevey Selected*, pp135-136

9 Mercer, p124

10 Mercer, p125

11 *The Dispatches [sic] of Field Marshal the
Duke of Wellington*, Vol.XII, p462, 13
June 1815

12 Mercer, p116

13 Badminton Archives, Fm M4/1/16(8)
Edward Somerset to Beaufort, 8 June
1815

14 Badminton Archives, Fm M4/1/16(9)
Edward Somerset to Beaufort, 13 June
1815

15 *The Capel Letters*, p105

16 *The Capel Letters*, p109

17 Madan, p103

18 Mackworth, p321

19 Jackson, p11

CHAPTER 18

1 Frye, p13

2 Hay, p203

3 *Supp. Despatches*, Vol.X, p84

4 *Supp. Despatches*, Vol.X, p130 quoted in
Miller, *Lady De Lancey at Waterloo*,
pp55-56

5 Miller, p105

6 Miller, p105

7 Quoted in Havard, *Wellington's Welsh
General: a Life of Sir Thomas Picton*,
p224

8 Stanhope, p50

9 Quoted in Robinson, *Memoirs of Sir
Thomas Picton*, Vol.II, p324

10 Quoted in Robinson, Vol.II, p327

11 Havard, p225

12 Badminton Archives, Fm M4/1/11(1)
FRS to Beaufort, 14 January 1815

13 Robinson, Vol.II, p322

14 Quoted in Robinson, Vol.II, p323

15 Havard, p229

16 Havard, p229

17 Quoted in Robinson, Vol.II, p336

18 Robinson, Vol.II, p337

19 Robinson, Vol.II, p338

20 Havard, p232

21 Gronow, p66

22 Gronow, p65

23 Gronow, p65

24 Gronow, p66

25 Gronow, p66

26 Robinson, pp340-341

27 Robinson, p341

28 Gronow, pp66-67

CHAPTER 19

1 Ross-Lewin, *With 'The Thirty-Second'
in the Peninsula*, p252

2 Quoted in Richardson, *Long Forgotten
Days*, p373

3 Quoted in Richardson, p373

4 Quoted in Stuart-Wortley, p235

5 Richardson, p373

6 Quoted in Stuart-Wortley, pp235-236

7 Stuart-Wortley, p235

8 De Ros in *Murray's Magazine*, p39

9 *Surgeon James's Journal*, p11

10 De Ros in *Murray's Magazine*, p39

11 Eaton, p13

12 Mackworth, p324
13 De Lancey in Miller, pp106-107
14 Kincaid in Fitchett, p117
15 Richardson, pp373-374
16 W. Fraser, *The Waterloo Ball*, pp10-11
17 *The Waterloo Ball*, p15
18 *Country Life*, 11 December 1975
19 *The Waterloo Ball*, p14
20 Murphy, *A Mixed Bag*, p54
21 Murphy, p54
22 De Ros in *Murray's Magazine*, p40
23 *The Waterloo Ball*, p31
24 *The Waterloo Ball*, p31
25 Thornton, p94
26 Eaton, p16
27 Kincaid in Fitchett, pp117-118
28 James Gunn, MS, pp49-50
29 *The History of the Gordon Highlanders*, Vol.I, p349 fn
30 Circumstantial account of Waterloo quoted *in The History of the Gordon Highlanders*, Vol.I, p349 fn
31 Letter from Lady Louisa Tighe, 13 January 1889 quoted in *The History of the Gordon Highlanders*, Vol.I, p349 fn
32 De Lancey in Miller, p43
33 Jackson, p12
34 Jackson, p13
35 Ross-Lewin, p253
36 Ross-Lewin, p253
37 Frazer, pp533-535
38 *Creevey Selected*, p137
39 De Lancey in Miller, p45
40 Stuart-Wortley, p236
41 De Ros in *Murray's Magazine*, p40
42 De Ros in *Murray's Magazine*, p40
43 Mackworth, p324
44 Richardson, p374
45 Richardson, p374
46 Richardson, p374
47 De Ros in *Murray's Magazine*, p43
48 De Ros in *Murray's Magazine*, p43
49 De Ros in *Murray's Magazine*, p43
50 Mackworth, p324
51 Mackworth, p324
52 Jackson, pp13-14

53 Hay, p159
54 Hay, p160
55 De Ros in *Murray's Magazine*, p40

CHAPTER 20

1 Vallance, *A Narrative of the Battles of Quatre Bras and Waterloo by a Soldier of the 79th Regiment of Foot*, p3
2 *Letters of Private Wheeler*, p164
3 *The Journal of Edward Heeley*, p104
4 *The Journal of Edward Heeley*, pp104-105
5 *The Journal of Edward Heeley*, p105
6 *The Journal of Edward Heeley*, p105
7 *The Journal of Edward Heeley*, p105
8 Vallance, pp2-3
9 *The Journal of Edward Heeley*, pp105-106
10 *The Capel Letters*, p106
11 Vallance, p3
12 *The Journal of Edward Heeley*, pp105-106
13 Eaton, p21
14 Eaton, p21
15 *The Journal of Edward Heeley*, p106
16 Eaton, p21
17 Kincaid, *Adventures*, p154
18 De Lancey, *A Week at Waterloo*, p45
19 Costello, p150
20 Mercer, p134
21 Costello, p151

CHAPTER 21

1 Eaton, pp21-22
2 Eaton, pp23-24
3 *The Journal of Edward Heeley*, p107
4 Eaton, p24
5 Eaton, p24
6 Burney, Vol.VIII, p212
7 De Ros in *Murray's Magazine*, p43
8 Kincaid, p154
9 Eaton, p24
10 Eaton, pp24-25
11 *Creevey Selected*, p137
12 Eaton, p25
13 Eaton, p26
14 *Creevey Selected*, p137
15 *The Journal of Edward Heeley*, p107

16 *Creevey Selected*, p137
17 De Lancey in Miller, p109
18 Eaton, p26
19 Eaton, p27
20 Eaton, pp28-29
21 *The Journal of Edward Heeley*, p107
22 A Near Observer [George Jones], p13
23 *The Journal of Edward Heeley*, p109
24 *The Capel Letters*, p111
25 *Creevey Selected*, p137
26 Eaton, p30
27 *The Journal of Edward Heeley*, p109
28 Haythornthwaite, *Waterloo Men*, p20
29 Simmons, p366
30 Havard, p238
31 Kincaid, *Adventures*, p158
32 Picton quoted in Havard, p242
33 *The Capel Letters*, p113
34 Lennox, *50 Years'*, Vol.I, p246
35 Lennox, *50 Years'*, Vol.I, p246

CHAPTER 22

1 Madan, p105
2 *The Journal of Edward Heeley*, p109
3 Jackson, p22
4 Vallance, p8
5 Vallance, p9
6 Haythornthwaite, *Waterloo Men*, p31
7 Jackson, p31
8 Capt. W.B. Ingilby (Lieut. at Waterloo) in Siborne, *Waterloo Letters*, p195
9 Kincaid quoted in Fitchett, p123
10 Ingilby to Siborne, Siborne, p195
11 Kincaid quoted in Fitchett, p125
12 Mercer, p148
13 Mercer, p149
14 Mercer, p149
15 Mercer, p149
16 Mercer, p149
17 Mercer, p153
18 *The Journal of Edward Heeley*, p113 fn
19 *Surgeon James's Journal*, p16
20 Roberts, *Waterloo*, p51
21 Mercer, p155
22 *Creevey Selected*, p138
23 *Creevey Selected*, p138

24 *Creevey Selected*, p138
25 Creevey, *Life and Times*, p77
26 Official bulletin quoted in Uffindell, *On the Fields of Glory*, p252
27 Eaton, p54
28 *The Journal of Edward Heeley*, pp109-110
29 De Lancey in Miller, p109
30 A Near Observer [George Jones], p15
31 Eaton, p49
32 Eaton, p50
33 Eaton, p57
34 Eaton, p58
35 Eaton, p59

CHAPTER 23

1 Vallance, p11
2 Creevey, *Life and Times*, p77
3 Creevey, *Life and Times*, pp77-78
4 *The Journal of Edward Heeley*, p110
5 *The Journal of Edward Heeley*, p110
6 *The Journal of Edward Heeley*, p110
7 *The Journal of Edward Heeley*, p110
8 *Supp. Despatches*, Vol.X, p501
9 Thornton, p95
10 Siborne, p197
11 Smith, *Autobiography*, pp266-267
12 Siborne, p195
13 Siborne, p195
14 Tomkinson, p286 fn
15 Mercer, p157
16 Mercer, p158
17 Morris, *Recollections*, p219
18 Gronow, p141
19 Gronow, p141
20 Frazer, p543
21 Frazer, p544
22 Gronow, p68
23 Gronow, p69
24 Gronow, p141
25 Shaw, p36
26 Stanhope, p136
27 Hay, p183
28 Gronow, p141
29 Lennox, *50 Years'*, p240
30 Lennox, *50 Years'*, p240
31 Lennox, *50 Years'*, p241
32 Madan, p106

33 Lennox, *50 Years'*, p241
34 Lennox, *50 Years'*, p241
35 Lennox, *50 Years'*, p242
36 Madan, pp106-107

CHAPTER 24
 1 Burney, Vol.VIII, p213
 2 *Creevey Selected*, p138
 3 Frye, p25
 4 Frye, p25
 5 Burney, Vol.VIII, p214
 6 *Creevey Selected*, p138
 7 *The Capel Letters*, pp114-115
 8 *The Capel Letters*, p115
 9 Jackson, pp35-36
10 *The Capel Letters*, p115
11 *Creevey Selected*, p138
12 *Creevey Selected*, p139
13 *The Journal of Edward Heeley*, p111
14 *The Journal of Edward Heeley*, p112
15 *The Journal of Edward Heeley*, p113
16 *The Journal of Edward Heeley*, p112
17 *The Journal of Edward Heeley*, p112
18 Smith, *Autobiography*, pp281-284
19 Tomkinson, p318
20 Tomkinson, p318
21 Frye, pp25-26
22 *Creevey Selected*, p141
23 Creevey, *Life and Times*, p78
24 Madan, p107
25 *The Journal of Edward Heeley*, p113
26 *The Journal of Edward Heeley*, p113
27 *Creevey Selected*, p139
28 Creevey, *Life and Times*, p79
29 *Creevey Selected*, p139
30 *Creevey Selected*, p139
31 Creevey, *Life and Times*, p79
32 *Creevey Selected*, p140
33 Creevey, *Life and Times*, p80
34 *Creevey Selected*, p141
35 Burney, Vol.VIII, p216
36 *Creevey Selected*, p141
37 *Creevey Selected*, p141
38 *Creevey Selected*, pp141-142
39 *Creevey Selected*, p142
40 Madan, p107
41 *Supp. Despatches*, Vol.X, p531

CHAPTER 25
 1 Adkin, p39
 2 Adkin, p53
 3 Vallance, p12
 4 Vallance, p12
 5 *The Wheatley Diary*, pp63-64
 6 *The Wheatley Diary*, p64
 7 *The Wheatley Diary*, p64
 8 Adkin, p53
 9 Adkin, p39
10 *Chatterbox* reproduced in Chandler, p96
11 *Chatterbox* reproduced in Chandler, p96
12 *Chatterbox* reproduced in Chandler, p96
13 W. P. Lennox quoted in Siborne, p36
14 W. P. Lennox quoted in Siborne, p36
15 Siborne, p89

CHAPTER 26
 1 Jackson, p60
 2 Jackson, p60
 3 Jackson, p65
 4 Jackson, p65
 5 *One Leg*, p149
 6 Stanhope, p136
 7 *Supp. Despatches*, Vol.X, p351
    Wellington to Lady F. W-W
 8 Badminton Archives, Fm M4/1/12
    Wellington to Beaufort, 19 June 1815
 9 Badminton Archives, Fm O1/11/6
    Wellington to Lord Aberdeen, 19 June
    1815
10 De Ros in *Murray's Magazine*, p45
11 Lennox, *50 Years'*, p246
12 *The Capel Letters*, p120
13 Tomkinson, p319
14 Quoted in Longford, *The Years of the
    Sword*, p483
15 Goodwood MSS, Chichester Record
    Office, Ms 599 ff.p1
16 Wildman quoted in *One Leg*, p150
17 *One Leg*, p150
18 Costello, p156
19 Costello, p156
20 Smith, *Autobiography*, p273
21 Costello, p156
22 William Hay, p212
23 Smith, *Autobiography*, p275

24 William Hay, pp200-201
25 Smith, *Autobiography*, pp286-287
26 De Lancey, p53
27 De Lancey, p66
28 De Lancey, pp66-67
29 Hay, p195
30 Gronow, p72
31 *Flying Sketches*, p26
32 Mercer, p189
33 Mercer, p189
34 Frye, p27
35 *Creevey Selected*, p142
36 Frye, p27
37 Hay, p211
38 Eaton, p129
39 Eaton, p137
40 Eaton, p138

CHAPTER 27

1 Eaton, p116
2 *One Leg*, p366 *end note*
3 West Sussex Record Office, Goodwood Ms, Ms 599 ff.pp 10-12, Charlotte Uxbridge to her daughters, 26 June 1815
4 WSRO, Goodwood Ms, Ms 599 ff.pp 10-12
5 WSRO, Goodwood Ms, Ms 599 ff.pp 10-12
6 WSRO, Goodwood Ms, Ms 599 ff.pp 10-12
7 WSRO, Goodwood Ms, Ms 599 ff.pp 10-12
8 WSRO, Goodwood Ms, Ms 599 ff.pp 2-3, Charlotte Uxbridge to her daughters, n.d. June 1815
9 WSRO, Goodwood Ms, Ms 599 ff.pp 10-12
10 WSRO, Goodwood Ms, Ms 599 ff.pp 2-3
11 *The Capel Letters*, pp117-118
12 WSRO, Goodwood Ms, Ms 599 ff.pp 2-3
13 WSRO, Goodwood Ms, Ms 599 ff.pp 2-3
14 WSRO, Goodwood Ms, Ms 599 ff.pp 2-3
15 WSRO, Goodwood Ms, Ms 599 ff.pp

17, Anglesey to his children, 30 June 1815
16 WSRO, Goodwood Ms, Ms 599 ff.pp2-3
17 Badminton Archives, Fm M4/1/11(15) John Somerset to Beaufort, 5 July 1815
18 Badminton Archives, Fm M4/1/11(14) FRS to Beaufort, 3 July 1815
19 Gwent Record Office MS D3135/1.29
20 Badminton Archives, Fm M4/1/11(14)
21 WSRO, Goodwood Ms, Ms 599 ff.pp 19-20
22 WSRO, Goodwood Ms, Ms 599 ff.pp 19-20
23 Thornton, pp110-111
24 Thornton, p110
25 *The Capel Letters*, p131
26 *The Capel Letters*, p149
27 *The Capel Letters*, p149
28 Rev. G.G. Stonestreet quoted in Miller, *The Duchess of Richmond's Ball*, p190
29 *Edinburgh Review*, Vol.CXII, July–October 1860, no. 288, p213 quoted by Miller in *The Duchess of Richmond's Ball*, p184

EPILOGUE

1 *Illustrated London News*, 19 June 1852
2 Stratfield Saye MS
3 *The Times*, 19 June 1852
4 *The Times*, 19 June 1852
5 *The Times*, 19 June 1852
6 *The Times*, 19 June 1852
7 Alicia Robinson, in *Elegant Eating*, p127
8 *The Times*, 19 June 1852
9 Wilson, *The Victorians*, pp145-146
10 Wilson, p179
11 Quoted in Wilson, p192
12 Quoted in Wilson, pp195-196
13 De Lancey in Miller, Appendix A, p123
14 De Lancey in Miller, Appendix A, p125
15 Tomkinson, p286
16 Knollys, pp7-8
17 Knollys, p8
18 Knollys, p45
19 Knollys, p45
20 Morris, *Recollections*, pp217-218

BIBLIOGRAPHY

Articles and Books

Adkin, Mark, *The Waterloo Companion*. London: Aurum Press, 2001.

Albemarle, G.T., Earl of, *50 Years of my Life*, Vols I & II. London: Macmillan & Co., 1876,

Allen, T., *The Panorama of London or Visitor's Guide*, 1828.

Anton, James, 'Recollections of a Military Life' in Fitchett, *Wellington's Men*.

Assche, Comtesse d', *Extracts from the Notebook of the Comtesse d'Assche'*.

Avery, Harold, *With Wellington to Waterloo*. London: Wells Gardner, Darton & Co., 1901.

Becke, A.F., *Napoleon and Waterloo*, London: Greenhill Books, 1995.

Bessborough, G.C.M.G., Earl of, and A. Aspinall, *Lady Bessborough and her Family Circle*. Edited by the Earl of Bessborough, G.C.M.G, and A. Aspinall. London: John Murray, 1940.

Breteton, Capt. F.S., *On the Field at Waterloo*. London: Blackie and Son Ltd, 1915.

Brett-James, Antony, *Life in Wellington's Army*. London: George Allen and Unwin Ltd, 1972.

Brett-James, Antony, *The 100 Days: Napoleon's Last Campaign from Eye-witness Accounts*. London: Macmillan and Co. Ltd, 1964 [re-edition].

Brocklebank, Beatrice, 'Home of the Waterloo Ball' in *Country Life*, 11 December 1975.

Broughton, Lord [John Cam Hobhouse], *Recollections of a Long Life*. Edited by his daughter, Lady Dorchester. 6 Vols. London: John Murray, 1909.

Brownlow, Countess Emma Sophia, *The Eve of Victorianism: Reminiscences of the Years 1802–1834*. London: John Murray, 1940.

Burney, Fanny, *The Journals and Letters of Fanny Burney* (Madam d'Arblay), Vol. IX. Edited by Warren Derry. Oxford: Clarendon Press, 1982.

Burney, Fanny, *The Journals and Letters of Fanny Burney* (Madam d'Arblay), Vol. VIII. Edited by Peter Hughes, Joyce Hemlow, Althea Douglas, Patricia Hawkins. Oxford: Clarendon Press, 1980.

Bury, Lady Charlotte, *Diary of a Lady in Waiting*. London: John Lane, The Bodley Head, 1908.

Byrant, Arthur, *The Age of Elegance, 1812–1822*. London: Collins, 1950.

Capellen, Baron van, *Baron van Capellen, Memoirs*. St Germain: Baron Sirtema de Grovestins, 1852

Chalfont, Lord, Ed., *Waterloo – Battle of Three Armies*. Book Club Associates, 1979.

Chandler, David G., *On the Napoleonic Wars: Collected Essays*. London: Greenhill Books, 1994.

Chandler, David G., *Waterloo: the Hundred Days*. London: Osprey, 1980.

Chateaubriand, François René, *Memoires d'Outre-Tombe*. Paris: Livre du Poche, 2000.

Cornwell, Bernard, *Sharpe's Waterloo. London*: HarperCollins, 1997.

Corrigan, Gordon, *Wellington: a Military Life*. London: Hambledon and London, 2001.

Costello, Edward, *The Peninsular and Waterloo Campaigns* [also called *Adventures of a Soldier*], Edited by Antony Brett-James. London: Longmans, 1967.

Cotton, Edward, *A Voice from Waterloo: a History of the Battle*. Mont-St-Jean: 1854.

Creevey, Thomas, *Creevey Selected and Re-edited by John Gore*. London: John Murray, 1949.

Creevey, Thomas, *Life and Times. A Further Selection from the Correspondence of Thomas Creevey*. Edited by John Gore, London: John Murray, 1934.

Creevey, Thomas, *The Creevey Papers: a Selection from the Correspondence and Diaries*. Edited by The Rt Hon. Sir Herbert Maxwell. London: John Murray, 1933.

Croker, Rt Hon. John Wilson, *The Croker Papers. The Correspondence and Diaries of the Late Right Honourable J.W. Croker*. Edited by Louis J. Jennings. 3 Vols. London: John Murray, 1884.

Cronin, Vincent, *Napoleon*, London: Fontana, 1990.

Dallas, Gregor, *1815: the Roads to Waterloo*. London: Richard Cohen Books, 1996.

Dallas, Gregor, *The Final Act – The Road to Waterloo*. New York: Henry Holt & Co., 1996.

Dalton, Charles, *The Waterloo Roll Call*. London: Willian Clowes & Sons, 1890.

d'Arblay, Frances, *Diary and Letters of Madame d'Arblay*. Edited by Charlotte Frances Barrett. Vol. 4. London: Hurst & Blackett, 1854.

d'Arblay, Frances, *The Journal and Letters of Fanny Burney* [Madame d'Arblay]. Edited by Peter Hughes et al. Oxford: Clarendon Press, 1980.

Davies, Norman, *Europe: a History*. London: Pimlico, 1997.

Dawnay, M.A., Major N.P. & Major J.M.A. Tamplin, T.D., 'The Waterloo Banquet at Apsley House, 1836' in *Journal for the Society of Army Historical Research*, Vol. 49, 1971.

De Lancey Lady Magadalene, *A Week at Waterloo in 1815. Lady De Lancey's narrative. Being an account of how she nursed her husband, Colonel Sir William Howe De Lancey ... mortally wounded in the great battle.* Edited by Major B.R. Ward. London: John Murray, 1906.

Deane, Agnes Trevor, *Harry the Drummer.* London: Ward, Lock & Co., c.1882.

Delavoye, Alexander Marin, *Life of Thomas Graham, Lord Lynedoch.* London: Richardson & Co., 1880.

Dobson, Julia, *They Were at Waterloo.* London: William Heinemann, 1979.

Douglas, John, *Douglas's Tale of the Peninsula and Waterloo.* Edited by Stanley Monick. London: Leo Cooper, 1997.

Dwelly, F.S.A.E., *A Muster Roll of the British Non-commissioned Officers and Men Present at the Battle of Waterloo.* Fleet: privately printed, 1835.

Eaton, Charlotte Anne [An Englishwoman], *The Days of Battle: or, Quatre Bras and Waterloo.* London: Henry G. Bohn, 1853.

Ellesmere, Earl of, *Personal Reminiscences of the Duke of Wellington.* Edited by Alice, Countess of Strafford. London: John Murray, 1903.

Erckmann-Chatrain, M.M., *Waterloo: a story of the Hundred Days.* London: Smith, Elder and Co., 1870.

Fitchett, W.H., *Wellington's Men.* London: Smith, Elder & Co., 1900.

Fleischman, Theo & Winand Aerts, *Bruxelles Pendant la Bataille de Waterloo.* Brussels: La Renaissance du Livre, 1956.

Fletcher, Ian, *A Desperate Business: Wellington, the British Army and the Waterloo Campaign.* Staplehurst: Spellmount, c.2001.

Fletcher, Ian & Rod Poulter, *Gentlemen's sons: the Guards in the Peninsula and at Waterloo, 1808–1815.* Tunbridge Wells: Spellmount, 1992.

Forty, Simon, *Historical Maps of the Napoleonic Wars.* London: Brassey's, 2003.

Francois, Capt. Charles, *From Valmy to Waterloo.* Translated and edited by Robert B. Douglas. London: Everett & Co., 1906.

Fraser, Sir William Augustus, Bt, *Words on Wellington. The Duke, Waterloo, the Ball.* London: J.C. Nimmo, 1889.

Frazer, Sir A.S., *Letters of Colonel Sir A.S. Frazer, K.C.B., Commanding the Royal Horse Artillery in the Army under the Duke of Wellington. Written during the Peninsular and Waterloo Campaigns.* Edited by Major-General Edward Sabine, London: Longman, Brown, Green, Longmans & Roberts, 1859.

Frye, Major W.E., *After Waterloo: Reminiscences of European Travel, 1815–1819.* London: William Heinemann, 1909.

Gill, Eli, *A Narrative of the Life and Adventures of Eli Gill, Private in His Majesty's 52nd. Regiment of Light Infantry.* Barnard Castle: Thomas Clifton, 1826.

Gleig, R., *The Story of the Battle of Waterloo from Authentic Sources.* London: John Murray, 1907.

Godwin, John Beaudesert, *The Pagets and Waterloo*. Staffordshire County Library Authority, 1992.

Gomm, Sir William Maynard, G.C.B., *Letters and Journals ... from 1799 to Waterloo 1815*. Edited by F.C. Carr-Gomm. London: John Murray, 1881.

Granville, Castalia, *Lord Granville Leveson Gower, First Earl Granville, Private Correspondence: 1781–1821*. London: John Murray, 1917.

Granville, Harriet, *Letters of Harriet, Countess Granville*. Vol. 1. London: Longman, Green and Co., 1894.

Greenhill Gardyne, Lt.-Col C., *The Life of a Regiment; The History of the Gordon Highlanders, Vol. I, 1794–1816*. Edinburgh: David Douglas, 1901.

Griffiths, Major Arthur, *Wellington & Waterloo*. London: George Newnes Ltd, 1898.

Gronow, Rees Howell, *The Reminiscences and Recollections of Captain Gronow*. Edited by John Raymond. London: Bodley Head, 1964.

Guedalla, Philip, *The Duke*, London: Hodder & Stoughton, 1931.

Guedalla, Philip, *The Hundred Days*. London: Peter Davies, 1934.

Hamilton, Lt.-Gen. Sir F.W., *The Origin and History of the First or Grenadier Guards*. Vols 3. London: John Murray, 1874.

Harris, Benjamin, 'Recollections of Rifleman Harris' in Kincaid, *Adventures* ....

Hart, J.W., *1815: A Romance of Waterloo*. London: H. Kell, 1915.

Havard, Robert G., *Wellington's Welsh General: a Life of Sir Thomas Picton*. London: Aurum, 1996.

Hay, William, *Reminiscences 1808–1815, under Wellington*. Edited by Mrs S.C.I. Wood. London: Simpkin, Marshall & Co., 1901.

Haythorthwaite, Philip J., *Waterloo Men: the Experience of Battle, 16–18 June 1815*. Marlborough: Crowood Press, 1999.

Haythorthwaite, Philip J., *Who Was Who in the Napoleonic Wars*. London: Arms and Armour Press, 1998.

Heeley, Edward, 'Journal of Edward Heeley' in *Journal of the Society for Army Historical Research*, Vol. 64. Summer & Autumn 1986, nos 258–9.

Hellman, George S., tr., *Memoirs of the Comte de Mercy Argenteau*. New York: G. P. Putman's Sons: The Knickerbocker Press, 1917.

Henty, G.A., *One of the 28th: a tale of Waterloo*. London: Blackie & Sons, c.1898.

Hibbert, Christopher, *Wellington: a Personal History*. London: HarperCollins, 1997.

Hibbert, Christopher, Ed. *The Wheatley Diary: a Journal and Sketchbook kept during the Peninsular War and the Waterloo Campaign*. Gloucestershire: Windrush Press, 1997.

Hills, Robert, *Sketches in Flanders and Holland ...* London: 1816.

Hofschröer, Peter, *1815, the Waterloo Campaign: Wellington, his German Allies and the Battles of Ligny and Quatre Bras*. London: Greenhill, 1998.

Holmes Richard, *Redcoat the British Soldier in the Age of Horse and Musket*. London: HarperCollins, 2001.

Holmes, Richard, *Wellington: the Iron Duke*. London: HarperCollins, 2002.

Howard, Martin, *Wellington's Doctors: the British Army Medical Services in the Napoleonic Wars*. Staplehurst: Spellmount, 2002.

Howarth, David, *A Near Run Thing: the Day of Waterloo*. London: Collins, 1968.

Hunt, Eric, *Charging Against Napoleon: Diaries and Letters of Three Hussars, 1808–1815*. Barnsley: Leo Cooper, 2001.

Jackson, Lt-Col Basil, *Notes and Reminiscences of a Staff Officer, chiefly relating to the Waterloo Campaign and to St Helena matters during the captivity of Napoleon*. Edited by R.C. Seaton. London: John Murray, 1903.

James, John Haddy, *Surgeon James's Journal, 1815*. London: Cassell, 1964.

James, Lawrence, *The Iron Duke: a Military Biography of Wellington*. London: Weidenfeld & Nicolson, 1992.

James, Walter Haweis, *The Campaign of 1815, chiefly in Flanders*. Edinburgh and London: William Blackwood & Sons, 1908.

Jones, George [A Near Observer], *The Battle of Waterloo with those of Ligny and Quatre Bras, described by the series of official accounts published by Authority . . . .* London: L. Booth, 1817.

Keegan, John, *The Face of Battle: a Study of Agincourt, Waterloo and the Somme*. London: Pimlico 2004.

Kelly, Christopher, *The Memorable Battle of Waterloo*. London: Thomas Kelly, 1817.

Kincaid, Captain Sir John, *Adventures in the Rifle Brigade and Random Shots from a Rifleman*, London: MacLaren & Company, n.d.

Knight, Corporal, *Adventures in Holland and at Waterloo; and Expedition to Portugal*. Sydney: F. Cunninghame, 1867.

Knollys, Major, *The Life of Shaw*. Deeds of Daring Library, 1876.

Lagden, Alan & John Sly, *The 2/73rd at Waterloo*. Privately published, 1988.

Lamington, Lord, *In the Days of the Dandies*, Eveleigh Nash, 1906.

Lancey, Lady de, *A Week at Waterloo in 1815*. London: John Murray, 1906.

Lawrence, William, *The Autobiography of Sergeant William Lawrence*. Edited by G.N. Bankes. London: Sampson Law, Marston, Searle & Rivington, 1886.

Leach, C.B., *Sketch of the Field Services of the Rifle Brigade, from its formation to the battle of Waterloo*. London: T. and W. Boone, 1838.

Leach, Lt-Col J., *Rough sketches of the life of an old soldier, during a service in the West Indies, at the siege of Copenhagen in 1807, in the Peninsula and the south of France in the campaigns from 1808 to 1814, with the light division, in the Netherlands in 1815, including the battles of Quatre Bras and Waterloo: with a slight sketch of the three years passed by the army of occupation in France*. London: Longman, Rees, Orme, Brown, and Green, 1831.

Leek, The Rev. William, *The History of Lord Seaton's Regiment (The 52nd Light Infantry) at the Battle of Waterloo*. London: Hatchard and Co., 1866.

Lennox, Lady Sarah, *Life and Letters of Lady Sarah Lennox*, London: John Murray, 1902.

Dancing into Battle

Lennox, Lord William Pitt, *50 Years' Biographical Reminiscences*, London: Hurst & Blackett, 1863.

Lennox, Lord William Pitt, *Celebrities I have Known*. London: Hurst & Blackett, 1877.

Lennox, Lord William Pitt, *Drafts on my Memory*. Vol. I. London: Chapman & Hall, 1866.

Lennox, Lord William Pitt, *Percy Hamilton, or the Adventures of a Westminster Boy*. 3 Vols. London: W. Shoberl, 1852.

Lennox, Lord William Pitt, *Three Years with the Duke, or Wellington in Private Life*. London: Saunders and Otley, 1853.

Lennox, 5th Duke of Richmond, Charles Gordon, *Memoir of C.G. Lennox, fifth Duke of Richmond*. London: Chapman and Hall, 1862.

Lockhart, J.G., *Memoirs of Sir Walter Scott*. 5 Vols. London: Macmillan and Co., 1900.

Longford, Elizabeth, *Wellington: Pillar of State*. London: Weidenfeld & Nicolson, 1969.

Longford, Elizabeth, *Wellington: the Years of the Sword*. London: Weidenfeld & Nicolson, 1969.

Low, Edward Bruce, *With Napoleon at Waterloo and other unpublished documents of the Waterloo and Peninsular Campaigns*. London: Francis Griffiths, 1911.

Mackworth, Sir Digby, 'The Waterloo Diary of Sir Digby Mackworth' in the *Army Quarterly*, Vol. XXXV (October 1937 and January 1938). London: William Clowes, 1938.

Maden, Spencer, *The Letters of Spencer Madan, 1814–1816*. Edited by Beatrice Madan. London: Private printing, 1970.

Malmesbury [James Harris], Earl of, *A Series of Letters of the First Earl of Malmesbury*. London: Bentley, 1870.

Mann, Michael, *And They Rode On: the King's Dragoon Guards at Waterloo*. Salisbury: Michael Russell, 1984.

Matthey, Cyril G.R., *Practical Information for Visiting the Battle-Fields of the Campaign of Waterloo*. Privately printed, 1908.

Maxwell, W.H., *Life of Field-Marshal His Grace the Duke of Wellington*. 3 Vols. London: A.H. Baily & Co., 1839–40.

Maxwell, W.H., *Stories of Waterloo*. London: Richard Bentley, 1834.

McGrigor, Sir James, *The Autobiography and Services of Sir J. McGrigor*. London, 1861.

Mercer, General Cavalié, *Journal of the Waterloo Campaign kept throughout the campaign of 1815*. London: Greenhill Books, 1985.

Miller, David, *Lady de Lancey at Waterloo: a Story of Duty and Devotion*. Staplehurst: Spellmount, 2000.

Miller, David, The Duchess of Richmond's Ball, 15 June 1815. Staplehurst: Spellmount, 2005.

Monsarrat Anne, *An Uneasy Victorian: Thackeray the Man, 1811–1863*. London: Cassell, 1980.

Morris, Thomas, *Military Memoirs*. Edited by John Selby. London: Longmans, 1967.

Morris, Thomas, *Recollections of Military Service*. London: James Madden & Co., 1847.

Morris, William O'Connor, *The Campaign of 1815, Ligny: Quatre Bras: Waterloo*. London: Grant Richards, 1900.

Mudford, William, *An Historical Account of the Campaign in the Netherlands, in 1815, under His Grace the Duke of Wellington, and Marshal Prince Blücher, comprising the battles of Ligny, Quatrebras, and Waterloo; with a detailed narrative of the political events connected with those memorable conflicts down to the surrender of Paris, and the departure of Bonaparte for St Helena*. London: Henry Colburn, 1817.

Muffling, General C., *Passages from My Life: the Memoirs of Baron von Müffling*. London: Greenhill Books, 1997.

Muffling, General C., *Sketch of the Battle of Waterloo . . . .* Brussels, 1833.

Murphy, Charles C.R., *A Mixed Bag, etc*. London: William Clowes, 1936.

Navez, Louis, *La Campagne de 1815*. Brussels: J. Lebègue & Co., 1910.

North, René, *Regiments at Waterloo*. London: Almark Publishing Co. Ltd, 1971.

Oman, Sir Charles, *Wellington's Army, 1809–1814*. London: Greenhill Books, 1986.

O'Riordan, Conal, *Soldier of Waterloo: a Story of Manhood*. London: W. Collins Sons & Co., 1918.

Owen, Edward, Ed., *The Waterloo papers: 1815 and beyond*. Tavistock: AQ & DJ Publications, 1997.

Page, F.C.G., *Following the Drum: Women in Wellington's Wars*. London: Deutsch, 1986.

Paget, George Charles Henry Victor, Marquess of Anglesey, *One-Leg. The life and letters of Henry William Paget, first Marquess of Anglesey, K.G., 1768–1854*. Jonathan Cape: London, 1961.

Paget, George Charles Henry Victor, Marquess of Anglesey, *The Capel Letters: Being the correspondence of Lady Caroline Capel and her daughters with the Dowager Countess of Uxbridge from Brussels and Switzerland, 1814–1817*. Edited by the Marquess of Anglesey. Jonathan Cape: London, 1955.

Pakenham, Sir Edward Michael, *Pakenham Letters: 1800–1815*. London, 1826.

Parkinson, Roger, *The Hussar General: the Life of Blücher, Man of Waterloo*. London: Peter Davies, 1975.

Pattison, Lt Frederick Hope, *Personal Recollections of the Waterloo Campaign*. Upton: Gosling Press, 1992.

Picton, G.W., *The Battle of Waterloo*. London: R. Edwards (1816).

Pococke, Thomas, *A Soldier of the Seventy-first. The Journal of a Soldier of the Highland Light Infantry, 1806–1815*. Edited by Christopher Hibbert. London: Leo Cooper, 1975.

Ponsonby, Sir John, *The Ponsonby Family*. London: The Medici Society, 1929.

Prawer, Siegbert Salomon, *W.M. Thackeray's European Sketch Books: a Study of Literary and Graphic Portraiture*. Oxford: Peter Lang, c.2000.

Rae, John, *Stanley Gordon, a Historical Tale of the Peninsular War*. London: Walter Scott, 1889.

Ramsden, Lady Guendolen, *Correspondence of Two Brothers: Edward Adolphus, Eleventh Duke of Somerset, and his Brother, Lord Webb Seymour*. London: Longmans, Green & Co., 1906.

Ray, Gordon, *Thackeray: the Uses of Adversity*. 2 Vols. London: Oxford University Press, 1955.

Redway, Major G.W., *Wellington and Waterloo*. London: T.C. & E.C. Jack, c.1913.

Richardson, Ethel, *Long Forgotten Days*. London: Heath Cranton Ltd, 1928.

Roberts, Andrew, *Waterloo*. New York: HarperCollins, 2005.

Robertson, Sgt, *Journal of the Gordon Highlanders*, London, 1911.

Robinson, Alicia, *Elegant Eating*. Edited by Philippa Glanville and Hilary Young. London: V&A Publications, 2002.

Robinson, Heaton Bowstead, *Memoirs of Lieutenant-General Sir T. Picton, including his correspondence, etc.* 2 Vols. London, 1835.

Romberg, J.B., *Brussels and its Environs*. London: Samuel Leigh, 1816.

Ros, Georgiana, Lady de, 'Personal Recollections of the Great Duke of Wellington' in *Murray's Magazine*, Vol. V. London: John Murray, 1889.

Ross-Lewin, Harry, *With 'The Thirty-Second' in the Peninsula and other Campaigns*. Naval & Military Press, 2004.

Rothenberg, Gunther E., *The Napoleonic Wars*. London: Cassell, 1999.

Saw, Philip, *Waterloo and the Romantic Imagination*. Houndsmill and New York: Palgrave Macmillan, 2002.

Scott, John, *Paris re-visited in 1815, by way of Brussels: Including walk over the field of battle at Waterloo*. London: Longman, Hurst, Hess, Orme, and Brown, 1816.

Scott, Lt-Gen., *An Authentic Narrative of the late Sanguinary Conflict on the Plains of Waterloo*. London: E. Cox and Son, 1815.

Scott, Sir Walter, *The Letters of Sir Walter Scott: 1787–1828*. 10 Vols. Edited by H.J.C. Grierson. London: Constable & Co., 1932–1936.

Shaw Kennedy, General Sir James, *Notes on the Battle of Waterloo*. London: John Murray, 1865.

Shelley, Lady Frances, *The Diary of Frances, Lady Shelley*. Edited by Richard Edgcumbe. London: John Murray, 1912–13.

Shillingsburg, Peter L., *William Makepeace Thackeray: a Literary Life*. Basingstoke: Palgrave, 2001.

Siborne, H.T. Ed., *Waterloo Letters*. London: Greenhill Books; Pennsylvania, Pa.: Stackpole Books, 1993.

Sidney, Rev. Edwin, *Life of Lord Hill*. London: John Murray, 1845.

Simmons, Major George, *A British Rifle Man. The Journals and Correspondence of Major George Simmons*. London: A. & C. Black, 1899.

Simpson, James, *A Visit to Flanders, in July 1815, being chiefly an account of the field of Waterloo*. Edinburgh: William Blackwood, 1815.

Simpson, James, *Paris after Waterloo*. Edinburgh: William Blackwood & Son, 1853.

Slessor, *The Backbone: Diaries of a Military Family in the Napoleonic Wars*. Edited by Alethea Hayter. Edinburgh: Pentland Press, 1993.

Smith, G.C. Moore, *The Life of John Colborne, Field-Marshall Lord Seaton*. London: John Murray, 1903.

Smith, Harry, *The Autobiography of Lt. Gen. Sir Harry Smith*. Vol I. Edited by G.C. Moore Smith. London: John Murray, 1902.

Smith, Newman, *Flying Sketches of the Battle of Waterloo, Brussels, Holland &c. in June 1815, by a young traveller*. London: W. Bennett, 1852.

Stanhope, Earl, *Notes of Conversations with the Duke of Wellington*. London: Prion, 1998.

Stanley, Edward, Bishop of Norwich, *Before and after Waterloo: Letters from Edward Stanley . . .* (1802; 1814; 1816). Edited by Jane H. Adeane and Maud Grenfell. London: T. Fisher Unwin, 1907.

Stickland, Margaret, *The Byron Women*. London: Peter Owen, 1974.

Stuart-Wortley, C.B.E., *The Hon. Mrs. Edward Highcliffe and the Stuarts*. London: John Murray, 1927.

Sutherland, John Patrick, *Men of Waterloo*. London: Muller, 1967.

Swinton, The Hon. J. R., *A Sketch of the Life of Georgiana, Lady de Ros with some reminiscences of her family and friends*. London: John Murray, 1893.

Talleyrand, Prince de, *Memoirs of the Prince de Talleyrand*. Edited by Duc de Broglie, tr. Mrs Angus Hall, 6 Vols. London: Griffith, Farran, Okeden and Welsh, London, 1891.

Thackeray, Wm Makepiece, *Selected letters of William Makepeace Thackeray*. Edited by Edgar F. Harden. London: Macmillan, 1996.

Thackeray, Wm Makepeace, *Thackeray: Interviews and Recollections*. Edited by Philip Collins. London: Macmillan, 1983.

Thackeray, Wm Makepeace, *The Letters and Private Papers of William Makepeace Thackeray*, Vol. I. Edited by G.N. Ray. Oxford: O.U.P., 1945–1946.

Thackeray, Wm Makepeace, *Vanity Fair*, London: Everyman, 1991.

Thackeray, Wm Makepeace, *William Makepeace Thackeray: Memoirs of a Victorian Gentleman*. Edited by Margaret Forster. London: Quartet Books, 1980.

Thompson, John, *Report of Observations made in the British Military Hospital in Belgium after the Battle of Waterloo: with some remarks upon Amputation*. Edinburgh: William Blackwood, 1816.

Thornton, James, *Your most obedient servant, cook to the Duke of Wellington*. Exeter: Webb and Bower, 1985.

Tomkinson, William, *The Diary of a Cavalry Officer in the Peninsular War and Waterloo Campaign, 1809–1815*. Edited by James Tomkinson. London: Frederick Muller, 1971.

Tupper, Carrey, '*Reminiscences of a Commissariate Officer*', in *Cornhill Magazine*, 1899.

Uffindell, Andrew, *The National Army Museum Book of Wellington's Armies*. London: Sidgwick & Jackson, 2003.

Uffindell, Andrew, *Women of Waterloo*. www.thehistorynet.com

Uffindell, Andrew & Michael Corum, *On the Fields of Glory: the battlefields of the 1815 campaign*. London: Greenhill Books, 1996.

Vallance, Dixon, *A Narrative of the Battles of Quatre Bras and Waterloo by a Soldier of the 79th Regiment of Foot* in *79th News*.

W.C., *Some Particulars of the Battle of Waterloo in a Letter from a Serjeant in the Guards*. London: J. & T. Clarke, 1816.

Weale, G., *An Interesting memoir of George Weale, From the Time of Leaving his Father ... until the Memorable Battle of Waterloo*. Leamington: Dewe, n.d.

Weller, Jac, *Wellington at Waterloo*. London: Longmans, 1967.

Wheeler, Pte William, *Letters of Private Wheeler*. London: Michael Joseph, 1951.

Woodberry, George, *Journal du Lieutenant Woodberry: campagnes de Portugal et d'Espagne, de France, de Belgique et de France (1813–1815)*. Translated by Georges Hélie. Paris: E. Plon, 1896.

Young, Julian Charles, *A Memoir of C.M. Young ....* London, 1871.

Anonymous Accounts

Account of the Battle of Waterloo, fought on the 18th of June 1815 ... by a British Officer on the Staff. London: James Ridgeway, 1815.

Britain Triumphant on the Plains of Waterloo, being a correct and circumstantial narrative of the memorable battle .... Burslem: John Tregortha, 1817.

Bulletin de la Société Belge d'Etudes Napoleoniennes.

Feuille d'Annonces et Avis de Bruxelles.

History of the 42nd Regiment. www.42highlandregt1815.co.uk

Journal de la Belgique.

The Battle of Waterloo, from the tradition of the Scots Greys and Highlanders. Glasgow and London: W.R. Mphun, 1859.

The Battle of Waterloo, or a faithful and interesting history of the unparalled events .... Manchester: J. Cleave, 1816.

The Waterloo medal roll compiled from the Muster Rolls. Dallington: The Naval and Military Press Ltd, 1992.

Westerton's Hand Book to the Duke's Funeral. The Order of Proceeding in the Public Funeral of the Late Field-Marshall Arthur Duke of Wellington, K.G. etc. London: Charles Westerton, 1852.

Documents and Manuscripts
Badminton Archive: Mss Letters to the Duke of Beaufort.
Gwent Record Office: Letter from Fitzroy Somerset.
Historical Record of the Second Regiment of Life Guards, unpublished ms at
    Household Cavalry Museum, Windsor.
Unpublished ts of the memoirs of James Gunn, Black Watch Archive.
West Sussex Record Office: Goodwood mss.

Newspapers and Periodicals
The *Illustrated London News*.
The Times.

ACKNOWLEDGEMENTS

Tedious for the reader yet vital for the author, the acknowledgements show that although my name appears on the cover, this book is really the product of many people, not all of whom can be named here. First I have to thank one of literary London's great double acts, Alan Samson and Luigi Bonomi. Luigi has been my agent for ten years or so and I value his professional opinion, his wit and his friendship. I would find it hard to manage without him. *Dancing into Battle* is the second book that I have been lucky enough to have Alan edit – he is a joy to work with and his is a light yet authoritative touch. He has the gift of exercising his considerable skill and conveying his immense wisdom in a manner that is both encouraging and enlightening. Weidenfeld & Nicholson is a great publishing house because of the people who work there. In particular I have to thank Lucinda McNeile for making the editing process such a civilised experience and Tom Graves for his humour and hard work in putting together the illustrations. Similarly tireless is my research assistant Sophie Robinson: resourceful, vigilant and highly versatile. I am delighted that she continues to work with me. While on the subject of research, I must also thank Lisa O'Sullivan who helped in the early stages of this book, before becoming a curator at the Science Museum. I would like to thank Charles March, without whose ancestors there would have been no ball on the eve of battle, for his cooperation and hospitality. Together with his delightful wife Janet, he has turned Goodwood into a model of what a stately home should be in the early twenty-first century. At Goodwood Rosemary Baird was generous with her time and insight. I am similarly grateful for extracts from various documents which appear by courtesy of the Trustees of the Goodwood Collections, the West Sussex Record Office and County Archivist. And while on the subject of County Record Offices, Gwent Record Office was immensely helpful too, and Lord Raglan, who gave his permission 'gladly' to use a letter from the first Lord Raglan. There are certain letters, to my knowledge previously unpublished, which appear by kind permission of His Grace the Duke of Beaufort. I am extremely grateful to be able to use this illuminating correspondence, and for the help of Margaret Richards and Elaine Milsom. The British Army should be proud of its wonderful regimental archivists who were so generous with their time and their collections, and without whose pride in their history and anecdotes this book would be greatly the poorer. I would like to single out the The Black Watch Regimental Archive for allowing me to make use of the unpublished memoirs of James Gunn and the Regimental Archive of The Highlanders (Seaforth, Gordons and Camerons) for Dixon Vallance's *A Narrative of the Battles of Quatre Bras and Waterloo by a Soldier of the 79th Regiment of Foot*. The National Army Museum was unfailingly helpful. The London Library is a wonderful institution which contributes to London's standing in the world; it is staffed by some of the most patient and helpful people you could care to meet. Mark Finch worked hard to transcribe some barely legible letters. Andras Bereznay turned my jumbled and messy estimations into a handsome map of Brussels in 1814-15.

Others to whom I owe my thanks for their friendship and support include Andrea Riva, Andrew Roberts, Andrew Wilson, Charles Finch, Edward Sahakian, Fabien Fryns, Franz Larosee, Jean Pierre Martel and Simon Sebag Montefiore.

I am deeply grateful to my wife Alexandra for remaining with me, creating what stability there is in my life and, most of all, for our two children.

INDEX

>⌒⌒⌒